The Good Society

BY THE SAME AUTHOR

The Spirit Level (with Richard Wilkinson)
The Inner Level (with Richard Wilkinson)
Act Now (with Common Sense Policy Group)
Basic Income (with Common Sense Policy Group)

The Good Society

And How We Make It

KATE PICKETT

THE BODLEY HEAD
LONDON

3 5 7 9 10 8 6 4 2

The Bodley Head, an imprint of Vintage, is part of the
Penguin Random House group of companies

Vintage, Penguin Random House UK, One Embassy Gardens,
8 Viaduct Gardens, London SW11 7BW

penguin.co.uk/vintage
global.penguinrandomhouse.com

First published by The Bodley Head in 2026
Copyright © Kate Pickett 2026

The moral right of the author has been asserted

Every effort has been made to contact all copyright holders. The publisher will be pleased
to amend in future editions any errors or omissions brought to their attention.

Penguin Random House values and supports copyright. Copyright fuels creativity, encourages diverse voices, promotes freedom of expression and supports a vibrant culture. Thank you for purchasing an authorised edition of this book and for respecting intellectual property laws by not reproducing, scanning or distributing any part of it by any means without permission. You are supporting authors and enabling Penguin Random House to continue to publish books for everyone. No part of this book may be used or reproduced in any manner for the purpose of training artificial intelligence technologies or systems. In accordance with Article 4(3) of the DSM Directive 2019/790, Penguin Random House expressly reserves this work from the text and data mining exception.

Typeset in 12.8/16pt Dante MT Std by Six Red Marbles UK, Thetford, Norfolk
Printed and bound in Great Britain by Clays Ltd, Elcograf S.p.A.

The authorised representative in the EEA is Penguin Random House Ireland,
Morrison Chambers, 32 Nassau Street, Dublin D02 YH68

A CIP catalogue record for this book is available from the British Library

ISBN 9781847928726

Penguin Random House is committed to a sustainable future
for our business, our readers and our planet. This book is
made from Forest Stewardship Council® certified paper.

For Richard Wilkinson –
with love, gratitude and admiration

Contents

Note on References in the Text ... ix
Prologue: What is a Good Society? ... 1

PART ONE
The Blueprints for a Good Society

1 In Sickness and in Health ... 25
2 All the Kinds of Care We Need ... 72
3 Educating a Good Society ... 137
4 Imprisoned by Injustice ... 184

PART TWO
How to Build a Good Society

5 Time for New Economic Thinking ... 239
6 The Building Blocks: Evidence and Equality ... 270

Epilogue: Living Proof ... 315
Acknowledgements ... 319
Note on Methods ... 321
Notes ... 327
Index ... 365

Note on References in the Text

This book uses a single, continuous numbering system for references and endnotes, rather than restarting numbering in each chapter. You will find every source featured just once in the Notes section at the end, with the full reference details. Every time that reference is quoted or used, the same number will be cited in the text to take you back to the relevant reference in the Notes; this means the numbering will sometimes be out of sequential order, but it is intentional. A single reference may appear more than once in the text, but its number remains the same wherever it occurs, ensuring consistency between the text and the endnotes.

PROLOGUE

What is a Good Society?

> 'We are at times too ready to believe that the present is the only possible state of things.'
>
> Marcel Proust

On a beautiful spring weekend, I went to look at some pictures being exhibited in open studios near my home, in York. So far, so middle class: I wandered happily between artists' garden sheds and spare bedrooms and bespoke ateliers, looking at landscapes, portraits, and still lifes. And then I had an accidental encounter with political protest. Stephen John Bottrill is a printmaker who incorporates political iconography and phrases into intricately patterned etchings and linotypes. Displayed in a suburban living room, I spotted Wat Tyler, leader of the 1381 Peasants' Revolt in England, Marx and Mandela, subverted advertising slogans, the Last Supper. There too was the quote, above, from Proust, a man most often remembered for dipping a little cake into his tea, which I think I knew but had forgotten. It brought me up short.

Throughout my life I've heard the phrase 'the good society', and through my research and writing I've believed I've been working in service of it. But do I really think that the present state of things is moveable? Do I really believe that change – profound change on a grand scale – is possible?

Well, yes. I do believe that, and I hope to convince you too.

That same weekend, I took part in a shoot for a feature film which tells the story of a young woman of today discovering William Beveridge's groundbreaking report, which led to the founding of the modern welfare state. Beveridge famously laid out a plan to slay the five 'giant evils' of Want, Disease, Squalor, Idleness and Ignorance.[1] Which all sounds a bit Victorian, but re-reading the Beveridge Report brought me up short for the second time that weekend. Pretty much everything that we need to do to create a good society was set out, in practical detail and sometimes surprisingly modern language, in 1942. But although we got the National Health Service, we didn't get most of what Beveridge envisioned, and we certainly haven't been making anything like steady progress in the right direction since. It's been one step forward, one decade back; there have been times of progress and times when things have become worse.

So why am I hopeful that another 'state of things' is possible (and indeed, desirable)? The simple answer: it's the evidence. There has always been theory and ideology underpinning any number of versions of what we might be aiming for in a good society. Now there is a wealth of evidence as well. I'm not averse to a bit of theorising, and I hold fast to certain values, but evidence is my trade, and so I rest my case for a good society on evidence as much as on values and vision.

My perspective comes from a research career grounded in social epidemiology, the branch of science that concerns the social determinants of health, and more recently from working within large, interdisciplinary research programmes on the environment, on economic development, and on wellbeing. In this book I use my own expertise, knowledge and experience and pull in the work of a very wide network of researchers and thinkers to show what a good society could look like, if we could only close the gap between what we've got and what we want, using a vast body of evidence that has too long gone unheeded.

My Good Society stall

Here, in a nutshell, is my version of a good society – this is what I think we should be aiming for, and this is what this book is about.

I want a society where everyone's physical and mental health is as good as it could be, because prevention is prioritised by the public health system and the health service, and health inequalities are levelled out by addressing the wider determinants of health. I want those who need care – whether children, those with disabilities, or the elderly – to be looked after without incurring financial stress in settings where their emotional and social wellbeing are as important as their physical needs. I want our children and young people to flourish in an education system that engages their imaginations, inspires their creativity, equips them with skills for life and leaves no one behind. I want a society where the focus is on preventing crime and rehabilitating those who commit crimes so that they can contribute to society rather than weighing it down. I want us to adopt new economic thinking and make serious strides towards tackling the climate emergency and protecting the environment, always keeping in mind how well we ensure the wellbeing of future generations.

That's it. Your priorities and desires might differ from mine entirely, in which case this book probably isn't for you – although if you'd like to see if I can change your mind, you are very welcome to stay. Or you might be in broad agreement with me but have some other issues close to your heart that I'm not going to be tackling here, such as the housing crisis or our transportation woes. For detailed solutions on those you'll need to look to other experts (although some of my solutions will be relevant to these problems too). I'm going to stick to the issues where I know the evidence and the arguments, through my own research or through my collaborations with others.

For me, these are the big and significant issues. If we can tackle and improve health, social care, education and the criminal justice system, and protect our environment within a sustainable economy then, I believe, our quality of life will be improved immeasurably. And I do mean the quality of life for *all of us*, young and old, all genders and identities, in all regions, and at all social class and income levels. This is proper 'big society' and 'levelling up', but without a left/right ideological stance or a party-political affiliation. Some of the changes I envision for a good society would benefit you (and me) directly – perhaps it would be easier to find good care for your parents, or a school that nurtures your child's development? But some of the benefits would be indirect: your community would feel safer and more cohesive; your surroundings would be cleaner and greener. And – and this is hugely important – if fewer other people were poor and fewer other people were rich, you would benefit from that too. This is the opposite of what we were promised by the 'trickle down' of neoliberal economics: instead of a misplaced belief in society improving because of (or in spite of) a few people becoming fabulously rich, the evidence tells us that tackling poverty and inequality is advantageous for our society as a whole.

Society is a big word. Prime Minister Margaret Thatcher famously didn't believe in it, stating in an interview with *Women's Own* magazine in 1987 that there was 'no such thing . . . there are individual men and women and there are families'.[2] She was wrong. Society is more than individual men and women (and families); it is bigger than the sum of its parts, and so a good society can't just be about what serves individual interests.

The good society is instead, as journalist Zoe Williams once put it, 'a landscape that we're proud to look at', that we are willing to work towards because we know that we can't truly prosper when others do not.[3] If you are as shocked as I am by tech oligarch Elon Musk's declaration that 'the fundamental weakness of Western civilization is empathy',[4] this book is for you, because it shows, emphatically, that he is also wrong.

A theory of (not quite) everything

Some years ago, I was presenting to the Treasury Executive Institute at the US Department of the Treasury, setting out, alongside Richard Wilkinson, some of our research on the impacts of inequality, on which this book is firmly grounded. During the question and answer session that followed, a sceptical audience member stood up. 'Do you mean to tell me,' he asked, somewhat belligerently, 'that if we simply reduce economic inequality, all those things – health, education, rates of imprisonment and so on – will all get better?'

Well, yes. That's exactly what we meant to tell him. I suggested that perhaps the US could try just a smidgeon more equality and see where that got them.

When I started to work with Richard in the early 2000s, we were building on his earlier research that began with a landmark study of income inequality and death rates, published in the *British Medical Journal* in 1992.[5] By 1998, the editors of that journal, commenting on further studies, noted that 'the more equally wealth is distributed the better the health of that society', declaring this a 'big idea'.[6]

Together, Richard and I widened our epidemiologic lens to look beyond health to a broader set of social outcomes, and in our 2009 book, *The Spirit Level*, we drew together a large body of evidence linking income inequality – the gap between rich and poor in a society – to social cohesion and children's life chances, as well as health and wellbeing.[7] This research is foundational to this book.

We showed that people in societies with bigger income gaps between rich and poor are much more likely to suffer from more premature mortality, higher rates of infant mortality, more mental ill health, more illicit drug use and more obesity, and that greater inequality also damages social relationships (more unequal societies have more violence, higher rates of imprisonment, weaker community life and less trust). As well as social capital, human capital is diminished: in more unequal places there are lower levels of child wellbeing and educational attainment, more teenage births and less social mobility. In addition to seemingly causing a wide range of problems, the differences between societies are large. Just to give a few examples, in the more equal Scandinavian countries, over 60 per cent of people think other people can be trusted, but it's less than 20 per cent in the more unequal Greece and in Portugal. The homicide rate in the very unequal USA is thirty-four times higher than the rate in Japan, which at the time was the most equal nation, and the US rate of imprisonment is ten times higher than that of Finland or Norway (we're talking about rates and not absolute numbers, of course). In Italy, Greece and Israel more than 40 per cent of young people lack basic skills in maths and reading, but it's only 22 per cent in the more equal Ireland. And although the poor are affected most deeply, even affluent and well-educated people have better outcomes in more equal societies. If we reduce inequality, we can improve life for everyone.

The basic mechanism that links inequality to these myriad outcomes is chronic social stress. Living in a more unequal society changes how we think and feel and how we relate to each other. In our 2018 book, *The Inner Level*, Richard and I set out a robust body of evidence to show that inequality increases the grip of class and status, making social comparisons more insidious and increasing the social and psychological distances between people.[8] Inequalities of wealth, income and power strengthen the tendency to believe that those at the top are hugely important and those at the bottom are almost worthless. In more unequal societies we come to judge each other more by status and worry more about how others judge us.[9]

Although it appears that the vast majority of the population are affected by inequality, we don't all respond in the same way. One common response in more unequal societies is to feel oppressed by a lack of confidence and low self-esteem, leading people to withdraw from social life, which in turn leads to higher levels of depression and anxiety. A second is to try to flaunt or exaggerate your own worth and achievements, to 'self-enhance' and become narcissistic. Part of the process of self-aggrandisement is through conspicuous consumption and consumerism. We use what we buy to present ourselves in a positive light; we try to show we are not 'second-class people' by owning 'first-class things'.[10] And a third response to the anxieties, caused by what psychologists call the 'social evaluative threat' of living in a more unequal society, is to try and tamp down the stress with drugs, alcohol or gambling, or to seek solace in comfort eating.[8]

Although it has at times been characterised as a 'theory of

everything', our research actually focused on problems with *social gradients*, problems that are more common at the bottom of the social hierarchy but that are, surprisingly, a little bit more common just below the very top income, education and social class brackets. For example, if you live in the poorest 10 per cent of areas of England, average life expectancy is 8–10 years shorter than for those living in the richest 10 per cent of areas, but you'll also live on average about a year less than the very topmost group if you're in the group just below it, in the second-richest areas. That's twelve months less life, even if you're pretty well off and highly educated . . . Inequality is killing us, even the affluent.

In recent years, we have come to realise that inequality is a major roadblock, not only to health and wellbeing, but also to creating sustainable economies that protect the planet.[11]

I'll come back to that later in the book, but here, before we make the deep dive into the big issues, is our most up-to-date

Health, social and environmental problems are more common in more unequal rich countries.

picture of the links between income inequality and health, social and environmental problems, published in *Nature* in 2024.[12]

The more equal countries are on the left of the graph, the more unequal ones on the right; the countries with more problems are higher up, the countries with fewer problems are lower down. If you know a country's level of inequality, you can do a pretty good job of predicting its infant mortality rate, or prevalence of mental illness, or levels of homicides and imprisonment and so forth. All of the big problems which must be solved to create a good society are intrinsically linked to inequality: it's the bedrock around which our current society teeters and crumbles.

I should add that if we had been given £1 for every time someone reacted to our research by saying that correlations do not prove causations, Richard and I could have joined the top 1 per cent and stopped worrying about inequality. In fact, just because correlations don't always show causal relationships, sometimes that *is* exactly what they are showing.[13] Great inequality characterises the societies that are struggling with poor population health, social dysfunction, restricted life chances for children and young people, and environmental degradation, and it looks as if inequality is a root cause of them all. It is the most unequal countries that are most in need of a reset – a recognition that things have gone awry, that they are not on a path towards sustainable prosperity and wellbeing – and that need a new blueprint for a good society.

Imagining Goodland

I've always been a bit suspicious of attempts to paint a picture of, or envision, a future good society. Such imaginings can seem trite, like school-age essays about what you want to be when you grow up. But in 2013, I came across an article in the *Guardian* newspaper by political economist Andrew Simms, in which he played what he called 'fantasy economics', inviting us to 'come to Goodland', where we might want to live. He went on to describe a country where:

> Its president refuses the state mansion. He gives away 90 per cent of his pay, living on the national average wage to share in the struggles of his people. Goodland has a new constitution, written by citizens. When its financial sector fell apart, speculators had to take their losses and the guilty were taken to court, not given a public bailout. The country has a dynamic, largely mutually owned, local banking system. It avoids bad risk and bends over backwards to help small businesses. In Goodland, human wellbeing is more important than economic growth. There is a national plan for good living, free health and education services, subsidised childcare allowing for a more equal workplace, and support for the elderly. It has a law enshrining protection of its life-supporting ecosystems that stands above all other laws. Goodland's cities are green and grow healthy, organic food for the inhabitants. A phase-out of most fossil fuels is planned by 2017, and its business sector has large, intelligently connected and productive cooperatives. A shorter working week is available by choice.

It sounds good, albeit fantastic and utopian. But the point about Goodland is, Simms says, that '[it] exists. It is just a little, well, spread out.'[14]

Every aspect of Goodland is already happening, somewhere in the world. Simms says it is like playing fantasy football, where you make up a perfect team by choosing actual players from real teams. In his fantasy Goodland, the president is actually the then-president of Uruguay (José Mujica), who chose to live modestly.

WHAT IS A GOOD SOCIETY?

The country that managed its financial crisis and banks well was Iceland. Citizens directing public spending through participatory budgeting actually happens in Brazil. Germany thrives on small and community banks. The successful €14 billion Mondragón cooperative in Spain has more than 70,000 employees. There is a shorter working week in the Netherlands. Bhutan famously measures its success by Gross National Happiness rather than Gross National Income,* and so forth.

As Simms points out, while 'Britain agonises about the affordability of services, Denmark's tax system pays for free health and education, home help for the elderly, and about three-quarters of the cost of childcare. Far from harming the economy, higher taxes stimulate investment in infrastructure, education and R&D.' He then challenged readers to build Goodland or create their own.[14]

This approach – which I'm calling 'fantasy society' because it encompasses far more than just economics – is fundamental to everything that follows in this book. The core insight is deceptively simple, yet revolutionary: the societies we dream of aren't fantasies at all. They already exist, in whole or in part, scattered across the globe. When we see Finland's education system, Costa Rica's approach to the environment, or Denmark's work–life balance, we're not looking at impossible utopias – we're looking at proof of concept. These examples ground our vision of a more perfect society in contemporary reality, transforming aspiration into achievable policy.

This is why I play 'fantasy good society' throughout these pages, seeking out places where good things are actually

---

* Gross National Income represents the total income earned by a country's residents, whether at home or abroad, minus income earned by non-residents within the country, whereas Gross Domestic Product measures total production of goods and services within a country.

happening, examples of good societies in action. If it can happen elsewhere, what exactly are the barriers to it happening wherever we might be living? The question shifts from 'Is this possible?' to 'What can we learn from those who've already figured it out?' The desirable becomes feasible precisely because the evidence shows it's already working somewhere else. I've used the fantasy society rubric twice before for framing what a good society could look like, including in the report of the Greater Manchester Independent Inequalities Commission, which I chaired in 2021 – it's always illuminating and so worth repeating the exercise.[15, 16]

Lifting the veil

Alongside the 'fantasy society' conceit, it's instructive to reflect on a thought experiment proposed by philosopher John Rawls. A key idea in this is what's called the 'Veil of Ignorance'.[17] Imagine that you are behind a blindfold, unaware of your own social status, intelligence, health, or personal circumstances. You don't know if you're rich or not, male or female, clever or not, and so on. From this position of ignorance, you are asked to design the principles of a just society. Rawls' argument is that, without knowing your own future place in society, you would choose fairness and equality – because you could end up in any position.

This mental exercise challenges us to consider: should social worth be based solely on attributes that can be influenced by circumstances, or should every individual be valued equally, regardless of their starting point? The Veil of Ignorance encourages us to focus on creating a society rooted in compassion, fairness, and respect for all. It highlights how social and economic inequalities distort our perceptions of worth and contribution, and why justice requires us to see beyond those divisions.

Rawls himself called his thought experiment, designing a society in which you don't know your own status, 'the original position'.[17] He believed that most people would design a society that balanced freedom (personal and political liberties) and equality (of opportunity), while protecting the material resources and ecosystems on which we and future generations depend. The power of the exercise is that it forces us to empathise, to look beyond our own interests and to construct a society, from first principles, that can look after the wellbeing of all. Economist and philosopher Daniel Chandler points out that everyone who fully engages in Rawls' thought experiment will find themselves challenging their preconceptions, biases and prejudices.[18]

It occurred to me that this would make an excellent video game and then I found, of course, that someone has already thought of the gaming potential, although *Veil of Ignorance* is a tabletop role-playing game, rather than a video game.[19] Set in a post-apocalyptic time, when the survivors of an uninhabitable Earth are heading to a new planet, players have to write the laws for their new society during the journey through space. In an interesting development of Rawls' idea, players can propose new laws or suggest removing old ones, but propositions are only accepted if all players agree. At the end of the game, players can find out about their character's individual history, temperament and personality, and have to say how they think that character would manage and feel in the new society they have co-created. I tried playing with a group of friends who think about these sorts of issues in their day jobs and almost immediately they proposed leaving all law- and policy-making to a randomly selected assembly of citizens on the new planet, which left them free to have another drink and chat about lighter matters . . . but see Chapter 5.

The Veil of Ignorance concept makes us think hard about inequality. Would we be happy to be on the bottom rungs of society? Would we be content only if we were to find ourselves in a position of privilege? Would we design a society where a very small number of people at the top (and with a vanishingly small probability that we would be one of them) could become unimaginably wealthy at the expense of everyone else, or at the expense of the environment? The difficulties and suffering experienced by those who have least in our current society will become clear throughout this book, as will the problems caused by allowing those at the top to accumulate vast wealth by extracting it from everyone else and from the natural environment. A good society is going to need us to tackle poverty and inequality, and so the Veil of Ignorance underpins this book; I'll be circling back to the issues of poverty and inequality repeatedly as the evidence points again and again to their central importance.

The Good Society has no boundaries

It's important to recognise that all societies can undergo profound transformation. America, in the 1970s, used to be as equal a society, in terms of incomes, as Sweden is today. When I was living and researching in the United States for sixteen years, until 2003, the idea that there would be a Black president in my lifetime seemed remote, but President Obama was elected just five years later. There is always hope. This book is shaped by my perspective as a UK-based researcher and citizen, but it has insights to offer for a good society anywhere. Fundamentally, our needs and dreams are not place-dependent.

Moving to action

In the very first episode of *The Thick of It*, the brilliantly dark TV satire of British politics that ran from 2005 to 2012, civil servants, spin doctors and special advisors brainstorm policies in the back of a car because they have just forty-five minutes to come up with something that the minister can announce to a waiting press conference. The show's creator, Armando Iannucci, asked the actors to improvise the policies, and they came up with some truly bonkers but very funny ideas. In an interview in 2020, Iannucci described how three of those 'joke-policies' – everyone should have a plastic bag of their own, ASBOs for pets, and a national spare room database – spookily presaged the carrier bag charge (the Single Use Carrier Bags Charges (England) Order 2015), criminal behaviour orders for dog owners (2014 amendment to the Dangerous Dogs Act) and the Bedroom Tax (the under-occupancy charge for housing benefit claimants introduced in the Welfare Reform Act 2012).

Is policy-making truly that haphazard? Iannucci believes politicians really are winging it. He went on to recall 'at some BBC event the then-Culture Secretary coming up to me and saying, "I've been in the back of that car" . . . people [are] saying it's so true. You think that policies are products of massive research and deep minds thinking about it but it's sitting down in a room going "well there's an election, we're going to call the election tomorrow. I mean, I need ideas for publishing the manifesto. What've we got? You, what you got? You know, something [that] costs £10 million. Come on, hit me!" '[20]

But what seems to happen more often than policy-making on the hoof is what has come to be known as 'policy-based evidence-making' – looking for, using or commissioning research, or reviews of research, to back policies that have already been decided upon. There is no doubt that this happens, and this was explicitly acknowledged (and discouraged) by the UK House of Commons Select Committee on Science and Technology in 2006. But it isn't, of course, what government thinks it is doing; government likes to think it is 'following the science' and doing the right thing.

Guided by the science . . .

During the Covid-19 pandemic, the British public was told consistently by the government that this is what they were doing: they were 'following the science'. That was a welcome pivot from being told that people had had enough of experts – as Michael Gove, then Lord Chancellor, had claimed in 2016 – even if it wasn't actually the case that the government was following all the scientific advice it was presented with (as the Covid Inquiry has brought to light). But at least government was acting as if the scientific evidence was important, as if following it was the best that could be done.

In the UK, the Scientific Advisory Group for Emergencies (SAGE) is convened to provide expert information and advice to the government in times of crisis. In the decade leading up to the Covid-19 pandemic, SAGE was convened several times to provide advice during domestic and international crises, including during the Ebola outbreak in West Africa in 2014, and the grounding of air traffic following the eruption of Eyjafjallajökull volcano in Iceland in 2010. SAGE feeds its coordinated, independent scientific advice to COBRA, the government committee that is convened to handle matters of national emergency or major disruptions, and SAGE also answer questions asked of it by COBRA. Other scientists may at times question the advice that SAGE gives, or the exact composition of its members at any time – and during the pandemic we saw some scientists group together to create their own independent version of SAGE – but it is clearly a good thing that government has a mechanism in place to listen to science when it feels it needs the input. During the Covid crisis, SAGE enabled the government to do some evidence-based policy-making, and an unusual degree of transparency developed around SAGE's workings in response to public concern and pressure. The membership of SAGE became public, and from May 2020 onwards the Government Office for Science published the minutes of SAGE meetings online for public scrutiny.

Despite all of this – which looks like good practice – the UK had a bad pandemic (I will come back to this in Chapter 1). Some of the explanation lies in government not having acted as fast or as fully as SAGE advised, but a much more important reason lies in the fact that there are all kinds of relevant evidence that successive governments have been ignoring for decades. The UK's high Covid-19 death rate was in large part due to pre-existing and intractable health inequalities and widespread and entrenched poverty and deprivation. And these problems might not have existed, and certainly not to the same extent, if government had been following different kinds of 'science'.

Clear evidence, clear opportunities

Much of the research that has the most to say about the workings of society and what would make things better comes from the social sciences. These include the disciplines of anthropology, business studies, criminology, demography, economics, education, human geography, law, political science, social psychology, social policy, social work, and sociology. My own discipline is a bit of a hybrid; known as social epidemiology, it's really a combination of science and social science. Very often using scientific methods applied to social issues, robust and rigorous research from these disciplines has a huge amount to offer.*

Social science research describes how things are in our society, suggests what works and what doesn't, what it costs to make change (and what it costs to not do things), and tells us how people feel about the world and how they want it to look. The social sciences are a veritable treasure trove of 'good society' evidence. We have facts, data and evidence about how to improve our society at our fingertips, and on a scale unimaginable even as recently as the start of my own career. There is a vast library of evidence-based blueprints for a good society, ready and waiting to be implemented.

This book is informed by all of that evidence, which is often hidden in plain sight, sitting on the shelves of our universities, civil service departments, think tanks and charities. The solutions for a good society that are woven throughout this book don't depend on us doing further research or setting up new commissions, reviews or inquiries, and this evidence belongs to all of us: it has usually been paid for, in one way or another, by us as taxpayers. It is typically contained in reports which are publicly available (and these days usually instantly available as a downloadable document), and which have been put together by committees of experts, often based on rigorous academic research, often conducted in our research-intensive universities, and published – after scrutiny by other experts – in scholarly

---

* If you want to know a bit more about the methods used in this kind of endeavour, take a look at the 'Note on Methods' at the end of this book.

journals. The reports synthesise and condense the research, usually put it into fairly plain language, and make recommendations for policy. They can act as a funnel, targeting research to exactly the people who need to see it and should act upon it.

I've written and taken part in quite a few of these sorts of reports over the years, contributing my own research, and helping to review and analyse research from other people and other disciplines. I've been part of reports for, and sometimes commissioned by, institutions as varied as government departments, all-party parliamentary groups, royal societies, political parties, think tanks and charities. And I've served on local, national and international commissions. I've lost count of the number of times I've heard someone assert that *this* report will make a difference, *this* report won't be left on a shelf. But they have been. I have copies of some of them on a shelf above my desk; raising my eyes I can see blueprints for tackling poverty and inequality, addressing health inequalities, implementing a proper living wage, mitigating the climate emergency and transforming capitalism, among others. Some made a bit of a media splash when they were first published, some have been cited in parliamentary debates, but none have been fully acted upon.

And so, this book is mostly about what we already know: the solutions we already have access to, for tackling some of our biggest problems. It's about the evidence that we could be guided by, if we took those blueprints off the shelf, dusted them off, and thought carefully about how they can help us change things for the better. But it is not just about what is often called an 'evidence gap'; this book is also very much about filling the 'action gap'. The best possible blueprints for a good society are of no earthly use if they are never implemented.

Part One of the book is my deep dive into some of the most serious problems we face: health, social care, education and prisons. We'll see clear and consistent evidence of how things could be better, and where improvements are drastically needed. I'm asking why men born in the poorest areas of the UK now live almost ten years less than those in the richest areas, and women eight years less, and looking at what the evidence tells us about how to reduce that gap. I look at the looming demographic and economic crisis of us not having worked out how to provide and fund care for either adults or children who need it. Two facts illustrate the magnitude of this crisis. More than 2.5 million older people have unmet social care needs because of shortages of care workers and nursing home beds. And in the city of Blackpool, a shocking 1 in 45 children are in care, each of them costing the local council close to £300,000 per year, which means that the council is spending close to half of its total budget on children's services. I also ask why we rank 26th out of thirty-eight rich countries on young people's skills – with 37 per cent of our children reaching the age of fifteen without having basic maths and reading skills – and look at what the evidence says about how we can help our children thrive. And I ask why the UK has the highest rate of imprisonment in Western Europe – with numbers having almost doubled over the past twenty years and costs spiralling so that it costs more to keep someone in prison than the average UK salary – when all the evidence suggests that imprisonment doesn't work to reduce crime. These four big issues – health inequalities, social care, education, and criminal justice – are a central focus of the book because if we could get them right, we would have the foundations of a very much better quality of life for everyone.

In Part Two, I look at the blueprint that has actually been dominating policy-making for the past few decades, the particular flavour of economics known as neoliberalism, and ask what the alternatives are. New economic thinking extends far beyond the economy itself and can help us look after the wellbeing of people and planet. I end the book by showing how we can make sure that policy is directed towards the society that we, the people, want, and how we can make sure that the best evidence for a good society is flowing into the pipelines that feed policy. I want to make sure that we keep our best evidence off the shelves, and in the hands of those who can put it into action.

The time is right

Where I'm standing, things are sadly and badly off-kilter right now. In the UK we seem in many ways to have stopped making progress towards a good society and to have lost the hope that life will be better for our children and our grandchildren. Even leaving aside the existential threat of the climate emergency, progress in longevity first stopped around 2010/11, and then life expectancy fell between 2017 and 2022.[21] Child poverty increased *by* 20 per cent *to* 20.7 per cent between 2012 and 2021, more than in any other OECD country;[22] that's 650,000 *more* poor children.[23] And 1.28 million children are persistently absent from school,[24] a number largely driven by high levels of anxiety. In 2022/23, local authorities in England and Wales received around two million new requests for social care, expenditures on care rose to £28.4 billion, and yet a third of those asking for help got nothing.[25] And this is in one of the biggest economies in the world.

Across the Atlantic, things are getting rapidly and frighteningly worse – the scale and speed at which human rights have been attacked, democratic institutions have been destroyed, the environment has been put at risk and the wellbeing of the world has been threatened shows us that some ideologues were certainly not sitting back and thinking that the present was the only possible state of things – they were ready; they had a plan for the moment when they could seize power and act. We must do the same: we must have a plan; we must be ready.

We are faced with existential war and climate crises, political divisions run deep, inequalities divide us, and progress across multiple areas of life has ground to a halt and in some cases reversed. We often hear that we should be having grown-up conversations about the challenges we face and that we need a vision before we can have a strategy to achieve it. The time feels right for this kind of debate and discussion. This book is my interjection into those conversations, and I hope that you will read it with growing conviction and enthusiasm for a better *possible state of things*.

Thinking together, acting together, writing a new social contract needs to start with conversations about the kind of future we want. Here is my Good Society. What is yours?

PART ONE

The Blueprints for a Good Society

CHAPTER 1

In Sickness and in Health

> *'Why treat people and send them back to the conditions that make them sick?'*
>
> Sir Michael Marmot

A friend of mine was suffering the mental and physical distress of burnout: she couldn't sleep, couldn't work well, was exhausted by caring for elderly parents and by a demanding relationship; none of her usual survival strategies were working. This is the kind of chronic stress that is linked to a whole raft of mental illness, chronic diseases, catastrophic health events and premature mortality. Luckily, my friend didn't succumb. Instead, her GP gave her a prescription for a month-long stay at a rehabilitation and health clinic where she could walk in nature and use the gym; eat organic, mostly vegetarian, food; swim and use the sauna and steam room; take part in psychological therapies; rest and learn coping skills. My friend says her treatment saved her sanity. She recovered her health and wellbeing and almost a decade later still has good connections with people she met there. My friend's treatment incurred a cost to the health system, sure, but in the long run probably saved a lot more than it cost, and also benefited her family, her employer, her society.

Before you seek a referral, I have to tell you: my friend lives in Iceland. And while that was an excellent way to look after an individual in a time of need, we need to think about how to look after the health of a whole society.

It turns out that Iceland is exemplary on that front too. It is one of a small number of countries, including New Zealand, Finland, Wales, Scotland and Canada, that have joined the Wellbeing Economy Governments alliance, dedicated to prioritising the wellbeing of their populations. Over everything else. None of them are perfect but they are trying to grow the right things that make a *healthy* good society. What could this look like?

Let's imagine a good society that prioritises the health and wellbeing of its population. Health care is free to everyone, including visits to doctors, hospital, and mental health care – providing high-quality services, minimal waiting times and free prescriptions. As well as a universal, publicly funded healthcare system, a strong emphasis on the social determinants of health and a focus on prevention keep the population healthy and in less need of care. Many people live to a hundred years in good health, and rates of chronic diseases are low. Those suffering from stress and exhaustion can be prescribed a month-long therapeutic break (at a spa, like my friend!), but chronic stress, fatigue and burnout are mostly prevented through a strong social security net and an emphasis on work–life balance, including a right to a shorter working week and a Minimum Income Guarantee. Active transport is encouraged, and more than half of all trips are by walking or cycling. A starter kit of bedding, clothes and toys is provided free to newborns. All school children of all ages receive free school meals, designed by nutritionists and based on food from local farms; free fruit, vegetables and milk are also provided. Mental health is supported by ensuring access to high-quality housing, income support and leisure facilities. All policy-making is geared towards optimising wellbeing and all public bodies are required to adopt transparent and effective measures to address the inequalities, including health inequalities, that result from differences in occupation, education, place of residence or social class.

We're in fantasy society territory – there is nowhere that all of this is happening – but all of it *is* happening somewhere, and it sounds very attractive. For most of us living in the UK, we have just a single piece of this healthy utopia: we have the free universal health care (although our satisfaction with it has fallen drastically[26] and it has a £37 billion shortfall compared to similar countries[27]). Elsewhere, there are so-called Blue Zones of people living exceptionally long and healthy lives – in Okinawa, Japan; Sardinia, Italy; the Nicoya Peninsula of Costa Rica, and the Greek island of Ikaria. You'll need to move to Germany or Iceland to be prescribed a residential spa treatment, or to Denmark for a 33-hour working week, or the Netherlands for a 29-hour one and the right to work part-time. More than half of all journeys are by bike or walking in the Netherlands and Switzerland, and Paris is the top cycling-friendly city for children. Finland has been providing a baby box of useful stuff (and the box doubles as a little bed) to all expectant mothers since 1938. Free school meals for all are provided in India; universal free school meals are designed by nutritionists using local farmed food in Brazil; and free fruit, vegetables and milk are on offer in schools in Estonia. The city of Trieste in Italy has pioneered successful community housing and support for those with severe mental illness. New Zealand and Finland have joined Iceland as Wellbeing Economy Governments, along with Wales, Scotland, and with Canada actively participating. In 2019, New Zealand adopted a Wellbeing Budget to change the way its economic success was prioritised and measured. Instead of just trying to grow GDP, the budget was aimed at improving the climate and environment, and at growing productive work, Māori and

Pacific opportunities, child wellbeing, and mental and physical health. The budget included $1.9 billion for mental health and more money for schools and hospitals, as well as climate-related projects, with investments less siloed within government departments and made with longer time horizons. Although a subsequent change of government has led to the Wellbeing Budget label being dropped, wellbeing objectives seem to have remained central to New Zealand's governmental strategy.

A gloomy picture in the UK, then, in comparison to other places? Health inequalities expert Sir Michael Marmot has said that 'our country has become poor and unhealthy, where a few rich, healthy people live'[28] and some of our health statistics are pretty appalling, as we'll see later in this chapter. The number of people dying before their time in the UK because of health inequalities is slightly more than if a plane carrying 250 people crashed with the loss of all life on board, every single day. We'd certainly be sitting up and paying attention if that happened. But, in fact, it's not all doom and gloom. Regionally and locally in the UK, additional pieces of that healthy good society are already in place, and they could certainly be scaled up if we chose. What follows isn't an exhaustive list, by any means, but there are some very encouraging examples.

Scotland and Wales are prioritising wellbeing as members of the Wellbeing Economy Governments, just like New Zealand, Iceland and Finland, and Scotland is seriously considering a Minimum Income Standard.[29] Both Scotland and Wales also have free prescriptions, and Wales is piloting a basic income scheme for young adult care leavers. And they might not have a sauna but there is a shining example of wraparound restorative care in the London Borough of Tower Hamlets: the Bromley by Bow Centre is both community hub and health centre, offering everything from vaccinations to support for job-seeking, walking groups, arts classes, and help applying for social security. Since the 1980s, Bromley by Bow have also consistently evaluated what they are doing, to see whether it is effective, as well as always ensuring that their work is shaped by what matters to the local community. New mums in Scotland get a Finnish-style baby box, as do new mums in deprived areas of Wales. Many UK cities are becoming a lot more bike-friendly, with twice as many bicycles as cars in the City of London during the working week, and a third of Cambridge residents riding their bikes three times a week. Both Scotland and Wales have adopted the Socioeconomic Duty of the 2010 Equality Act to consider how their policy decisions impact people experiencing socioeconomic disadvantage, as have forty-seven local councils, including Newcastle and North Tyneside, and eight out of ten councils in Greater Manchester. All primary school children in state schools in London have received free school meals since 2023, and some London boroughs provide free school meals in secondary schools as well.

So, there are pockets of good health-promoting policy right on our doorsteps, as well as all the good examples we can look to further afield. We can do this. And we have a lot of great stuff to work with.

Professor Simon Szreter from the University of Cambridge says that public health research and the people who do it are part of a 'self-conscious social and scientific movement . . . that has conspired to act on the public's health, locally, nationally, and internationally, for at least the last 2 centuries'. He goes on to say: 'We literally create our public health, our understanding of it, and our capacities to monitor and improve it through a continuous historical practice of acts of political will to bring about, fund, and support this area of knowledge and to act on what we learn about it.'[30]

What I will show in this chapter is that we have evidence, gathered over decades, as well as expert evidence-based consensus among the UK's dedicated public health academics and professionals, to inform policy to improve the health of the population and reduce inequalities in health. It certainly hasn't been consistently embraced by government (we'll have a quick look at the history of that), and the nation's health is consequently in a pretty parlous state. What will become crystal clear is that the ultimate responsibility for prevention of poor health and the optimisation of population health lies with those who have power in society. Not with you or me deciding whether to buy a two-for-one ultra-processed ready meal over a bag of apples, or whether we go for a run or not, and not even with our health service, but with the government shaping the context which supports our wellbeing. That means confronting the ideology of those who use the scaremongering language of the 'nanny state' to divert us from the state's responsibility and accountability for our population health. A good society should have both an excellent health service *and* a healthy population who have the least possible need of that service. Luckily, we know the solutions. Spoiler alert: the big three are a focus on prevention, giving every child a good start in life, and sufficient livelihoods for everyone.

A public health perspective: prevention and root causes

What we first need to get our heads around, in thinking about how to create a healthy good society, are two of the core principles of public health. These are the bridge between scientific evidence and the social justice of a healthy society. Those same core principles are driving the good practice we've been looking at in all of the fantasy healthy society examples and we'll see them again in later chapters, because these two principles apply much more widely, far beyond just health issues.

The first is a preference for prevention over treatment. A common analogy used in public health training is one of people on the edge of a cliff. If we don't do anything to stop people falling over the edge and crashing to the ground, we will have to pick up the pieces and treat the complex injuries of the fallen. If you are the person who has fallen off the cliff, obviously you want an ambulance, with health professionals, to come and pick you up and take you to hospital and treat you. But as a society, we are surely keen to prevent that kind of harm happening as much as possible, for both ethical and economic reasons. It would be expensive to keep a fleet of ambulances near the bottom of the cliff, as well as to have enough hospital beds and medical care available for the injured.

We could put a safety net somewhere below the cliff edge so that at least people falling off the cliff don't fall so far. We could perhaps help them get back up the cliff from the safety net when they have fallen (ladders? trampolines? climbing gear?). Even better, we could build a fence at the edge of the cliff, although if a lot of people are pushing up against it, it will have to be a pretty robust fence – and there will always be someone who manages to climb over for kicks, or to take a selfie. Much better would be to move everyone away from the cliff edge.

In public health terms, the ambulance at the bottom of the cliff represents acute medical care and *tertiary prevention* – this means things like rehabilitation programmes after a stroke, or a heart attack, or injury, or the management of chronic diseases like diabetes and asthma. The net halfway down the cliff represents *secondary prevention*, detecting and treating disease or injury early to reduce its impact – things like screening for breast cancer, or tracking and treating the sexual partners of someone newly diagnosed with a sexually transmitted infection. The fence at the top of the cliff represents *primary prevention*, preventing disease and injury before it happens – such as with vaccinations, or making people wear seat belts in cars, or teaching them about the dangers of smoking. All of these healthcare interventions cost money, few are 100 per cent effective (and some are a lot less effective), but, generally speaking, primary prevention is more effective and cheaper than secondary prevention, which is more effective and cheaper than acute medical care and tertiary prevention. Society should have a strong interest in favouring prevention over treatment and preferring prevention at the earliest possible stage. And this applies in education and social care, and in criminal justice, just as much as it does in health care.

Moving everyone away from the cliff edge represents an even more effective strategy, analogous to acting on the wider determinants of health, which I'll come back to shortly.

And that leads us to the second principle learned from public health that underpins the good society envisioned in this book: we need to focus not only on prevention, but to get people as far back from the cliff edge as we possibly can we need to be tackling the *causes of the causes*.

I gave a keynote address at the European Congress of Psychology a few years ago, in a large auditorium filled with delegates. It seemed to go well; I could see people nodding and looking appreciative in the front rows. But when I came off the stage, a man came up to tell me that I was completely wrong to have been talking about inequality as a cause of mental health problems. 'I trained as a physicist,' he told me quite forcefully, 'and we know about causation. There are all kinds of things intervening between inequality and mental illness, like education and people's behaviour, so inequality is not the cause.'

Now I am not a physicist, but surely even in physics there is a recognition of causal chains? A causal chain is a series of events where each is caused by the previous one; it explains indirect and remote causes of events, and we can have causal networks too for more complex patterns of cause and effect. I robustly defended my presentation of inequality as a root cause on a pathway to mental health problems, but I went back to my hotel and googled 'causal chains in physics' for reassurance. I got the example of fire causing smoke, which causes an alarm to sound. The fire doesn't cause the alarm to go off; it is mediated by the smoke. Similarly, a lot of physical processes happen between me flicking a switch and a light turning on, but I think it is fair to say that, at some level, I caused the light to come on, and if I didn't want it on, I shouldn't have flicked the switch. I then read a philosophical treatise on causality for further reassurance and found myself happily in agreement with Professor Nancy Cartwright that 'there is a great variety of different kinds of causes'.[31] So, if inequality leads to an uneven provision of quality education and affects some children's capacity or even inclination to learn, and that makes them withdraw from the learning environment and then become anxious or depressed, then for me, inequality has caused the mental illness. And if I tackle the root cause, the cause of all the subsequent causes in the chain, there will be less likelihood of some people missing out on the benefits of my preventive strategy and thus more problems will be prevented and more money will be saved, and more wellbeing created.

There is also a happy collateral benefit of tackling root causes – which is that the causes of the causes are generally causes of multiple outcomes; each root has multiple stems. If we lower levels of child poverty, for example, we will not only improve children's health, both physical and mental, but also their learning, their social wellbeing, their adult productivity and lifelong quality of life. You get more bang for your buck when you deal with root causes.

The health paradox: health care is LESS important than you think

As soon as we get to grips with the importance of prevention, and of acting on the causes of the causes, it ceases to seem so paradoxical that we Brits are not a healthy lot, despite having a National Health Service that is still ranked among the best in the world, and of which we are overwhelmingly proud (even if we're feeling more let down by it than usual at this time), and despite having a good level of spending on health care compared to other countries. We certainly all want the ambulance and medical professionals to show up if we medically and metaphorically fall off a cliff and need urgent care – and we also want healthcare services to treat our chronic illnesses and to screen us to detect disease, and to vaccinate us to prevent it – but the cliff analogy helps us to distinguish between the benefits of health services and medical treatments vis-à-vis the impact of prioritising prevention. This is why, perhaps surprisingly, health services play a much more modest role in ensuring population health than anyone might guess.

This was first pointed out back in the 1960s, by Thomas McKeown, a British doctor who argued, in the face of much opposition from his medical contemporaries, that the population had got healthier since the Industrial Revolution because of better economic conditions, rather than because of improvements in clinical medicine and public health interventions. McKeown was fond of pointing out that Britain started to get healthier long before modern medicine had anything like its later arsenal of antibiotics, effective surgical techniques and clean hospitals. He was particularly fond of showing that deaths from a particular cause, such as deaths from tuberculosis, had been falling way ahead of effective treatments becoming available. In the case of tuberculosis, the decline not only predated treatments coming online in the 1940s; it even predated by a long chalk Robert Koch's discovery, in 1882, of the bacteria that causes tuberculosis.

McKeown bashed away at the medical profession with his charts, and the medical profession bashed back, including the public health professionals who felt that he was ignoring their contributions: what Simon Szreter, Professor of History and Public Policy at the University of Cambridge, calls the 'foot soldiers . . . sanitary inspectors, housing officers, lady health visitors, trained midwives, and school medical officers'.[30] Academics have been debating ever since whether McKeown was right or wrong, but the contemporary consensus is that he was basically on the money – he might have got some of the details awry but he was spot on in his basic claim: that changes in the environment rather than medical developments were behind the long decline in mortality rates. Professor Szreter feels that McKeown, working through the 1960s and '70s, didn't feel the need to champion the achievements of public health science and interventions. He probably thought that the economic conditions he was living amidst – greater economic equality alongside an economic boom – would go on improving the health of the population, hand in hand, and eventually those two forces would create optimal public health. Perhaps he would have given more credence to the positive contributions of those foot soldiers of public health if he could have peered into the future, to where we're standing today . . .

Since McKeown, lots of research has tried to tease apart exactly how much of our health is due to health systems and health care. In a large review of research in the late twentieth century, leading Dutch epidemiologist Johan Mackenbach, and his colleagues, looked at deaths from what they called 'amenable causes' – things that medicine can properly treat, like hypertension, pneumonia and rheumatic heart disease. Deaths from those causes were declining faster than deaths from other causes between the 1950s and the 1980s, but variations in those same deaths between different places were consistently related to socioeconomic factors, like income and unemployment, and only weakly and inconsistently to healthcare resources, such as the supply of hospitals and use of care.[32]

Estimates differ, but typically analyses find that health services account for as little as 10–20 per cent of our health, and that number would probably be even lower if we looked at well-being, quality of life and healthy life expectancy rather than the very narrow definitions of health – like mortality and various kinds of diseases – that are typically used in such studies.[33] There are all kinds of limitations and assumptions in the methods used to come up with these estimates, but there is no need to quibble over the exact contribution of health care to population health: all the studies at least agree that it is much lower than the contribution of factors *beyond* health care.

And it's of course no good relying on healthcare services to create a healthy population if those services don't reach the people who need them most. One group of researchers wanted to understand why Canada, which, like the UK, has universal health care but spends only half as much per person on health care as the United States, has *much* better health than the USA, with Canadians living, at the time, 2–3 years longer than Americans (the advantage is now 3 years and 5 months to Canada).[34]

The higher spend on health care in the US simply wasn't translating into good access to care: Americans were less likely to have a doctor, more likely to not get the medicine they needed and more likely to have unmet health needs, and the Canadian system had fewer inequalities in access for low income or ethnic minority groups. Even within our own UK National Health Service, free at the point of care, we've recognised – since Dr Julian Tudor Hart first articulated his 'inverse care law' in the 1970s – that there is paradoxically less health care available in the areas of the country and among the people where it is most needed.[35]

What is perhaps less surprising than the small contribution of health care to population health, although equally widely unknown, is that most of what we, as a society, spend on health is not on prevention, or even on treatments that give people extra years of healthy life. We spend less than a tenth of our health budget on prevention, while healthcare costs increase the closer to death we get (which is not the same as simply being older), and are particularly high in the final month of life.[36] I've seen estimates that suggest that medical care expenses in the last year of life account for 10–20 per cent of all spending on health. In summary, then, health care doesn't do as much for population health as you might think; it's unevenly distributed, those who need most get least, and the money we spend on it is not wisely balanced across prevention and treatment.

Over the rainbow: the social determinants of health are MORE important than you think

Instead of being so focused on the health service we need to change our policy mindset. The way that we've been thinking about population health within epidemiology and public health, for more than three decades, is with reference to what has become known as the 'rainbow model'.

This framework describes how, as well as being shaped by our genes, our constitutions, and our healthcare services, our health is also affected by our lifestyles, community influences, living and working conditions and more general social, cultural and environmental conditions. Public health doctors and researchers call these the 'social determinants of health'.

The rainbow model puts individual factors that influence our health at the centre (things like our age, sex and constitutional factors, such as our genetic makeup); then, radiating outwards, individual lifestyle factors (things like our diet, physical activity, whether or not we smoke); social community influences (such as friendships and social support); living and working conditions (our jobs and our livelihoods, but also material things like housing and resources such as the health system); and then

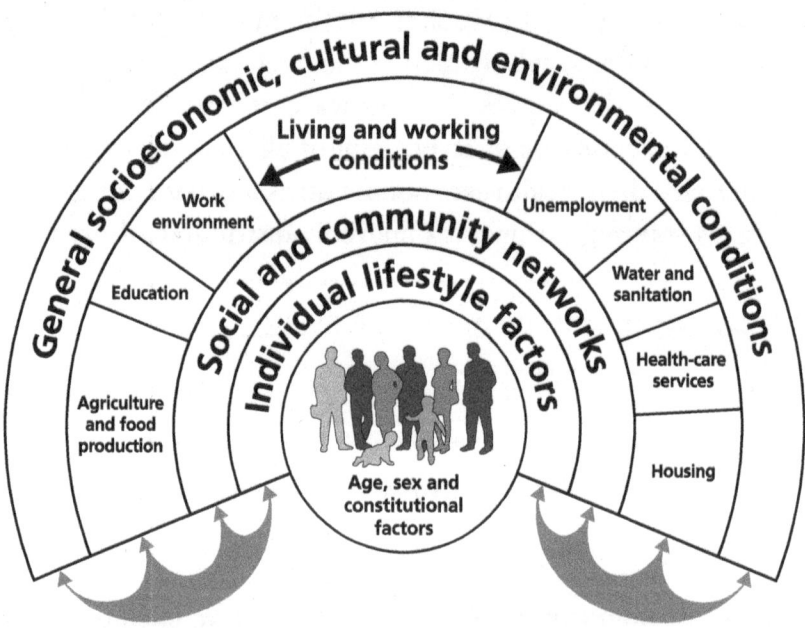

The Dahlgren and Whitehead 'rainbow model' of the social determinants of health.[37]

more general social, cultural and environmental conditions at the outermost layer (these are things like a country's level of development, the distribution of wealth and income, and the green environment).

Although the rainbow model is everywhere in public health, according to its originators it had 'a rather unpromising start to life'.[38] Researchers Göran Dahlgren and Margaret Whitehead had been commissioned by the World Health Organization Regional Office for Europe to produce a report to promote equity in health that would be easily accessible to politicians and policymakers. They came up with the rainbow model but were initially told it was too complicated for politicians and policymakers (!) and that they should leave it out of the report. So, the rainbow model was first published in some obscurity in a working paper by the Swedish 'Institute for Futures Studies' in 1991, where one of the authors was then working. But the model is actually so intuitively appealing that it quickly became ubiquitous in public health: everyone knows it, cites it, and understands it. Not so much outside of public health, though, even in clinical medicine. I once co-authored an opinion piece in the *New York Times*, drawing attention to the social determinants of mental health, only to receive an email from an academic psychiatrist who said he was going to have to rethink everything he had been taught. He was an expert on schizophrenia and had thought of it only in terms of a genetic disease, whereas there are clearly causes of schizophrenia embedded in the 'general socio-economic, cultural and environmental conditions' in that outermost layer of the rainbow. That's the layer where we find those 'causes of the causes' – the root causes of the causal chains and networks that lead to individual disease and population differences in the levels of different diseases.

Researchers and public health practitioners not only agree

on a social determinants of health model; they also agree on the importance of tackling those causes of the causes. In 2014 experts came together at a conference in Scotland to talk about the lack of progress in tackling health inequalities. Following the discussion, researchers at the University of Edinburgh put together a list of ninety-nine different proposals for addressing health inequalities. They sent the list to experts (I was one of them), asking which proposals would reduce health inequalities. Using those responses, they whittled the list down to the twenty proposals that had the most support, and then sent those to a larger group of experts to see what they thought. The consensus was that tackling inequality, poverty and deprivation had the highest likelihood of improving health and reducing inequalities.[39]

Drifting away from the causes of the causes

Despite this consensus, a lot of UK health policy over past decades has focused on targeting lifestyles and behaviours instead of the fundamental root causes. This is known as 'lifestyle drift' – the tendency for policy initiatives to drift from the broad social determinants (what we think of as upstream factors, away from the cliff edge, the causes of the causes) in the outer rings of the rainbow (to mix our metaphors), to the downstream, individual lifestyle factors in the inner ring.[40]

Focusing on individual lifestyles and behaviours is problematic for several reasons. It ignores or downplays the context that produces those lifestyles and behaviours in the first place, puts blame and responsibility on individuals rather than addressing the structural causes of their choices, and focuses on behaviours which are often extremely difficult to shift. Professor Len Syme at the University of California, Berkeley, used to teach us public health students to think about the effort it took to intervene to get one person to stop smoking; meanwhile, at the same time, somewhere else, a child would be trying their first cigarette. That's a good example of why public health experts agree that it is the wider social determinants of health that need to be fixed. I'm one of the many lucky social epidemiologists to have been trained by Professor Syme, who like all good teachers was as happy to share lessons he had learned the hard way as much as his successes. He had been part of the Multiple Risk Factor Intervention Trial (always abbreviated as MRFIT), which was set up to test whether or not changes in lifestyle could prevent deaths from heart attacks, the leading cause of death in the US in the 1970s. A vast number of men (but only men!), more than 350,000, were screened, and those considered to be at high risk of heart disease were recruited into the trial, where they were randomised to receive either a special programme of interventions, or just their usual care. The special interventions included counselling to help quit smoking, pharmacological treatment of high blood pressure, and dietary advice to lower cholesterol. The participants were then followed for seven years. To the investigators' surprise, there were no differences in death rates from heart attacks between the two groups. The way this is usually interpreted is that the social environment and health-related behaviours were changing in the general population over that time period (shades of McKeown). People were getting keen on physical activity (remember jogging and Jane Fonda demonstrating aerobics?); they were giving up smoking in droves, and switching from butter to olive oil. It's hard to pick up any impact of a behavioural intervention when the social and cultural context is changing everyone's behaviour.

To give just one more example, a lot of people focus on individual behaviours when they think about the problem of obesity.

They think people just need to be better educated about diet and nutrition and taught to cook healthy meals. Or more harshly, they need to stop being so lazy and eating so much junk food. But what we eat – what we choose and what we can afford – is shaped by culture, the food shops in the neighbourhoods we live in, the time we have available, how stressed we are feeling, as well as how much money we have. Some blame also lies with insufficiently regulated overproduction and marketing of energy-dense, low-nutrient foods, which make huge profits for the food industry. Supersized bag of crisps or chocolate bar anyone? Academic researchers describe this context as the 'obesogenic environment'. My colleagues, Dr Katie Pybus and Dr Maddy Power, at the University of York, working with parents on low incomes in the city of York, found that, contrary to tabloid portrayals, parents on low incomes knew all about healthy eating and wanted to buy good food and cook nourishing meals for their families. They just didn't have easy access to affordable, healthy foods.[41] Often living in inner-city neighbourhoods and without cars, they struggled to get to the supermarkets on the outskirts of the city, where better prices and more choice were available than in the city-centre convenience stores and shops oriented towards tourists. As one woman said: 'You have to spend time shopping around to get the best deals.' Many spoke of relying on debt (credit cards) to eat healthily and they used a high proportion of their incomes trying to feed their families well. Another woman said: 'The reality is that on Universal Credit I cannot provide the recommended amount of fresh fruit and vegetables per day for my children and I go without more times than not so they can have my share.' Far from being unknowledgeable or lazy, parents on low incomes were working hard and making sacrifices to try and do the right nutritional thing, but it's a hard struggle when you're poor in an obesogenic environment.

Nevertheless, we have more *experimental* evidence that we can change people's behaviours and thus improve their health. We have far less *experimental* evidence that we can change people's social and economic circumstances to improve health, which is clearly what we need to try and achieve. And it is experimental evidence that policymakers like best. Earlier, I described how researchers at the University of Edinburgh asked experts to select the interventions that they felt had the best chance of improving health inequalities, and they chose tackling inequality, poverty and deprivation. The top proposal was a more progressive taxation and benefits system; developing and implementing a Minimum Income Standard came second; and better support for more vulnerable populations, such as the homeless or those with mental illnesses, came third. As well as being asked to choose what they thought would work best, they were also asked whether or not their suggestions were *strongly* supported by available evidence. The experts still put a more progressive taxation and benefits system at the top, but second and third places were now given to smoking cessation programmes and to putting fluoride into residential water supplies. Out of the ninety-nine proposals that they were presented with, four economic proposals made the experts' top ten list for having the most potential benefit. There were no lifestyle-behavioural interventions in the list, but there were six proposals (three of which focused on tobacco) relating to lifestyle-behavioural change in the top ten list for having strong (i.e. experimental) evidence. A further question, about whether the policy proposals were 'appropriate' for the health inequalities research community to be promoting, suggested that the experts felt that the behavioural interventions were 'more politically and socially "feasible" than the kinds of "upstream", economic policies they felt were most likely to be effective'.[39]

A conundrum then. We're as certain as we can be that addressing the broadest and most upstream social and economic factors will do the most to reduce inequalities and improve the health of the population, but we haven't got a lot of *experimental* evidence that proves it, and it takes a lot of time and effort to generate relevant evidence through observing what happens to people in their day-to-day lives.

As just one example, researchers using a national study of people born in 1958 found that if they had even a small amount of savings in the bank at the age of twenty-three (just £200 in 1981, which would be £961 in today's money), ten years down the line they had a wider range of better health, social and economic outcomes than those who hadn't had those savings. For instance, at age thirty-three they had better mental wellbeing, were more likely to be employed, and were less likely to have had a marriage break-up. And this wasn't due to – among other things that might have differed between those who had savings and those who did not – differences in social class, being good at maths, having been ill as a child, having parents with financial problems, or not thinking there is much point in planning for the future. Although this analysis was first conducted with fairly traditional statistical analysis, it was re-analysed using state-of-the-art causal analyses (borrowed from economics), and the findings held up.[42] From this, policymakers could reasonably assume that if they could intervene to make sure that young adults had some savings, then good things would follow. This was exactly the research that underpinned the Child Trust Fund scheme that the UK Treasury ran for children born between 1 September 2002 and 2 January 2011. The government would put £250 into a tax-free savings account for the child, which family and friends could add to, with the money becoming available to the child at the age of eighteen. The first cohort of children to receive the money turned eighteen in 2020.

In 2022, the government reported that 6.3 million accounts were opened under the scheme, into which £2 billion had been paid; the value still in those accounts in 2022 was £9 billion.[43] This kind of evidence takes time to accumulate and sometimes we should clearly act on a balance of probabilities of not causing any harm and likely doing some good. The jury is still out on whether the Child Trust Fund scheme will have long-term benefits for health; it will be some years before we know that. Preliminary findings from the Child Trust Fund so far suggest only a modest impact on savings and saving habits, with many families seeming to have forgotten they even had the accounts.[44]

Best of intentions?

All governments, of course, claim to have the best interests of their citizens at heart and say they want to do what it takes to create a happy, healthy population working productively in a thriving economy. But just as all parents have their children's best interests at heart, while adopting widely different parenting styles, some of which work and some of which don't, so governments differ in their approaches, and their effectiveness, in promoting population health.[45] On the political right, broadly speaking, the ideological approach is to incentivise individual attainment, ambition, and healthy behaviour, spurring people on to help themselves to get ahead and believing that people's health is very much in their own hands. You could say that governments on the right have a preference for focusing on the inner rings of the rainbow. On the political left, the ideological focus is more on working to overcome relative disadvantage and perceived inequities, which sit more firmly in the outer rainbow. The right sees the state's job as empowering individual freedom to choose how to live. The left sees its job more in terms of intervening to get the context right to shape those choices.

We now have some fascinating long-term data from Australia, the UK and the USA, stretching back for more than a century, so that we can see which of these broad ideological approaches does best in terms of health.

Three studies focus on trends in suicide, which is one of the so-called 'deaths of despair' (drug overdoses, suicide, and alcoholic liver disease), in relation to changes in political regimes. The first to be published focused on the Australian state of New South Wales between 1901 and 1998, finding a significantly higher risk of suicide when both the federal and state governments were conservative, compared to periods with social democratic (Labor Party) governments.[46] This finding was replicated for Britain between 1900 and 1991, with significantly higher suicide rates during times of Conservative governments.[47] The third analysis examined both suicides and homicides in the USA from 1900 to 2007, finding that rates of both rise when the Republican Party is in power, and fall under Democratic Party administrations.[48]

Explanations of these patterns, from the social scientists who produced them, lie in causal chains that lead from the increases in unemployment and job losses common across these conservative administrations, through loss of status, and the experiences of feeling shame and inferiority, being disrespected, being regarded as worthless and 'redundant', and these in turn leading to the 'deaths of despair'.

To some extent, the health outcomes of those different regimes and political ideologies are collateral outcomes of broader economic policies. Governments aren't necessarily thinking about health except in terms of paying for health services, and so perhaps don't expect their wider economic and social policy to have these health impacts. This blind spot is largely structural: health departments focus on hospitals and treatments, while the Treasury designs tax policy, and housing ministries plan urban development – each operating in isolation from the others. Yet a finance minister's decision about benefit levels, or a transport secretary's choices about public transit, can have far more profound impacts on population health than many medical interventions. The departmental silos that characterise modern government mean that policies with major health consequences are routinely made without any consideration of those health impacts, creating a system where we treat the symptoms of poor health downstream, while inadvertently creating the conditions for it upstream. But historically, sometimes governments have acted with great intentionality to improve the health of the population.

Galvanised into action by the First World War, the British government responded to the poor health of the population that had been uncovered by the compulsory physical examinations of men who were being conscripted into the forces during the war. From 1916, successful mass programmes were put in place to reduce malnourishment and control tuberculosis.[49] Similarly, the Second World War spurred the foundation of the modern welfare state.[1] But the mass of research evidence on the 'causes of the causes' of good population health is still awaiting full implementation.

Uncovering the pattern

I'm turning now to some more recent history, because a theme that will run through this book is how governments use, or don't use, the best evidence available to them to improve society, and health inequalities are an object lesson in this regard. It is perhaps hard to imagine a time when health inequalities were not well known to the medical profession, to public health researchers, and to the government. But for a long time after the establishment of the National Health Service in 1948 it was assumed that making medical care and health services available to the whole population, free at the point of use, would eliminate any inequalities in health. Everyone assumed that there wasn't an issue to be addressed. If they thought about it at all, they tended to get the problem exactly upside down – there was a lot of talk about 'executive stress' and even doctors thought that there were more heart attacks at the top of society. This is a myth that hasn't been completely debunked in the popular imagination: one company's 'Executive Stress' vitamin and mineral supplement has only recently been rebranded as 'Unwind'.[50]

It was in 1976, when health inequalities were still widely unknown, that Richard Wilkinson, then studying epidemiology at the University of Nottingham, discovered widening class differences in health – with much higher death rates, including from heart attacks – at the bottom of society, not the top. Being short of money at the time, he entered his thesis for the annual 'Nutrition Award' run by a margarine manufacturer. He didn't win, but came second, and the excellent public relations machine of a major food company meant that the revelation of social class gaps in health, which were widening dramatically *despite* the NHS, got a lot of media attention. Taking advantage of that, Richard pointed out, in an open letter to the then-Secretary of State for Social Services, David Ennals, that Jim Callaghan's Labour government was presiding over the widest social class differences in mortality since the 1930s. The letter, published in *New Society*, asked the Secretary of State 'What can the government, and you . . . do about it'; and concluded: 'May I ask you to set up an urgent inquiry to look into these issues and to recommend action?'[51]

As a consequence of this and other calls to action, the UK government set up the world's first formal commission on health inequalities, a Department of Health working group under the leadership of Sir Douglas Black, which would result in the publication, in 1980, of the now-famous *Black Report*. This is a story widely known in public health but perhaps not beyond. Commissioned in 1977 by a Labour government, the working group completed its review in 1980, concluding that enduring social class differences in health ran across the whole lifespan and that the problem was not one which could be addressed by health services; rather, it needed to be addressed by 'radically improving the material conditions of life of poorer groups'.[52] Sound familiar? But that was not a message to suit the political ideology of the new Conservative government, led by Margaret Thatcher, which had been elected on a pledge to drastically cut income taxes and public spending. After much internal debate in government, the report was published in tiny numbers on a bank holiday, with a foreword from the new Secretary of State for Social Services, Patrick Jenkin, who thanked the group for its work, but commented that:

> It will be seen that the Group has reached the view that the causes of health inequalities are so deep rooted that only a major and wide-ranging programme of public expenditure is capable of altering the pattern. I must make it clear that additional expenditure on the scale which could result from the report's recommendations – the amount involved could be upwards of £2 billion a year – is quite unrealistic in present or any foreseeable economic circumstances.

He concluded by saying that he was making the report 'available for discussion, but without any commitment by the government to its proposals'.[53]

And that was that. What Jenkin did not consider, sadly, was how much those health inequalities themselves were actually costing society, in terms of productivity and spending on health and social care. Two billion pounds per annum, even in 1980, was not such a large portion of public spending, and it is highly likely that the right kind of investment for prevention would have saved money in the medium and long term. Trying to bury the issue backfired in the end, and the government's attempts to suppress the *Black Report* caused enough of a furore to ultimately put health inequalities firmly on the research agenda. From then on, British social scientists have led the world in producing evidence on the social determinants of health, furnishing us, over the years, with a wealth of evidence and blueprints for change.

Since the *Black Report* in 1980, we've had a repeated series of similar reports, including *The Health Divide* by Professor Dame Margaret Whitehead in 1987;[54] the report of the government-commissioned *Independent Inquiry into Inequalities in Health*, chaired by Sir Donald Acheson in 1998;[55] the 2010 government-commissioned Marmot Review, *Fair Society, Healthy Lives*, by Professor Sir Michael Marmot;[56] and *The Marmot Review 10 Years On* in 2020.[57] All of these were significant works of rigorous analysis and scholarship, laying bare, time after time, deep and entrenched inequalities in health.

And all, from the *Black Report* onwards, called for remarkably similar responses from government – the major calls to action have always been for investment in early childhood to give children a better, healthy start in life; a focus on prevention rather than treatment; and on ensuring an adequate income for all.

We've seen the reactions of the Thatcher government to the

Black Report, and their rejection of its recommendations, but from 1997, under New Labour, the government did develop a formal health inequalities strategy for England, which was put in place between 1999 and 2010. This strategy had targets: the aim was to reduce the relative gap in life expectancy between the most deprived local areas and the average, and to reduce social class inequalities in infant mortality. And what followed was indeed a slight decline in those inequalities.[58, 59]

What exactly were the policies that worked? There was actually a lot going on, so it's not easy to put a finger on which ingredients worked most effectively. We know that public spending increased, significantly, for both education and health services, with more health spending directed towards more deprived areas.

A key innovation was the introduction in the UK, in 1998, of Sure Start children's centres. These were centres funded by the government, located in disadvantaged areas and designed to offer one-stop support to families with children below school age. Parents could go to Sure Start centres and find a range of services, including health care and help with parenting, managing money, enrolling in training and getting help finding work.

Investment in early childhood is always high, and often top, of everyone's list for improving health because it is the most effective and the most efficient solution for which we have evidence. When I say the most effective, that's because we know, from a vast array of research, that what happens in early life (including in pregnancy) is foundational for lifelong trajectories of health and wellbeing. We know that children who experience physical and emotional abuse, neglect, and household dysfunction early in life have worse physical health, including heart disease and cancer, poor mental health, addictions, poor social functioning, and premature mortality. We also now know that the pathways linking these adverse early life experiences to later poor psychological and physical health work through the neurobiological effects of acute and chronic stress and through changes to the ways that genes are expressed (so-called epigenetic changes). Long-term epidemiological studies of health show us that pregnancy and early childhood environments influence the full lifespan risk of developing a wide range of chronic illnesses, like heart disease and diabetes, as well as mental health, with some effects even rolling over to future generations. For example, a baby born at too low a birth weight is at high risk of poor health for all of its life, but when that baby grows up, its own children and grandchildren also carry some higher risk for chronic disease. This means that the payoff from investing in support early on, like through Sure Start, rolls forward across generations, saving more and more as the years pass, leading to fewer and fewer families needing early intervention.

In Wales, the government has taken on board the idea of acting now for future benefit, passing the Wellbeing of Future Generations Act in 2015, with seven legally binding wellbeing goals, each with an attached minister, responsible for setting targets and reporting on progress. The Act requires all public bodies in Wales to consider the long-term impact of policy, to work better with people, communities and with each other, and to focus on goals which include making Wales more resilient and healthier. The Act works through public service boards in each local authority area, as well as the responsible ministers and a Future Generations Commissioner, and is credited with having influenced legislation, including banning single-use plastics; dropping a planned motorway extension and instead putting the money into sustainable transport; and creating a hospital-owned solar farm, which saves £1 million each year in electricity costs. In 2023 the Welsh government renewed its Future Generations strategy to try to do more and do it faster. The Act has certainly given a boost to Welsh pride in its ability to set a compass for a good society. As I completed this book, similar legislation was being introduced in the Scottish Parliament as a private member's bill, to promote consideration by public bodies of sustainable development and the wellbeing of future generations, including establishing a Future Generations Minister of their own.

Focusing on future generations might be one of the most effective ways to get people together in support for the sorts of solutions we need to build the good society. Even if we don't have children and grandchildren ourselves, we can see that there are strong social justice arguments to be made in favour of stewardship of our environment and a health-promoting society for those not yet born. Classical and neoliberal economic theory has always expected people to care more about short-term gains than the longer-term future. Economists call this discounting, expecting us to prefer to have goods and services today rather than be planning to have them in the future. But contrary to classic economic theory, most people are actually willing to pay to reduce future increases in climate-change-related deaths in Britain.[60] It seems that we do care about future generations. Sure Start was an intervention that got right to the heart of this issue.

By 2010, the Sure Start programme was receiving £1.8 billion a year in funding, but since then spending has fallen disastrously, by more than two-thirds, and many centres have been closed or scaled back. Of the 3,620 centres operating in 2010, only 2,204 were still going in 2023. The cuts and closures weren't evenly distributed: spending was cut by much more in the North of England – £412 per eligible child – than the £238-per-child cut elsewhere, increasing inequalities across the North–South divide.[61] Some areas hung on to their Sure Start centres (but had to make cuts to other services); others closed almost all their centres. Staffordshire, for example, lost 46 of 54, and Oxfordshire lost 37 of 45 centres. And this in spite of the fact that Sure Start worked as intended and was eventually shown to be cost-effective.

It takes time, of course, for something like Sure Start to show its true colours. It was based on a similar programme in America, called Head Start, which was known to have had a positive impact on children's health, their educational attainment and labour market participation, and to have reduced their involvement in the criminal justice system. For every dollar invested in Head Start, researchers estimated there was a return on investment of $7–9. But initial evaluations of UK Sure Start were disappointing. There seemed to be very small positive effects, and these were confined to the more middle-class families using the services. Children of single parents, teenage mothers or in families where no one was working didn't seem to be benefiting at first. But as the programme bedded in, the positive effects began to spread to even the poorest families: by 2019, the respected Institute for Fiscal Studies (IFS) had shown that there were significantly fewer hospitalisations among children who lived in a Sure Start area by the time they finished primary school;[62] the programme was preventing more than 5,000 hospitalisations every year, by age eleven, with the poorest children benefiting the most. By 2022 it was clear that centres like Sure Start were good for children's health, even in a country with universal health care – a fact which nobody had been sure of before – and that the effects were long-lasting: reductions in hospitalisations among teenagers were almost as great as among infants.[63, 64]

As well as improving health, by 2024 we could see that Sure Start was also improving children's educational outcomes, and this was especially true for children from the poorest families. The IFS reported that children who lived near a Sure Start centre had better communication and language scores when they started school; did better on standard tests throughout primary and secondary schools; and had almost a whole grade higher GCSE attainment at age sixteen.[65] Notably, Sure Start increased the prevalence of children with Special Educational Needs statements in primary school, but *decreased* them in secondary schools. This is exactly how it should have worked: access to Sure Start seems to have been increasing the likelihood that special needs were identified early, and addressed, and therefore there was less need for those services at later ages. All in all, looking across educational impacts, these alone returned almost a 10p in the pound benefit for every £1 spent, finally showing Sure Start centres were cost-effective, even without taking into account benefits on health, youth offending and children's social care.

The Nobel Prize-winning economist Professor James Heckman, of the University of Chicago, has shown that investing in early childhood, and the earlier the better, always pays off, and that it is the most cost-effective intervention we know of for reducing poor health, school dropout and crime, and promoting economic growth:

> The highest rate of return in early childhood development comes from investing as early as possible, from birth through age five, in disadvantaged families. Starting at age three or four is too little too late, as it fails to recognize that skills beget skills in a complementary and dynamic way. Efforts should focus on the first years for the greatest efficiency and effectiveness. The best investment is in quality early childhood development from birth to five for disadvantaged children and their families.[66]

The big idea to get hold of here is that investing in *other people's children*, and especially in other *poor* people's children, isn't just beneficial for them; it is good for us all. It isn't just the right thing to do; it's one of the best things we can do for a good society. We get a more productive economy, live in more crime-free communities, and because we save money in not having to treat health problems, we have more resources to spend on other things we might like in a good society (housing? public transport?). Our quality of life is better, even if we don't access Sure Start ourselves.

We need to get back to this kind of far-sighted investment, more funding for the Sure Start centres that still exist and the family hubs (very under-resourced) which replaced them in some areas, and which have a very similar model but serve children of all ages. We could go one better and expand the offering to create community hubs, like in Bromley by Bow, for people of all ages, everywhere. We may not be able to go as far as the Icelandic and German residential spa treatments for stress and burnout, but we could have community hubs in all communities, offering activities, skills training, therapy and social connections as well as preventive medicine, screening and other treatments. Remember that this *saves* money (perhaps if we did it for long enough we could have the spas as well!).

New Labour did more than just Sure Start centres; they introduced the minimum wage, which significantly increased the earnings of low-paid workers; 'Health Action Zones' were set up and funded as community-based multi-agency partnerships to tackle health inequalities. Child Benefit increased and Child and Working Tax Credits were introduced. Pensioners began to receive winter fuel payments. There's more . . . but the point is that a lot was happening, and with a purpose.

The biggest impacts of all of these policies were on child

and pensioner poverty. A million pensioners and around 600,000 children were lifted out of relative poverty during those years, mostly due to public spending on benefits and tax credits, with a smaller contribution coming from increases in employment. Relative poverty is usually defined as having 60 per cent or less of the median income within a country; it matters because relative poverty excludes people from full participation in society and is a psychological and social stressor. The IFS found that without that spending, poverty rates would not have fallen and might have increased, and although there was little change in income inequality over the period of New Labour, 1997–2010, it would probably have risen without those reforms to public spending.[67] But, sadly, following a dramatic fall in child poverty, and in poverty among working-age adults with disabilities after 1996, from 2010 onwards poverty began to rise again.[68]

New Labour got a lot right for public health, guided by their formal strategy, by changing the 'living and working conditions' that sit in the second-outermost ring of the rainbow, and through their focus on public spending and interventions such as Sure Start. However, by the end of their tenure there hadn't been time to accumulate all the evidence that would later come in, showing how effective their strategy had been.

With a change in government and the establishment of the Conservative–Liberal Democrat coalition in 2010, followed by Conservative governments from 2015 to 2024, came a change of focus, and the imposition of austerity: economic policy intended to reduce the national deficit. Deep cuts to public spending included cuts to local government, the education sector, and to the NHS. Austerity was then compounded by a cost of living crisis from 2021 onwards, and rapid rises in the costs of life's essentials – food, energy and shelter. Child poverty rates continued trending upwards and by the early 2020s there were growing numbers of poor children, poor pensioners and poor families. Close to a third of British children are now living in poverty, most of them in a home where someone is earning. In early 2024 the Joseph Rowntree Foundation reported that six million people were living in *very deep* relative poverty – that's living on less than 40 per cent of the median income: 1.5 million more than twenty years previously.[69]

The widest microscope

That is a short and very potted history of how we got to the state of health we have today. I don't want to club you over the head with a long catalogue of woeful health statistics (I could; there are a lot of them), but we do need to understand how low we have sunk. My colleagues in the ecological and sustainability sciences tell me that there is an ongoing debate as to whether people are more motivated to act by messages of climate apocalypse or by messages of optimism and agency. My aim here is to major on hope over pessimism, but we will need to occasionally look at some grim numbers along the way, to show us the baseline from which we can improve. And while some of the statistics might be depressing, because they come from comparing data across different countries, they do show us how much better things could be. This helps us to see what is feasible – a bit like the fantasy society constructions – and we can see which other countries have better outcomes, so that we know it isn't hopeless to aspire to something better.

Much of this data for comparisons comes from the Organisation for Economic Co-operation and Development. The OECD describes its purpose as building 'better policies for better lives'. For a researcher like me, it is a hub of high-quality data, providing evidence on social, economic and environmental issues for member countries. Sometimes called the country club of rich nations, the thirty-eight member countries are wealthy, developed market democracies – the set of countries that we'd expect to have the highest standards of living, and surely the set of countries that should be the benchmark against which we measure ourselves.

Let's turn our social microscope on to a few health indicators and see what they show us about what we need to turn around. Among those thirty-eight OECD countries, the UK ranked twenty-fourth for life expectancy, twenty-ninth for rates of infant mortality, and thirtieth for obesity.[70–72] Comparing mental health data is tricky, but on prevalence of depression we ranked ninth out of the fourteen OECD countries which had comparable data.[73]

We are obviously lagging far behind what we might think of as our peer countries. In Western Europe only people in Greece and Portugal have shorter lives, and we are living on average three years less than people in Japan, Spain and Switzerland.[70] After life-expectancy gains ground to a halt from 2010, we moved from having fairly average life expectancy among European nations to our present dismally poor standing. Then came Covid, and we all know how that went: the UK did badly, much worse than many other countries. Between the start of the real take-off of the pandemic in the UK, in March 2020, and the end of 2023, we lost 230,626 people to Covid.[74] And people do keep on dying with Covid. I thought I'd start writing this book about nine months before I actually got going, and more than 11,000 people died of Covid-19, just in that period. We've also fallen behind on infant deaths. The infant mortality rate is so sensitive to changing conditions that it is often described as a 'canary in a coalmine' for public health. We used to be quite high up in the international league table – in 1960 we ranked tenth best among OECD countries. Now we have dropped to twenty-ninth.[71] Even worse, the UK's infant mortality rate shockingly began to *increase* from 2010, at first for the most disadvantaged children,[75] then for everyone from 2014.[76] That downward trend then plateaued for a little while, but it is now increasing again: we saw more infant deaths in 2022 than in 2021.[77,78] This canary in the coalmine is squawking loudly.

Moving on to mental health. This is tricker to measure than other health issues because of debates about definitions, and variations in people's willingness to report mental ill health. Despite these difficulties it is clear that the trend is towards more mental illness of all kinds. Official figures are very out of date as I write: the most recent official UK survey is from 2014, with new data supposed to have been reported in 2023/24. Back then, 1 in 6 people over the age of sixteen in the UK were experiencing either depression or anxiety (the 'common mental disorders').[79] The World Health Organization claims that the pandemic has triggered a 25 per cent increase in depression and anxiety worldwide,[80] and in the UK many studies point to higher levels of mental health difficulties, including increases in suicidal thoughts. We have 1 in 5 children with a probable mental health condition, rising over recent years, with a particularly sharp rise for older teenagers. The pandemic really did make things worse: in just six months in 2021 there was an 11 per cent increase in referrals to mental health services for adults, compared to before the pandemic, and an 81 per cent increase for children and young people.[81] Over the same six months, there were 15,000 emergency/crisis care referrals for mental health for children, and admissions to acute wards in England for children in mental health crisis have risen 65 per cent in a decade.[82] Services are unable to cope and a group of charities have forecast that the crisis will cost the UK's young people over £1.1 trillion in lost pay over their lifetimes.[83]

Finally, obesity: more than a quarter of us are 'obese' (a body mass index greater than 30), going up to two-thirds when we include those who are 'overweight' (a BMI greater than 25), and rising to almost three-quarters among people aged forty-five years and above. The OECD estimates that we live, on average, two and a half years less in the UK due to our levels of obesity and overweight, that this accounts for close to a tenth of all our spending on health care and services, and reduces our labour market productivity by getting on for the equivalent of a million full-time workers every year.[84] All of this adds up to a hugely damaging impact on our national economy: GDP is lowered by 3.4 per cent (sounds small, but that's a loss more than three times what the entire agricultural sector contributes) and our taxes are raised by more than £400 per person per year. Our children are also too fat. All UK children have their height and weight measured when they start and finish primary school. In 2020/21, 10 per cent of 4–5-year-olds were obese and an additional 12 per cent were overweight; at ages 10–11 years that rises to almost a quarter who were obese and an additional 14 per cent overweight.[85] Overweight and obesity among children rose noticeably during the Covid pandemic and remains higher than before. This bodes extremely ill for our future population health and our economy. It's not an inevitable consequence of modern life: Japan, Belgium, Switzerland, the Netherlands and the Scandinavian countries all do much better.

Beyond average . . .

All of these average numbers mask the big inequalities in health between different groups of people that we first saw in the *Black*

Report in 1980, whether we look at different income groups, different ethnic identities or different parts of the UK. Inequalities of obesity are so stark that it is almost as if we had completely different tribes of people occupying high and low social classes. Nowadays, there are more adults and more children living with obesity in the most deprived, compared to the least deprived, areas of England – a gap that has grown over the past decade, and increased even more following Covid.[86]

There were inequalities of a similar scale in the not-so-distant historical past, but the body sizes typical of each class were completely reversed at that time. In Elizabeth Jane Howard's family saga, the Cazalet Chronicles, one of the characters describes being drawn towards socialism after observing how different men's bodies were when he was serving in the Navy during the Second World War:

> I noticed it when I was Number One on that destroyer. Men used to strip down, swabbing decks or in the engine room, or I saw them just when I was doing the rounds. I noticed that most of the Ordinary Seamen's bodies were a different shape: narrower shoulders, barrel-chested, bandy legs, scrawny-looking . . . They just looked as if they'd never had a chance to grow to what they were originally meant to be . . . compared to the officers they looked very different. It seemed to me then that except for our uniforms, we should have looked the same.[87]

There must have been a time when body size differences across social classes disappeared, before re-emerging as we see them today, this time with obesity and overweight and their negative health consequences concentrated in deprived areas. Really, we should all look the same. These changing patterns across time in our own country hammer home the point that health inequalities are not inevitable; they are tractable social injustices if we can just find the right levers to pull.

One final point to make about health inequalities is that they aren't simply a matter of the poor having bad health and the rest of us being okay. As mentioned in the Prologue, there is a finely graded socioeconomic gradient in health – running from worse health among the poorest, least educated or those with lowest social class in society, up to the best health for the richest, most educated, highest social class. Your health is likely to be somewhat worse than those at the very top, even if you're reasonably affluent, well educated, middle class. Every £1,000 increase in household income means a 3.6-month (a quarter of a year) increase in life expectancy, at each rung up the social ladder from bottom to top.[88] If you're on a high household income but just below the very top, you're still going to have a shorter life, on average, than those at the very top, and even those with average incomes are missing out on substantial numbers of years of life.

Obviously, people with very low incomes may be seeing their health suffer because they can't afford enough food or the right food, or warm, dry housing. These problems have increased with the cost of living crisis that began in 2021, but if only the very richest have optimal health, then it's clearly not only about the material resources your money can buy. We live shorter lives, in part, because of the psychological and social stresses of income inequality itself. That's one reason why, in the final chapter, I'll be proposing ways in which we can tackle inequality as well as poverty.

Putting our performance under the social microscope of international comparison shows us that not all rich countries have such deep and intractable inequalities, so there is no need for us to put up with them as some kind of inevitable consequence of modern life. A recent study looking at health measures, such as the number of people with multiple chronic conditions and mental health problems, found that Canada, Norway, and the Netherlands had *no* geographic inequalities in health.[89] Another up-to-date study found that the smallest disparities in men's deaths and deaths of younger people that were related to people's incomes were in the Nordic countries.[90] For women, such inequalities were smallest in the Central European countries.

Imagining a society with better health and without health inequalities, then, isn't a utopian pipedream: the international comparisons show that it's a realistic ambition towards which we can, and should, set our moral compass.

Money (That's What I Want) . . .

It's time to talk money. Not in the sense of whether or not we can afford to create a healthy population – remember that spending on prevention is cost-effective. But in the sense of whether or not some of us having more money, and some of us having less money, is good for health.

You'll have heard the old adage that money can't buy you health. Others would like you to think that it could, so they can sell you something. Aromatherapy to help you sleep? Crystals and gemstones to 'detoxify' your body? An infrared sauna to melt your body fat away? Wearable magnets to relieve pain? A DIY kit for some at-home cupping treatments? A vitamin supplement to improve your mental focus? On a well-known celebrity 'wellness' website I was able to add all of these to my shopping basket for a cool £1,268.25. Had I gone through with the purchases the only thing likely to have got healthier was somebody else's bank balance.

Most of what the so-called wellness industry would like to sell you is a pup. Most of what will really keep you healthy is non-commercial, free or cheap: friendship, doing things that give you a sense of purpose (preferably with other people), a walk or a run, a diet majoring on vegetables, fruits and wholegrains, laying off the tobacco and the booze. Those are the ingredients most likely to keep you, as an individual, well.

They are not, however, quite the same ingredients that keep a society healthy. To have a healthy society we, all of us, need to have enough money so that we don't have sleepless nights worrying about how to pay the bills. We all need to have enough money for a secure, warm, dry home that isn't overcrowded; we all need to have secure employment, with sufficient benefits available when we need them so that we don't feel precarious. We need to not be poor. What we need in our shopping basket for population health are the reports full of scientific evidence and a bagful of social justice.

It's perfectly possible to have a much healthier society, but it does require a mind shift. If we're really going to underpin health (and indeed productivity) through action on the social determinants of health, it is sufficient livelihoods that matter most. According to David Taylor-Robinson, Eric Lai, Margaret Whitehead and Ben Barr from the University of Liverpool, 'money is the ultimate personal medicine'.[76] We know that even short-term changes in financial circumstances have immediate consequences for mental health.[91]

After all, Sure Start centres in the UK, and Head Start in the USA, were located in poor areas because child development outcomes are worse in those areas and the evidence suggested that the return on investment would be greatest there. This is recognition of how much poverty matters. And if poverty matters so much, why not simply ensure that nobody is poor? If we take to heart the recommendations of the 2010 Marmot Review of health inequalities and the update published in 2020, among six areas of action to prevent inequalities in health, there is a repeated call for *ensuring a healthy standard of living for all*. There is a related call for action on *fair employment and good work for all*.[56, 57]

But calling for a healthy standard of living for all, for *everybody*, working or not, old or young, suggests we need a big and radical shift. It makes us ask what exactly we mean by a healthy standard of living and how we can make it available to everyone. There are existing standards that we could think about guaranteeing, including one called the Minimum Income for Healthy Living and another called simply the Minimum Income Standard. Both consider how much income people need to have to be able to eat a healthy diet (not just enough food), to exercise, and to have enough money for housing, transport, medical care and hygiene, and, crucially, to participate in society and social life, with dignity. As I mentioned at the start of this chapter, Scotland is seriously considering a Minimum Income Guarantee for all adult residents.

The two Marmot reviews stop short of recommending exactly *how* government should ensure a healthy living standard for all, but there are options. Some would focus on tweaks to current systems, such as tax credits or raising the minimum wage and social security benefits, to catch up the ground they have lost over time to inflation. But a truly radical shift could mean moving towards a universal basic income (sometimes called a citizen's basic income, or a guaranteed income), meaning that the state would provide some level of income to everyone (although the amount could vary with age) with no conditions attached. I'm going to come back to this later in the book, because some kind of basic income could be foundational for addressing more than just our public health woes.

Most importantly, I want to recognise the centrality of people's livelihoods to the health of our country and to emphasise the point that *other people's income sufficiency* underpins *your* health and wellbeing. At the risk of sounding like a broken record, less poverty and inequality equals more health, more productivity, less need to spend on medical care and other consequences of being poor, and so more money for good things.

Building a healthy society

What if, instead of organising government budgets around departmental spending, we structured them around wellbeing outcomes? This isn't a pipedream – New Zealand, Scotland, Finland, Iceland and Wales have already moved beyond GDP as their primary measure of prosperity, putting wellbeing at the heart of their policy-making. The Institute for Public Policy Research (IPPR) suggests we could allocate 5 per cent of public spending to a dedicated public health and wellbeing budget, creating a mechanism that would fundamentally reshape how we approach population health.

Such a wellbeing budget could be underpinned by comprehensive monitoring using tools like the new Office for National Statistics' Health Index, which tracks everything from life expectancy and infant mortality to happiness, life satisfaction, and access to nature. The IPPR suggests this index could be reported on in government budgets, spending reviews and fiscal statements, keeping population health firmly in the government's mind and at the forefront of public policy, and reaffirming the direct link between health outcomes and other social and economic factors.[92] With this framework in place, we could implement 'health impact assessments' for all new policies and spending decisions, ensuring that the health consequences of government action are visible before policies are enacted. This is another recommendation from the IPPR – and they point out that it can be done in advance, through modelling and simulation, for all and any new policies before they are enacted, and for all spending decisions above a set threshold.

In a nutshell, then, we could have a much healthier society by putting wellbeing at the heart of government policy, gearing towards prevention, investing to give children a healthy start in life, and focusing on making sure that everyone has sufficient income. I would recommend a national strategy, with targets and measures in place to make sure that we can monitor and evaluate progress. This contributed to the success of the 1999–2010 health inequalities strategy. The research institute Health Equity North, of which I'm an academic co-director, suggests expanding on the health outcomes that were targeted in that earlier period, so that they would include life expectancy and healthy life expectancy, the infant mortality rate, overweight and obesity, anxiety and depression and suicide rates.[93] These should be tracked in relation to deprivation and by ethnicity across regions and localities. As it can take at least a decade to see change in these measures, there should also be interim indicators to check that things are moving in the right direction. These could show early signs of progress – we should look at changes in household relative poverty rates and child poverty, inequalities in employment rates and educational achievement, and differences between groups in meeting recommendations for physical activity and eating five or more portions of fruits and vegetables every day. These data are already collected by national agencies and surveys, so we wouldn't have to set up new data systems to be able to track them. Health Equity North also recommends that targets be achievable, as well as aspirational:

they call for levelling up from the bottom-most 20 per cent of areas by deprivation to the national average, which would mean improving life expectancy by about five years for men and three and a half years for women in the most deprived areas.

None of this is technically difficult, but it does require political will. If we're going to commit to giving everyone a healthy standard of living, we'll need to have a highly visible and public conversation to increase understanding of the social determinants of health, and to create the space for discussion and debate to support healthy livelihoods. (In the final chapter of this book, I'll set out some of the mechanisms we could use to do this.) We're also going to need significant investment in the short term before we realise medium- to long-term savings, so that we can prioritise prevention and early childhood. (Again, in the last chapter, I'll set out where that initial investment might come from.) But we don't need new reviews or consultations. We could very quickly have a ten-year national strategy for action on the social determinants of health with the aim of reducing inequalities in health outcomes. We could then back this with a public health/wellbeing budget (the Institute for Public Policy Research's aforementioned 5 per cent of public spending), and monitor signs of progress on the causes of the causes. We would be kickstarting a virtuous circle which would raise the health and wellbeing of the nation, reduce inequalities and inequities, and lay the good health foundations for a good society.

Only connect

In his 1910 novel, *Howards End*, the author E. M. Forster used the epigraph 'Only connect!' to suggest that his characters could only live a life of good purpose if they could make a connection between the head and the heart, between thought and feelings. If we want, with good purpose, to create policies and institutions for our wellbeing, then we must also recognise the centrality of feelings, emotions, and of connections themselves, to any agenda for a good society.

So before moving on from thinking about health to looking at care, I just want to say a few things about one of the middle rings of the rainbow model, the one labelled 'social and community networks'. This chapter has focused on the importance of shifting policy towards the outermost rings as opposed to the inner ones, but it is in this middle ring that my own discipline of social epidemiology has perhaps made its biggest contributions over recent decades. We have found that poverty and inequality undermine social relationships, while learning that friendship is as protective of health as smoking is damaging,[94] that social support is vital to wellbeing,[95] and that loneliness is harmful.[96]

The evidence on social relationships and health is both striking and consistent. People with strong social connections have a 50 per cent increased likelihood of survival compared to those with weaker social ties – an effect size comparable to quitting smoking or losing excess weight. Yet we rarely talk about social isolation as a public health emergency in the same way we discuss obesity or smoking rates. When we do address loneliness, we tend to focus on individual solutions – encouraging people to join clubs or volunteer – rather than examining how our economic and social policies systematically fragment communities and undermine the conditions for meaningful connection. The closure of libraries, community centres, and local services; the design of housing that isolates rather than connects; work patterns that leave little time for relationships; the erosion of job security that forces families to move frequently – all of these policy choices flow from a fundamental structural problem: government departments operate with separate budgets, separate accountability frameworks, and separate success metrics. The Department for Work and Pensions measures benefit administration efficiency, not community cohesion. The Ministry of Housing, Communities and Local Government focuses on housing supply numbers, not whether neighbourhoods foster social connection. The NHS is held accountable for waiting times and clinical outcomes, not for addressing the upstream causes of ill health. Each department optimises for its own targets while inadvertently undermining the social fabric that underpins population wellbeing. Can we really expect joined-up health policy that addresses the economic and social determinants of health unless we radically restructure how government money, time and accountability are organised? Understanding these systemic barriers helps us to see why a health-focused society must also be one that prioritises community, relationships, and care – which brings us naturally to our next area of focus. The central importance of how we all relate to and look after one another is going to become even more visible and relevant as we start to think about care.

CHAPTER 2

All the Kinds of Care We Need

'Society should be organised around the assumption that it is normal for people . . . both to give and to receive care.'

Susan Himmelweit

I care, you care . . . who cares?

I've never been keen on essays that begin, in sophomoric style, with a dictionary definition of the subject, often excused by quoting Voltaire ('first define your terms'). And yet . . . when thinking about the terms 'care' and 'caring' it is perhaps useful to remind ourselves that as well as all the meanings related to providing for the health, welfare, maintenance and protection of someone or something, 'care' also has the meaning of doing something correctly, or to avoid damage or risk, as in 'she planned this chapter with great care'. And both kinds of care, nurturing and doing something right, can be what we mean when we use the words 'careful' and 'carefully'. Care also has the meaning of attaching importance to something, as in 'I don't care whether this is a rather hackneyed way to start a chapter'. Here's the question for this chapter: do we take care (in the third sense) to ensure that care (in the first sense) is provided with care (in the second sense) to those who need it?

Picture, for a moment, a room in a care home for the elderly. Older people are sitting in chairs, in a big room, doing nothing – I've seen depressing scenes like that in care homes I've visited. But what if the doors to the room opened, and in bounced a group of lively pre-schoolers, greeting their elderly friends with high-fives and hugs, before all ages get going on a day filled with exercise, dance, singing, games and story-telling? That's the daily scene in Kotoen, an intergenerational care facility, which also includes adults with disabilities, just outside Tokyo, Japan. In the Netherlands, university students live rent-free in an elderly care facility, Humanitas, in exchange for interacting with their older neighbours. The elderly residents are now just as likely to be gossiping about the young people's love lives and comings and goings as chatting about their own health problems; the arrangement has, says the centre manager, brought a twinkle back to the older people's eyes. Intergenerational care facilities are popping up worldwide and can be found everywhere from the USA, Canada and Australia to Denmark, Belgium and Singapore. Something similar got started in Wandsworth, London in 2017, where the Apples and Honey intergenerational preschool and day care is located in the garden of Nightingale House, a care home for older people, with young and old interacting every day. Belong Chester, in Cheshire, is another intergenerational care community with both a care home and a nursery, as well as apartments for older people, the whole enterprise being carefully evaluated by university researchers. This kind of care is explicitly based on values of connection, inclusion and care that have everything to do with human flourishing and nothing to do with squeezing out as much profit as possible from the care system.

It took me some time to recognise the importance of explicitly naming the values that I believe should be the foundations of a good society. I think that was primarily because I thought it was obvious – surely all right-thinking people hold the same values – but also because my own research is grounded in what can be found out and verified by observation or experience, and so I'm perhaps biased against arguments arrived at only by theory or pure logic. I've at times felt frustrated (or alienated?) by the efforts expended by philosophers on debating ethical principles, rather than simply looking at what works.

Some years ago, I was invited to take part in a series of workshops exploring the philosophical significance of economic inequality, and watched with bemusement the debates on the ills of inequality that took place without reference to, or seemingly much interest in, evidence. (It reminded me of the scene in the BBC's adaptation of Susanna Clarke's fantasy novel *Jonathan Strange & Mr Norrell*, when a would-be magician seeks answers from the Learned Society of York Magicians as to why magic has disappeared from England. Can they actually *do* any magic, he queries – whereupon they round on him with the retort that they are 'theoretical magicians' . . .) But I think I've become a little wiser, or disillusioned, over the years and I see that the values that I think underpin a good society are not necessarily a universal given and so *do* need to be stated clearly. That surely wasn't necessary in relation to health: who wouldn't agree that ensuring optimum levels of health is a priority in a good society? But looking at the quote which opens this chapter – 'it is normal for people . . . both to give and to receive care' – I'm not sure *that* would be a truth universally acknowledged.

I believe, based on both the evidence that I'll share throughout this chapter and on a normative ethical theory of care[97] (which simply means a theory which tells us what is right or wrong, and why), that a good society is a caring society as much as it is a healthy society. It recognises that we (our wellbeing and security) are shaped by other people as much as by our own actions and qualities, and so we need to embed principles of reciprocity into our systems. The good society places the importance of relationships, attention to vulnerability, attentiveness to one another, and care, firmly at its heart.

This chapter includes different kinds of care. It covers systems of formal care: childcare for babies and little children, mostly to provide them with care while their parents are working; social care for children who need something other than, or as well as, parental care; and social care for adults, often at the end of life. Social care systems are also needed for both children and adults with disabilities and/or neurodiversity, and with mental or physical health conditions who need something beyond medical care. It might not seem like these different systems have much in common, but they do, because how we prioritise them, value them, and fund them is driven by the moral weight we give them. And, practically, as in those intergenerational care facilities at Kotoen, Humanitas, Apples and Honey, and Belong Chester, they might be combined in ways that are good for everyone.

These systems can be structured quite differently. Social care is sometimes provided in people's homes, as when social workers visit homes to help parents who are struggling to look after children, or carers come to the homes of elderly people to help with personal care such as washing, dressing and getting up or going to bed. Sometimes care is provided in day centres or residential settings (children's homes and nursing homes). Some care is about providing material things, like mobility aids or adaptations to people's homes, or about imparting knowledge, giving information and advice. But across these different systems, 'care' is also about providing nurturance, support and, indeed, love.

There is much nostalgia for a time, viewed through very rose-coloured spectacles indeed, and located at various and nebulous times in the past, when families and communities supposedly cared for everyone, from cradle to grave, as a matter of course and without recompense, in extended family structures. That may well have worked for some, but it most surely didn't work for many with challenging needs, or without family (and remember George Burns' quote on the claustrophobia of some families: 'Happiness is having a large, loving, caring, close-knit family in another city'). This is anyway an irrelevant romanticism in our contemporary society, where most parents work, many children and adults have complex needs, and we have a rapidly ageing population. There are, of course, vast numbers of people providing informal and unpaid care to family members and others. The 2021 UK Census came up with a figure of 5.8 million, or about 9 per cent of the population, providing unpaid care, and this doesn't include parents caring for infants and children younger than school age. This chapter is also about the interconnections between unpaid care and formal care systems, and about how these forms of care interact to provide what is called the 'care economy'.[98]

There is no doubt that the formal care system in Britain, in its entirety and in its distinct parts (childcare, child and adult social care, formal and informal care), is broken – and I mean broken as in not working, not providing careful care, as well as fragmented so that it doesn't work coherently, either internally or in partnership with other systems, such as the healthcare system or the education system.

In the Prologue, I described how life expectancy stalled from around 2010–11 onwards. In 2017, I was one of a group of researchers looking at rising mortality rates from 2015, a period that had seen the biggest rise in death rates for almost fifty years.

Most of those deaths were among frail, elderly people. We found that delays in hospital discharges were accounting for up to a fifth of those excess deaths – about 8,000 every year.[99] And why were there delays in hospital discharges? Because there was nowhere for those patients to go. Not enough nursing homes, not enough intermediate or what is known as 'reablement' places, and long delays and lack of resources for arranging support for care at home. This is what is derogatorily described in the media as 'bed blocking' and at the time we were writing there were about 4,500 people trapped in hospital on any day, who were ready to be discharged but had nowhere to go. As well as having knock-on negative effects on people who could not be admitted to hospital because there were no free beds – and we've all seen the horror stories of patients dying on trolleys in hospital corridors or in ambulances parked outside – being in hospital when it is more appropriate to be receiving a different kind of care elsewhere is also bad. You might pick up an infection you wouldn't have been exposed to elsewhere; your cognition, resilience and ability to cope can decline in an unfamiliar environment; you might feel stress, anxiety, loneliness or despair. The NHS declined to comment on our findings and the Department of Health simply said that they were 'clear that no one should have to stay in a hospital bed longer than necessary'.[100]

But this, of course, is not really a health system problem; it's much wider than that. We should view those 8,000 or so excess deaths as the tip of an iceberg, or a canary in a coalmine, just as with the infant mortality data I laid out in Chapter 1 – our social care systems are not adequately meeting the needs of the most vulnerable in our society and those deaths give us a hint about the scale of the problem. For every death attributable to 'bed blocking', there are also countless numbers of people who are not in hospital but are trying to get care, as well as all those who *are* receiving social care but are being failed by its inadequacy. So the population I'm concerned about are all of those who cannot access *any* care, can't get *enough* care, or are not getting *good* care. And good care, of course, is preventive: it promotes and preserves wellbeing in ways that keep needs and costs from escalating. This is another reason, beyond values, for thinking about all these different kinds of care systems together – they have all been vastly undervalued, at great (if often hidden or ignored) cost. And so the fundamental solution to all of them lies not in creating agreement that they should be a priority (we're probably there already), but in how we use that consensus to unlock the means of paying for it all.

Caring for the next generation

Let's start with those who need to be cared for because of their very young age. For at least the last three-quarters of a century, scholars and parents have gone back and forth and round and round, debating whether little children should be at home – especially home with mother – or in some kind of group care, usually called nursery care, or just simply childcare in the UK. Ever since John Bowlby, psychiatrist and psychoanalyst, came up with attachment theory in the 1950s, suggesting that the social and emotional development of babies was dependent on them having a strong attachment from birth with a primary caregiver, everyone has wrestled with the question of who should be looking after infants, toddlers and preschool children. There has been serious controversy surrounding some research purporting to show that little children who spend more time, or more time from a very young age, in any kind of group childcare are more likely to have psychological and behavioural problems, including more aggression and perhaps later criminal involvement,[101–103] with other studies contesting these conclusions and finding no ill effects.[104] One large American study which took place between 1991 and 2009 found positive effects for cognitive development of being in group childcare after eighteen months of age, but negative effects for children who were in childcare at younger ages, and negative effects on behaviour of receiving group childcare at any age, although this diminished over time.[105]

These are the sorts of findings that fuel the views held by some groups, including some on the far right, some fundamentalist Christian sects, and also those who have been called the 'tech-influenced hypermasculine conservatives', that women really shouldn't be in paid work: they should be at home and looking after children (in the run-up to the 2024 US presidential election, candidates were asked about their plans for childcare; Donald Trump's running mate, vice-presidential candidate J. D. Vance, said parents should get help from grandparents and other relatives and suggested that childcare workers don't need as much training as they currently get. Trump himself simply rambled . . .[106]).

But for the most part, in most rich countries, there is little discussion in policy circles about support for stay-at-home parents – the assumption has firmly taken hold that society wants/needs everyone in employment and this is rarely challenged. The 'Wages for Housework' movement, which from the 1970s advocated for women's unpaid labour and caring work to be recompensed, feels like a very distant memory, despite still being an active campaign. And whether by choice or economic necessity (wage increases not having kept up with the rising cost of living), most parents in the UK are working: in official statistics for 2021, reported in 2023, 76 per cent of mothers and 92 per cent of fathers with children under eighteen were working.[107]

From 2020 onwards, in families where both parents were working, the most common pattern of employment was for both parents to be working full-time. Numbers are somewhat lower for single parents: only two-thirds of them are working, but government welfare and benefits policy is very much geared towards getting them into the labour force as well. Numbers are also lower for parents with babies rather than with older children, but still almost half of mothers with a child less than a year old are employed full-time (although they will almost all be on maternity leave for some of that year). The demand for childcare is clearly high.

There are good societal reasons for wanting a childcare system that supports parents, and especially mothers, to work if they want to, as well as a welfare system and labour economy that supports parents to choose not to work during their child's earliest years. Some of these reasons are to do with gender equality – good and affordable childcare enables women to access paid work and maintain their career progression, reducing the gender pay gap. This gap rises every year spent raising one's offspring, up to 33 per cent by the time a firstborn child is twelve years old, as mothers accumulate the impact of missing out on promotions and having less work experience.[108] Mothers who choose to work part-time after having children see virtually no progression in their wages and on average end up working below their skill level.[109] Only a third of working mothers say that they have some kind of special working arrangement, like flexible working hours, job-sharing or shorter working weeks, to help them balance paid work and unpaid childcare. If mothers leave the labour market or work less than they want to, the economy takes a productivity and capability hit. Governments also want parents to work because they want to keep down the cost of welfare and benefits paid to parents who are not working.

That's the demand side, then, with parents and governments aligned in needing widely available, affordable childcare. But is the supply of such childcare sufficient to meet the demand?

The baby balance sheet

I remember how quickly my pleasure at being awarded a scholarship to undertake a research degree at the University of California turned to dismay when I realised that it would not go far enough to cover even part-time childcare costs. (And what about rent! food!) Parents in the UK have access to at least some free childcare, but just like I found all those years ago, it simply doesn't stretch far enough to meet many families' needs. From September 2025, working parents are entitled to thirty hours of free care for children aged from nine months to starting school. But even so, on average, UK families spend more than 25 per cent of their household income on childcare, whereas the average for the OECD countries is around 10 per cent. If you're working full-time and need to get to and from a nursery to your workplace, you're actually likely to need as much as fifty hours of care per week; so even with recent boosts to the free childcare hours, you still might have to find the money for twenty hours of additional care every week, and that's going to cost, on average, something like £8,000–10,000 in 2024.[110] In the UK, a full-time nursery place for a child under the age of two currently costs around £15,700 a year, and can be much higher, well over £20,000 in some places, like London.

And good luck finding that free care. In their twenty-third annual survey of childcare, the charity Coram Family and Childcare asked local governments if they had sufficient availability of childcare for different groups of children.[110] Worryingly, local authorities saw a decrease in availability in *all* categories between 2023 and 2024, reporting that they only had 35 per cent of the places they needed for children under the age of two; only 16 per cent of what was needed in rural areas; and only 6 per cent (and I'm sorry to say that is not a typo) of the places they needed for children with disabilities, this latter kind of more specialised care having decreased by 12 per cent in just one year. And why are the numbers of childcare places declining? Because the costs of providing care have risen (costs for staff and energy most significantly) beyond what government provides to fund those free hours. Some childcare providers are charging families who are accessing free hours, which they shouldn't do; others are cutting costs by increasing staff-to-child ratios, which is also bad news.

Although there are still some ambiguities in the research evidence related to group childcare, what is not in doubt is that the quality of that care matters a lot. And quality means *how* children in childcare are cared for – whether or not the caregivers are kind and responsive to children, talking to them, reading to them, playing with them and showing affection. And that is difficult to provide if there are insufficient staff for the number of children, or poorly trained or inexperienced staff.

You might think that it would be a given that regulated childcare, staffed by trained providers, would be of good quality. But sometimes we get shocking stories of childcare settings that have failed to provide this kind of attentive and responsive care even though they have passed inspection (childcare settings, like schools, are regulated by Ofsted). Nurseries can be operating for up to thirty months before they are inspected, and after a first inspection need only be inspected again once every six years – this is a system lacking in capability to truly reassure parents about quality. In 2024, two childcare workers at the same nursery in Stockport, which had been rated as 'good' by

Ofsted five years earlier, were jailed: one for 'wilfully ill-treating children' and one for manslaughter, after nine-month-old Genevieve Meehan died there, having been tightly swaddled and strapped face down to a beanbag. What shocked as much as the heavy-handed physical ill-treatment of several babies caught on CCTV were the uncaring ways in which the two women spoke to and about the tiny children in their care. Most of the time, of course, infants and toddlers in regulated nursery settings will be cared for with tenderness and attentiveness, but that will be far more likely when the ratio of caregivers to children is high, when staff are well trained and supervised, and when the caregiving staff don't change frequently. That's the kind of care we want our children to experience in formal childcare and that's the kind of care that research consistently shows makes a difference for child outcomes.

The fantasy childcare game

If we widen our comparative research lens to look abroad to other countries, we find that, yet again, we're not where we should be as one of the richest economies in world. In the Netherlands, 70 per cent of children under the age of two are enrolled in childcare, compared to only 45 per cent of the UK's 0–2-year-olds; Dutch children are not, however, enrolled for a lot of hours, as many Dutch mothers work part-time and so don't need full-time childcare. Childcare enrolment rates *and* weekly hours are high in societies like Denmark and Norway, where the norm is for both parents to return to work full-time after parental leave and childcare is heavily subsided by the state. Some countries have fairly low enrolment rates for the under-twos because parental leave is generous – in the Slovak

Republic, for instance, parents are entitled to parental leave until their child is three years old and six years if the child has a long-term health problem; in Finland mothers get a month of pregnancy leave before a child is born and parental leave after the birth is for 360 days, split across both parents if a child has two involved parents. UK rates of enrolment are so low because our (regulated) childcare costs so much – parents seek out cheaper, informal and possibly lower-quality options or work less than they would wish to, because they can't afford to do anything else. And, of course, the negative impact of high childcare costs is felt most keenly by poorer parents.

Paul Lindley, author of *Raising the Nation*, writes that the case for quality universal childcare is 'so compelling . . . that if I had my last public pound to spend it would be in [that]'.[111]

Good childcare costs good money, of course. If, as a society, we want to make high-quality childcare universally available, that means having lots of nursery-care places available in all localities, sufficient to meet need; providing the hours and the flexibility that parents require in order to exercise their preferences about paid employment (and other activities that contribute to society); and ensuring that these care needs are provided by well-trained and committed staff, which means paying them properly. Childcare workers in the UK are among the lowest paid in society. According to Payscale, a company that provides salary data, the average pay is £9.22 per hour in 2024, which is less than the National Living Wage paid to those over twenty-one years old, because so many childcare workers are young and/or on apprenticeship schemes.[112]

Other countries clearly manage to afford good universal childcare without any damage to their economies or wellbeing, but we also know that it would be worth our financial while to invest in a national high-quality childcare offer, given the direct benefits to the economy. I made this point in relation to health in Chapter 1, but it bears repeating. The think tank New Economics Foundation (NEF) says that this is the 'highest returning investment a government can make', which is quite a statement, citing work by American economists published in *The Quarterly Journal of Economics*.[113] Investing in high-quality universal early childhood education and care pays off more than investing in health insurance, or any other kind of education, or training, or cash transfers, or in-kind transfers like housing vouchers. NEF estimates that for every £1 spent on good childcare, society gets a £7 return on that investment, mostly because outcomes are improved for poor families and this return means that, even if we fund it entirely through borrowing, the investment pays for itself.[114] Infrastructure projects, they say, are thought to be good value if returns on investment are greater than 4:1, so 7:1 for good childcare is stupendously good value. As NEF also says, 'ensuring every child has guaranteed access to early years education will lead to higher earnings, more growth and the Treasury gaining money in the long run'. NEF points out that, at the moment, as the free childcare offer is only for working parents *and* affordable childcare is hard to find, *and* it is extremely difficult for families on Universal Credit to claim for the childcare costs that they are entitled to (only a quarter of them do so), as a society we're losing out on the benefits to society of better social and economic outcomes for low-income children and their parents.

We (rightly) value our National Health Service, but we need to be thinking seriously and campaigning for other universal services that would create a good society. If universal early childhood education and care will pay for itself through returns on investment, and meet social justice targets, and improve the wellbeing of the whole society, then we must enable that to happen.

A National Children's Service

What could it look like, then, a system that met the needs of children and parents and society? Consider our pride in the National Health Service and its core values, which include quality of care, improving lives and ensuring that everyone is treated equally and that everyone's needs are met. A 'National Children's Service' would support the caring relationships within families that ensure optimal child development and wellbeing. It would also be the scaffolding on which professional standards and conduct, and the institutional infrastructure for child-centred public policy, could be built. Just as a National Health Service provides a framework for the consistent quality of care and services (well, that is at least the theory and the ambition), so could a National Children's Service – if integrated across national, regional and local government – begin to address the fragmented nature of current provision. A National Children's Service could give coherence to funding streams, content of care, equality of access, regulation and standards, accountability, and workforce development. The Scandinavian countries, which have very high levels of child wellbeing, put children at the heart of government, with departments and Ministers for Children, and representation of young people and their needs across different government departments (we don't, after all, want children's issues only addressed within a siloed 'Department for Children', even if we want such a department to keep these issues high on government agendas). The Nordic Council of Ministers has a transnational strategy that aims to make the whole region 'the best place in the world for children and young people'. There is something similar in the State of Victoria in Australia, where a Children's Services Coordination Board makes government departments – from the Treasury, to Justice, to Education, to Housing, to Health – all accountable for child wellbeing and development. No country in the UK has a Cabinet-level minister for children and families.

The Welsh government, however, does have the exemplary Wellbeing of Future Generations Act (2015), described in Chapter 1, which gives a legally binding common purpose to national, local, and other public bodies in Wales in pursuit of wellbeing goals. Many of their national wellbeing indictors focus on the needs of children, as well as addressing poverty and deprivation. A similar Act at UK level would give weight to a care agenda for children.

We used to call it women's work

Gender equality needs to be central to reforms to early life care and education.[115] This is because there is no such thing as free care and if society doesn't provide it then someone will have to look after the children and that has, now and in the past, mostly fallen to women. Whether women choose to look after their children full-time, or work part-time because full-time childcare is too expensive, their lifetime earnings and pensions are compromised. And because caring for children as paid work has traditionally been women's work, it is low paid and undervalued. The high cost of childcare is partially responsible for the falling birth rate which means that the UK will, in future, have the economic challenge of a smaller workforce and an unbalanced population age structure (more on that later in this chapter). Swedish journalist Katrine Marçal puts it well:

Feminism's best-kept secret is just how necessary a feminist perspective is in the search for a solution to our mainstream economic problems. It is involved in everything from inequality to population growth to benefits to the environment and the care crunch that will soon face many ageing societies. Feminism is about so much more than 'rights for women' . . . The next step is to realize what a massive shift this has been, and to actually change our societies, economies and politics to fit the new world we have created . . . We don't need to call it a revolution; rather, it could be termed an improvement.[116]

Professor Heejung Chung, of King's College London, reviewing the research on fathers' involvement in childcare, found that it is good for society for men to be more involved in looking after their children, both through impact on the children themselves – in terms of their emotional and psychological development, educational outcomes and future careers – and family relationships, with less family breakdown.[117]

It seems clear, then, that a properly functioning National Children's Service must rest on a firm foundation of paid parental (and adoption) leave for both mothers and fathers (or whatever combination of parents/guardians are caring for each child).[118] Some families are already entitled to good parental leave and support through their employers, but this is very uneven. Some of this support needs to kick in during late pregnancy, and men and other parents should have equal rights with mothers to attend pregnancy care and classes. Currently, pregnant women are entitled to paid time off for antenatal care, but dads are only entitled to attend two appointments, and without pay. If fathers and other parents can't access the same services as mothers in the lead-up to parenting, it will be harder for them to care as equals.

In families with more than one parent, we need to support them to be involved in parenting from the earliest possible stage. Some combination of statutory paid leave entitlement should cover the child's entire first year, and fathers/other parents need to be brought into the leave system by incentivising them to take their share of that leave. This could be achieved by splitting a thirteen-month leave entitlement across both parents on a use-it-or-lose-it basis (in other words, you get fewer months unless both parents take leave; the entitlement can't be transferred from one to the other). Parenthood would be given a good start by requiring *both* parents to be on leave for the first month of the baby's life and then providing a further eleven months of entitlement to split evenly. Paid parental leave should be for all parents and guardians whether they are employed full- or part-time, studying, training, unemployed, or whatever, and pay should be at some sensible level of normal salary or self-employed equivalent or a Minimum Income Standard level. These changes would start to take some of the gender inequalities out of the system, which is good for children, parents, the economy and society. It's not beyond the wit of policymakers to establish such a system and quickly. Think about how swiftly we put in place a national scheme for furlough payments during the Covid-19 pandemic.

To maintain parents' ability to choose to work or to continue to care for children, the end of a full year's entitlement of parental leave then needs to be aligned with the provision of state-supported and -regulated high-quality early childhood education and care, which will then seamlessly connect into primary school. And if we're really interested in supporting parents choosing to be in employment, then primary-school-aged children need high-quality, subsidised before- and after-school, and holiday care, as well, because hardly anybody's working hours fit neatly into the typical 9 a.m. to 3.30 p.m. school day. Parents may always want to use a combination of informal care (provided by themselves, grandparents, or others) and formal care, but the high-quality formal care needs to be there for those parents who need it.

'20 per cent of our population, 100 per cent of our future'*

Should this care be free? Offered on a sliding scale? To some extent this depends on how badly we want it. In *Raising the Nation* Paul Lindley suggests options to fund a 'National Children's Service'.[111] One mechanism could be for the government to issue so-called 'Children's Gilts' to raise money for investment in children's services, similar to the existing Green Bonds that successfully raise private money for investment in environmental sustainability. All the evidence I set out earlier, suggesting a good return on investment, means that these gilts could be offered by the Bank of England to commercial markets on attractive terms.

Another mechanism that has been successful in (so far limited) practice is Social Impact Bonds. These are public–private partnerships where social investors put money into a service delivery organisation to undertake a payment-by-results contract. In one example, young people at risk of not engaging with employment or further education were trained to become mentors to nursery-school-aged children; social investors provided funding for the programme and received a return

---

* An epigram generally attributed to the then-prime minister Tony Blair, but he was quoting his Chancellor of the Exchequer, Gordon Brown.

on investment when the programme succeeded in meeting its goals of improving school attendance and qualifications for the young people. Paul Lindley proposes that Social Impact Bonds could be scaled up to support a National Children's Service. He also calls for investment from a National Wealth Fund, like that proposed by the Labour government elected in 2024 – although the government's plans for this were focused on green infrastructure rather than children. But if we know that investment in a National Children's Service will bring about a worthwhile return, then we can ask the best financial experts to help us set up the most sensible and efficient capital-creation mechanisms to underpin it. Other countries manage, so we must too.

All experts agree on the need to invest more in the childcare workforce, improving their qualifications, pay, and working conditions. Raising the standards of the profession will raise the standard of care, as has worked (as we'll see in the next chapter) for raising standards of education in Finland when the status and training for teachers was prioritised. Care providers for our very young children should be as well educated and qualified (and paid) as our schoolteachers and university lecturers; nurturing the development of the very youngest minds needs just as much skill, specialist knowledge and experience as teaching older children and young people. In a properly integrated care and education system, with highly qualified staff for all age groups, we could expect optimal application of teaching and learning theory – this is what is called pedagogy – geared to children's developmental readiness, and we could expect that to smooth out some of the very early inequalities in children's development that go on to be entrenched and perpetuated in school and beyond.[119]

There is a striking consistency across the multiple and heterogeneous voices of researchers and campaigners for a better system of care and education for our children. Not only in the components of a system that would work better for our children (they *all*, for example, call for reform to parental leave; universal free or extremely heavily subsidised childcare; an integration across early years; and statutory schooling) but also in the need for a transformative overhaul. Nobody thinks that tweaks will be enough. All the experts worry, and write about, sounding 'utopian' or 'radical', but everything they call for has been tried and tested somewhere. None of this is really fantasy; we've just fallen out of the habit of thinking that we *can* choose to do what it takes to create the best society possible for our children (and therefore for all of us and for future generations as well).

The child in need of care

I'm turning now to a different kind of formal care – the care that is given to children who, according to the 'system', cannot be cared for by their parents. This includes what is called 'kinship foster care' – when children's social services place a child into the care of a relative, family friend or close connection – as well as foster care or adoption, where a child is placed with approved carers not connected with the child's family. In both cases, the state is taking over parental responsibility for the child (at least until a formal adoption is finalised), who is these days, therefore, often termed a 'looked after' child, as well as 'in care'. Sometimes these arrangements for children's care are made through agreement with the parents, such as when a parent voluntarily relinquishes their parental rights over a child, allowing for their adoption – close to 3,000 children were adopted in the UK in 2024[120] – or when a parent feels they can no longer manage a child's behaviour. More often, however, children become 'cared for' by the state because children's social services have asked a family court to make a care order on the grounds that the parent(s) cannot look after the child themselves. There are a great many reasons why social services will initiate care order proceedings, including neglect, abuse (emotional, physical or sexual) and abandonment, or when parents are ill or in prison, or have died. Children who come to the UK seeking asylum may be placed in care if they are not accompanied by parents or relatives. These are all obviously sad and, one would hope, extreme cases; I think most readers will be shocked to find out how many British children are 'looked after'. Every day, 107 children enter the care system; that's almost 40,000 a year, and around 105,000 children are looked after away from the parental home.[120]

'The point of being in care is to be cared for . . .'

Those are the words of Mia, and that's her real name because she is a brave young woman. Mia shared her story, and became a co-author, with a group of researchers (I was one of them) – practitioners and others with lived experience – on a report on children in care in the North of England.

Social care workers had been involved with Mia and her family from when she was a young age, and she was taken into foster care at the age of fourteen. She described how her long-standing mental health problems 'spiralled' after being taken into care, at which point of acute crisis she received mental health care for the first time in her life. Mia described her mum having received inadequate support to leave an abusive relationship with Mia's father or to take care of her three daughters, one of whom, Mia's twin sister, was belatedly diagnosed with autism. After being deemed unable to look after her children, Mia's mum was hit with the so-called 'bedroom tax', as she now had empty rooms: with the loss of Housing Benefit and no longer receiving Child Benefit, she felt unable to cut financial ties with Mia's dad, as she was desperate to maintain her home in case her children could return to her. Mia feels that she, her mother and her sisters were neglected by the 'care system', both before and after the children entered formal residential social care, becoming 'looked after' children.

In Mia's experience, the system is itself a 'neglectful parent'. Mia's younger sister now comes home for visits, without any financial support for this, and Mia's mum worries that if she asks for support, she will be viewed as an inadequate parent. Mia herself was in five foster placements in three years and has now spent eight of her twenty-one years separated from her twin sister. At one stage she was told that if she requested to leave an emotionally damaging placement, she would have to leave her younger sister there. Child protection orders, said Mia, 'do not seem all that protective . . . The point of being in care is to be cared for; underfunding, corrupt systems, and scarce prevention strategies, in my opinion, is not care . . . My mother was neglected.'[121]

The quality of our care

Outcomes for children who have had experience of the UK care system are appallingly bad; they have worse educational, employment, income, housing and health (physical and mental) outcomes than other children and are far more likely to have involvement with the criminal justice system. And the effects are long-lasting. In one study, researchers looked at people's health over ten-, twenty- and thirty-year periods, comparing those who had spent time in different kinds of care.[122] Adults who had been in residential care (children's homes) in childhood were three and a half times more likely to report that their health wasn't good than adults who had no care experience. Those who had been looked after by relatives, or in foster homes, were twice, and two and a half times, respectively, more likely to report poor health. And that's after the researchers took account of other characteristics that might account for the findings, such as the parents' economic and educational status. After another period of follow-up, the researchers found that those who had been in care were 62 per cent more likely to have died prematurely, with the excess deaths mostly attributable to self-harm, accidents and mental and behavioural causes.[123] This mortality risk appears to be rising, as do inequalities in health between those who experience care and the rest of the population.

The same set of data was used to look at other kinds of outcomes in adulthood, including social class, educational qualifications and employment, home ownership, marrying and having children, and living alone. Once again, those who had been in children's homes had the worst outcomes, those who had never been in care the best outcomes, and those who had been cared for by relatives or in foster care were somewhere in the middle.[124] Ninety per cent of those who had been in residential care ended up with educational qualifications lower than what would be expected at age eighteen (that means A levels/NVQ Level 3s). This is an often hidden inequality: in an otherwise comprehensive and excellent report on educational inequalities from the Institute for Fiscal Studies Deaton Review of Inequalities, there was not a single mention of the poor educational outcomes related to being in care. Few will know that only 6 per cent of children who have been in care go to university, compared to almost half of all other children. Why are these children's educational outcomes so bad? Part of the answer, of course, has to do with the reasons why children are in care in the first place. The assumption is that children in the care system would have worse outcomes if they were not taken into care, but of course we can't actually analyse that counterfactual. What we need to be aiming for is to reduce the harm done by the care system itself by improving the system, *and* supporting families to stay together with better preventive interventions to limit the trauma of separation wherever possible.

Care can be positive for educational outcomes, if we compare those in care to children who are being supported by social care but are not 'in care'. However, some of the poor outcomes are because children in care often move (both residential settings and schools) a lot and the kinds of educational settings that such children often end up in can be problematic. Many children, like Mia, are moved from placement to placement, and each change of placement after age eleven has been linked to one-third of a grade less at GCSE.[125] But children in care are also more likely to be outside the normal school system: they are twenty times more likely to be in special education and eighteen times more likely to be excluded from school and attending a Pupil Referral Unit.[126] Children in care are supposed to be given priority in admission to schools, which ought to mean that they are more likely than other children to be going to good schools, but the sad reality is that they are *less* likely to do so, with only 76 per cent of them in 'good' or 'outstanding' schools, compared to 84 per cent of other children. The *Huffington Post* news website, using freedom of information requests, uncovered a scandal of UK academy schools, who control their own admissions, blocking the admissions of children in care.[127] Government ministers had been asked, seventy-two times in three years, to intervene to force them to admit children in care. Almost 1 in 10 children in care are having some kind of schooling that is outside of Ofsted regulation because there is nothing else suitable for them – this might mean them receiving online classes only, or tutoring. This 1 in 10 estimate comes from a study sample; we don't actually have comprehensive tracking data for children not in regulated schools.

Pathways to prison and the streets

I'll be coming to prisons and the criminal justice system in Chapter 4, and the role of adverse childhood experiences and vulnerabilities – including being known to children's social services, being 'in need' or in care – in shaping trajectories of criminal involvement and imprisonment. Here, I'll just point out that children with experience of the care system are two to sixteen times more likely to have some kind of involvement with the youth justice system than other children.[128] This involvement varies a lot by ethnicity: a third of White British children who have experience of the care system have a 'youth justice caution' (a formal warning given to a young person who has admitted a minor criminal offence) or a conviction, but that figure is closer to a half for children in care from Gypsy, Roma and Irish Traveller communities. If we look at custodial sentences among children who have been in care, being sentenced to a secure children's home (a locked environment for children who have been remanded or sentenced to custody) is twice as likely for Black and Mixed ethnicity children as for White British children.[128] This problem seems to be getting worse: just as health inequalities are increasing between those who've been in care and those who haven't, the proportion of the prison population who have been in care is increasing.

Homelessness is also extremely common among young people leaving care. Although children in care can now be supported through the transition to adulthood, up to the age of twenty-five, more than a third experience homelessness when that care ends,[129] and a quarter of homeless adults are care-experienced.[130] Katelin, another young woman who had been in care, and who contributed to our report on the care system, slept on friends' sofas for months after leaving the care system – she had only been offered lettings in what she described as 'deprived and dangerous areas of Liverpool', unsuitable for a seventeen-year-old young woman living on her own. Two years later, she was living with her partner's family, feeling 'homeless and anxious'. She had heard from her social care support team only twice in two years; 'they clearly don't care about me', she said.[131]

Anyone who knows anyone who works in social care knows how deeply most care workers do care, and how distressing it is for them, as well as for those who are cared for, that the system is stretched so far that they have neither time nor other resources to offer the quality of care they would wish. At the start of this chapter, I described how an 'ethics of care' should be foundational to a good society. Such an approach would pay attention to the injuries caused both to those who are cared for *and* carers by the way society is organised, and aim for the prevention of harm and the promotion of flourishing to both.[97]

How much?

Optimal social care should cost a lot of money; that's a given. And we should willingly pay for it if cared-for children, and society, benefit. What we actually have is a system which costs more than it should, while providing less than it ought, for the primary benefit of private equity investors.

It costs ... wait for it ... £1.2 million pounds in lifetime social costs for each child in care, double what it costs to support with a social worker a child who has not been taken into care (and five times what it costs parents to raise a child to age eighteen[132]). This is according to the Independent Review of Children's Social Care, which published its final report in 2022.[133] At that time, children's social care was costing the UK about £10 billion each year, and the review predicted that, if the number of children in care continued to increase in line with recent trends, it would be costing the nation £15 billion per year by 2032.

It is local authorities who are responsible for providing and paying for social care for children. Over a six-year period, from financial years 2015/16 to 2021/22, local authority spending on children's residential care alone more than doubled. The cost varies in different parts of the country, but as many as 1 in 10 local authorities face significant debt and possible bankruptcy, just due to children's social care costs. Reflecting what was happening in many other local authorities, the city of Bradford's children's services had a predicted £45 million overspend on their annual budget in 2024, as numbers of children needing care kept increasing. Some of that budget was being spent on bringing in additional social workers from private agencies as the council simply didn't have enough, and paying for expensive children's home places in other districts – about £6,000 per week per child – because there were insufficient places locally.

The variation in costs across different regions means that some local authorities in regions where placements are more expensive pay for children to be placed outside of their own borough. This has led to unintended (but surely not unimagined?) consequences of children being placed far from family and friends (this is sometimes, of course, the best solution for children who have become enmeshed in things like county lines drug-running). Although the local authority of origin is responsible for the child even when placed elsewhere, they are not having to cover the additional costs to the health, welfare, education, justice and children's services of the localities where the child is placed. In our report on children in care in the North of England, we found that the North, where property is cheaper, now has 40 per cent of all children's homes in England, despite having only 28 per cent of the child population.[131] The higher rates of children in care in the North can be partly attributed to deprivation (of which more later), but also partly to this practice of placing children outside of their local authority borough for cost reasons.

If a local authority has to spend more and more on children's social care – for which it has a statutory responsibility and so *cannot not* spend money on – it has less and less money to spend on the kinds of preventive services for children and families that might avert them from needing to be taken into care in the first place. This is a truly vicious circle. In terms of our public health cliff-edge metaphor, we're spending almost all the child social care budget on the ambulances picking up people at the bottom of the cliff and have less to spend on building the infrastructure to prevent them from falling off in the first place. In the decade from 2011 to just before the pandemic, total spending on preventive services for families declined by 25 per cent. Cuts to adolescent services of £58 million pounds are estimated to have ended up costing the taxpayer £60 million, because of the increase in the number of sixteen- and seventeen-year-olds being taken into care.

As Dr Davara Bennett from the University of Liverpool reported from her interviews with local authority policymakers, children's services have been:

ALL THE KINDS OF CARE WE NEED

'stripped', 'restructured', 'consolidated', 'slash and burned'; investment 'dwindled' and there was 'under-investment', 'de-investment', and investment not 'sustained'. Funding for early help was 'lacking', 'cut', 'redirected', 'removed', 'reduced', 'significantly contracted', 'tiny', 'lost', 'taken out' and 'taken away'. Children's centres were 'closed', 'cut', 'lost', 'condensed', 'let go', 'mothballed', 'restructured', 'hollowed out', 'morphed into something else', their offers 'diluted'. Children's centre staff and managers were 'cut', 'reduced', placed on 'temporary or fixed term contracts'. Family support was 'reined in', 'whittled down', 'pared back'. Youth services 'cut significantly', 'decimated', staff 'removed'. Drug services were 'annihilated', 'cut', 'withdrawn'. School improvement budgets were 'significantly reduced', school effectiveness officers 'cut'. Third sector investment programmes were 'cut to the bone'. Disability support was 'halved', the scope of health visiting 'reduced'.[131]

Why does children's social care cost so much? I'm not saying it should be cheap, but how can it cost an average of £6,000 a week for a child to be looked after? One reason is that foster care (which is cheaper) is no longer as well supported, financially, as it used to be, and so foster carers are leaving the system in increasing numbers, about 3,000 in the last three years, and more are leaving than are signing up. Children who need to be cared for but can't be placed in foster care end up in the much more expensive children's homes. The shortage of foster carers is most acute in deprived regions of the country, where the need is greatest. The cost of living crisis has hit foster carers as hard as everyone else, with some resorting to food banks, turning down the heating, and worrying that they are no longer able to support the children they are caring for.[134, 135] As one foster parent told the organisation FosterTalk: 'will likely have to sell the car and take part-time work which will impact on the childcare, resulting in stopping fostering [soon]'.[126]

Residential children's care used to be provided almost entirely by local authorities; now it is increasingly provided by profit-making private companies, with profits for 2023 estimated at the very least to be £310 million.[136] Half of these companies are at least part-owned by private equity or foreign sovereign wealth funds. It's bad enough that there is a market at all in looking after vulnerable children, but this is a broken market, which the Competition and Markets Authority says has higher profits than it should have, doesn't reinvest in things like staff training and support, and carries rickety levels of debt, such that children's stability is constantly at risk of care home providers exiting the market.[137]

A (largely) preventable problem

On 17 April 2024 we presented our report on children in care to the Child of the North All-Party Parliamentary Group. There was a fair amount of media interest, and by the time the request came through for one of us to appear on Nigel Farage's evening show on GB News Radio, we were all tired and some were still on their way home from Parliament. I drew the short straw. I talked to Farage about poverty as a driver of rising numbers of children in care, a widely recognised issue, of course, but GB News had managed to find probably the only right-wing children's social worker in the UK to also come on the programme, who said he had never seen a child taken into care because of poverty. Well, here we are back on the clifftop of causation again, with someone not recognising (or refusing to see) poverty, deprivation and inequality as underlying or upstream causes of the neglect, abuse, addiction, mental illness and so forth that are the causes of children needing to be taken into care.

In fact, recent research has linked rises in child poverty to increases in children entering care, estimating that between 2015 and 2020 more than 10,000 additional children were taken into care – equivalent to 1 in 12 of all new cases – because of that increase in poverty.[121]

In cities and regions with high rates of deprivation, more and more families are coming into contact with social care. In England as a whole, 1 in 5 children born in 2009 and 2010 had been referred to children's services before they turned five, and in the city of Liverpool it was half of those children. Close to, or more than, 1 in 50 children are in care in Stoke-on-Trent, Blackpool and North-East Lincolnshire. Regionally, the highest rates are in the North West, then the North East, followed by the West Midlands, and Yorkshire and the Humber.[131]

I described some child poverty statistics in the Prologue, including the rise in child poverty from 2010 onwards. In fact, in 2023 UNICEF (the United Nations Children's Fund) reported that, of all forty countries in the OECD and EU, the UK had the biggest increase in child poverty over the previous decade – a 20 per cent rise – at a time when some countries, including Poland, Canada and Portugal, were managing to reduce their child poverty by about the same percentage or more.[22] And all of those countries had lower rates of child poverty than the UK even before those reductions.

We know, from robust research, that poverty and inequality affect parents' mental health, stress and exposure to domestic violence.[8] They are also strongly related to child maltreatment.[138–141] I've never been keen on the way economists talk about parents 'investing' in children, but think of all the ways in which financial resources help parents to care for them: as we described in our Child of the North report on children in care, parents invest in 'people (babysitters, nannies, tutors, quality time with parents), places (safe and healthy homes, nurseries, schools, neighbourhoods) and things (heat, food, clothes, toys, technology, transportation to and from school, extra-curricular activities)'.[131, 121]

Local authorities often do give financial support to families to help get children *out* of care, providing housing support for example. But putting support in place *before* children enter care is the kindest, most caring, and most cost-effective solution to prevent children being in need of social care in the first place. If we were good at state 'caring' the issue wouldn't be so critical; but children in care do so poorly as a consequence of being in the care system that we need to be looking for all the solutions we can to support families to be together.

Before moving on to potential solutions, I need to mention racism in relation to the social care system for children. Children of Black and Mixed heritage, as well as Gypsy, Roma and Irish Traveller children, have much higher rates of being taken into care than White British or Indian, Pakistani or Bangladeshi heritage children – twice as high for Black Caribbean children, and two and a half times as high for some Mixed ethnicity children. And this is despite there *not* appearing to be higher rates of self-reported abuse in these groups. There is a disturbing intersection between ethnicity and deprivation in relation to children being taken into care: in rich neighbourhoods in England, children from ethnic minorities are the most likely to be in care. In poor neighbourhoods, it's the White British children most likely to be in care. What is going on? Underpinning this phenomenon is the fact that there is a steep social gradient for White British children, as in, the poorer their families are, the more likely they are to be taken into care, which fits with what we would expect. For children in Indian, Black African, Bangladeshi and 'Black – Other' (not nice terminology but these are census categories) families, there is no social gradient, suggesting that structural racism might be playing an insidious role.

Research also shows us that ethnic minority children are more likely to be placed far from home, to have to move around a lot from placement to placement, to come back into care after being reunited with families, to be NEET (not in education, employment or training) after leaving care, and to be involved in the criminal justice system. A form of racism known as 'adultification bias' has been described within systems like social care and the justice system, referring to ways in which Black and other ethnic minority children are perceived as more mature than they are – disciplined more harshly, held (inappropriately) as more accountable for their actions, viewed as less 'innocent' or vulnerable. In effect, says leading expert Dr Jahnine Davis, these children 'are more likely to be met with suspicion, assumed deviance and culpability', leading to them being perceived as in less need of protection.[142]

The blueprints for children's social care

To reform children's care we need to take on board the recommendations of the 2022 Independent Review of Children's Social Care.[133] This is packed with examples of good practice from across children's care services and costed recommendations. This is a true blueprint for reform of the system, including early preventive help for families and reforms of the child protection system and workforce. Nevertheless, this otherwise excellent and comprehensive report does not focus on the need to tackle the most upstream determinants of children needing care. As with early childhood education and care, this is a field without dissenting expertise: social workers, child psychologists and psychiatrists, economists and policy experts line up to call for a revolution in children's social care, but they are not always looking at the same parts of the causal chain.

First and foremost, and again, if we're thinking about a good society where parents are enabled and supported to look after their children, we must return to the need to tackle poverty and inequality. I know I keep repeating the point, but it makes good economic sense, as well as being better for the whole of society and the right thing to do from a social justice point of view and from an ethics of care perspective. Government needs to acknowledge the causal links between poverty, child poverty in particular, *and* inequality, on parents and children and the need for care. This means that social security and welfare need to be increased in line with inflation, with punitive sanctions removed, not just for families with children but especially for them. It means attention to livelihoods more broadly, to housing, and to all the material provision, like free childcare and free school meals, that can help to support families. It means making sure that families are actually getting the benefits they are entitled to, as well as ensuring that those benefits are sufficient. At all levels of government, poverty and inequality need to be viewed as the primary social determinants of health and wellbeing because tackling them unlocks short-term and long-term benefits across health, education and social care.

Second come all the solutions that move the focus upstream to prevention, intervening with families in supportive and meaningful ways as early as possible. This means listening to what parents and children need, of course, and working to remove the stigma of needing help as a parent. This is about putting more resources into children's centres, family hubs, health visiting, parenting interventions and all the universal and ordinary services that families access. Mental health support is crucial here, both for children and for parents.

The third set of critical reforms are to do with moving away from a fragmented system that is warped and dysfunctional through a dependence on profit-making privatised 'care', with all the ridiculous distortion that creates. Just to give a couple of examples, cutting staff numbers or training or reducing the hours of care workers will increase profits but lead to reduced quality of care and fewer resources going to children who need support. More profit can be extracted by driving down staff wages, leading to higher turnover and lower morale – which of course impacts the quality of care provided to children. Experienced and motivated staff are crucial for providing consistent and high-quality support. We simply can't afford to have a system where private equity and foreign sovereign wealth funds make (big) money from 'care' that delivers such poor outcomes for our most vulnerable children. It's mad and has to stop. The Independent Review of Children's Social Care calls for a network of 'Regional Care Cooperatives' to be established, with the duty of ensuring sufficient care (of the right kind and for the right numbers); creating and running public-sector-provided fostering services, children's homes and secure children's homes; and commissioning care. The review does not call for this commissioned care to be entirely not-for-profit, but it could be, with sufficient prevention-oriented investment from government.

It is a common trope for experts writing about children's social care to excoriate its exceptionally poor outcomes, including the risks of children being exposed to criminal and sexual exploitation, financial abuse and experiencing severe mental health problems, by pointing out that if a parent did the same, they would be accused of neglect or abuse and the system would remove their children. That point is well made, should be more widely known, and should be a basis for radical reform.

I'll be discussing basic income in more depth in Chapter 6, but it's worth saying here that the Welsh government is piloting a basic income for all young people leaving care, giving them an unconditional basic income of £1,600 every month for two years from their eighteenth birthday. This bold and brave policy was born out of the government's recognition of how hard it is for care leavers to make a successful transition to adulthood. I'm part of an evaluation team led by researchers from Cardiff University to look at how this impacts outcomes for care leavers and whether or not this intervention – which is expensive – is cost-effective.[143] Results are expected in 2027 but already care leavers have told us about the opportunities and choices the income has given them, including being able to take driving lessons, buy an instrument for a music course, eat more healthily and save money for the future: all things that are perfectly normal for middle-class children. As one young person, attending college and working a part-time job, commented:

> I think eighteen is the perfect age to receive this, because you're going into adulthood, you gain the responsibility, and it's good to have that financial support when you turn into an adult, because most care leavers, in their childhood, they never had anything that was completely theirs on their own. That they could control. So, I suppose it helped us with feeling in control, and that.

And a head of children's social care service told us:

> . . . with one young person, she's been able to reduce her hours in the full-time occupation to be able to train for . . .

something that she really wants, and she really wants to move forward. And she's a really difficult young person to work with, but actually, it's got to a level where we're having very adult conversations, and very future-focused conversations, which is something that we've never had [before].[144]

Extra care needed: supporting people with disabilities

Nobody watching the fabulous opening ceremony to the London 2012 Summer Paralympics could have failed to feel moved by the joyous celebration of disability and diversity that marked the 64th year of the Paralympic movement, and the start of the biggest-ever international sporting event for athletes with disabilities. The ceremony show, titled 'Enlightenment', played to a live audience of 80,000 people in the Olympic Stadium and 7.6 million people on television in the UK alone, and prominently featured performers, directors, narrators and volunteers with disabilities. Themed on Shakespeare's *Tempest* and the advances of the scientific enlightenment, it paid tribute to the contributions that science has made to the lives of those with disabilities and sought to challenge audience perceptions of human possibility. The ceremony was attended by many grandees, including the then-prime minister, David Cameron, and Boris Johnson, then Mayor of London. The Paralympic Games that followed were watched by 36.1 million people all over the world, including almost 70 per cent of the British population. Audiences watched more than 4,000 Para athletes from 164 countries compete in 503 medal events across twenty sports. It felt like a triumph for progress.

But in 2012, the proportion of adults with disabilities who were living in poverty in the UK had started to rise again, after falling dramatically from the mid 1990s. By 2014, Professors David Taylor-Robinson, Margaret Whitehead and Ben Barr from the University of Liverpool were calling this the 'Great Leap Backwards'.[68]

This worrying trend should have been a serious wake-up call to government, and we should have been able to expect that the government would immediately implement course corrections to make sure that the most vulnerable people in our society were properly cared for. Not so. Instead, in all the years since, poverty has remained stubbornly high – at around 30 per cent – for adults who report having a disability or are claiming disability benefits.[145] Post-pandemic, but even before the cost of living crisis hit, the proportion of families with one or more children with disabilities living in poverty rose by nearly a third.[146] In fact, the majority of families in poverty include either a child with disabilities, an adult with disabilities, or both.[147] Disability benefits have been cut by recent governments from both sides of the political aisle, including changes announced in March 2025 that will mean 400,000 fewer people will be eligible for Personal Independence Payment and that a quarter of a million more people will be pushed into poverty, including 50,000 more children, with more deprived areas feeling the biggest pinch.[148]

Some aspects of living with disability have undoubtedly improved over recent decades, mostly as a result of the tireless campaigning and advocacy of disability rights groups. Access to public places is better than it used to be, although a continuing trickle of horror stories of people struggling and humiliated while trying to access public transport and buildings shows that there is still some way to go. Protections against discrimination and bias against people with disabilities are built into the

2010 Equality Act, and the Access to Work programme supports people with physical or mental health conditions and disabilities in work – this can include paying for special equipment, communications support, travel costs, and alterations to work environments – although it doesn't actually help individuals find work. We will see in the next chapter some of the educational challenges faced by children and young people with disabilities, but there has been progress there as well, with better awareness of needs, much more inclusive provision now within mainstream schools (although some would argue this is not always a good thing), and better assistive (albeit expensive) technologies and support services in many schools, all improving outcomes over time. The proportion of people with disabilities with no educational qualifications dropped from 15 per cent to 13 per cent between 2020 and 2021, which is a percentage not dissimilar to people without disabilities. The proportion with a degree increased from 23 per cent to 25 per cent, but this is significantly lower than among people without disabilities, about a third of whom have a degree.

Nevertheless, despite all this progress, people with disabilities do still face discrimination and bias in the workplace, and rates of unemployment, under-employment and low pay are high: 53.5 per cent of disabled people are employed, compared to 82 per cent of people without disabilities.[149] There are also acute shortages of suitable housing for many people with disabilities: 25 per cent are in social housing, compared to 10 per cent of the population without disabilities (and we all know about the crisis in availability of social housing). These two challenges alone, combined with stigmatisation and the byzantine and labyrinthine complexity often involved in accessing support of all kinds, lead to high levels of isolation, anxiety and stress, both for disabled people and their families, high levels of social exclusion and loneliness, and the avoidable high costs to society of not preventing these problems.[149] Families are often the ones who have to manage the consequences of there being insufficient employment and housing opportunities for people with disabilities, with impacts on their own ability to work full-time, to build up pension and savings, and to avoid poverty and deprivation.

The right to work: employment as the foundation of independence

I have a lovely niece, Imogen, who is in her mid-twenties and is deaf and has a moderate learning difficulty. Imogen was well supported by a scheme run by the charity DFN Project SEARCH as she prepared to find her first job. She was excited by the idea of working and earning her own money. When she started a supported administrative apprenticeship in a large hospital trust, she enjoyed getting ready for work and travelling by bus to her new job; she was pleased to have a wage and a purpose. But although Imogen ended up passing her apprenticeship assessment with a distinction, the hospital trust did not provide a permanent role at the end of it, and through their lack of proper support for her needs caused her sufficient mental stress that she developed a stammer. Her parents and her trade union were burdened with many months of difficult negotiation with her employer, trying to get them to fulfil their obligations. A real lack of 'care' created trauma for both Imogen and her family. She is, as I write, now more happily and securely employed in a retail role which she started through a scheme run by the Prince's Trust (now known as the King's Trust) in partnership with Marks & Spencer – an exemplary inclusive employer – where she is experiencing real empathy and is once again working hard and delighted to be working. As I'm writing this, it feels as if Imogen is in a good situation and she is about to take the next step in her growing independence, making a home away (but not too far) from her parents, where, with support, she can control her own life and thrive as an adult. But she has travelled a long and difficult road to get to get to this good place and it has been so much harder on her, and her family, than it should have been.

One of the primary problems people with disabilities face is not being able to work, which in turn deprives them of the income and independence that they need, compounding all of the adverse effects of poverty and undermining their sense of self-worth, agency, and wellbeing. Given the high rates of poverty, unemployment/under-employment, social exclusion and loneliness among adults with disabilities, making sure that everyone who can and wants to work is able to find properly remunerated and purposeful employment has to be a priority of any good society.

Good employment would go a long way to prevent these problems. The transition out of childhood and education is absolutely key to this, and in 2024 the Public Services Committee of the House of Lords published its blueprint for supporting young disabled people into work.[150] Their report is based on expert evidence, as well as being co-produced with people with disabilities. The committee titled its report *Think Work First*, acknowledging that – while some people with disabilities will likely not be able to work and must be properly supported by the welfare system – most young people with disabilities 'yearn to work' and 'the presumption has to be, at every stage of a young disabled person's development, that they are fully capable of thriving in work, as long as they have the appropriate support'. Some of what is needed for the proper support of people with disabilities lies within health and social care, education, the benefits system, housing and transport; but getting employment right will reduce pressures on *all* of these public services, as well as being the best solution for individual well-being for so many people with disabilities.

Research from the University of Warwick shows that approximately 35 per cent of young people with disabilities are not in employment at age twenty-five, compared to 18 per cent of young people without disabilities; this is the age by which most young adults have finished their education and training and established themselves in employment. The capability of young people with disabilities to make this transition turns out to be sadly dependent on their social class – young disabled people from upper- and middle-class families have much higher rates of employment than those from low social-class groups.[151] We clearly need a system of support for this important transition into adulthood that mitigates the misfortune of not having been lucky enough to escape being born poor.

So, what did the Public Services Committee want to see? They want support for employment to be happening well before young people with disabilities leave full-time education and call for 'vocational profiling', where a specialist job coach works one-to-one with a young person to find out about them, their skills and aspirations, and what they need to support their job preferences. There are not enough job coaches to meet the need and they are often inadequately trained, inexperienced and poorly paid. The committee called for far more supported internships and special work programmes, such as ThinkForward (which provides coaching), and DFN Project SEARCH (which is for young people with a learning disability or autism or both). These only provide work experience, though, not a long-term job. The House of Lords Committee also called for wider awareness and reduced delays in getting support through the Access to Work programme.

I know, however, from my own family's experience that all the work preparation schemes in the world come to naught unless there are sufficient employers committed to creating inclusive workplaces and fully supporting in practice as well as in principle the employment rights of workers with disabilities. And my sister, Imogen's mum, points out that it should be someone other than the parent who is responsible for applying for and managing Access to Work support. There are some reassuringly good examples out there, but too many counter-examples of poor practice and discrimination and employers still not understanding or making 'reasonable adjustments' for workers with disabilities, even though the 2010 Equality Act enshrined this duty in law more than a decade ago. 'Reasonable adjustments' are not defined in the Act, only by case law, and so are often contested.

The right to housing: home as the foundation of care

Imagine you are a parent with a child with a disability approaching adulthood, and you want to explore independent housing and living options for them, because that is what the young person wants; and it's what you want, after caring for them throughout their lives up to now – it's better for everyone. You do an online search and find a useful website from a trusted source — for example, the NHS has relevant information. You feel relieved, and even more relieved to read about all the options they describe. The website describes how young people (two-thirds of whom will be unemployed, remember) might buy or rent an adapted property. Or, it says, they might prefer to go into a sheltered housing scheme especially for younger people or live in supported housing in the community. There are supported living services, where carers visit people in their homes to perhaps help them get out to college or work in the morning, or help with shopping, housework, managing bills and organising repairs. Then there are 'shared lives' schemes where the person with disability is matched with a carer who lives with them, providing emotional as well as practical support.

It all sounds great – the website talks about these as 'options' that a young person might 'consider'. But just how available are these options, in reality? So far, it seems, there are no suitable housing solutions available for Imogen, although she lives in a large city, and to look at the local authority website, you'd think all the 'options' they list might actually be available. This is why official statistics show that adults with disabilities are more likely to be still living with their parents after the age of twenty-five, and they are much less likely to own a home at any age: only 4 per cent of adults with learning disabilities own a home.[152]

The Equality and Human Rights Commission found people consistently reported that navigating the complex systems for housing allocations and adaptations was stressful and challenging, and that not having an accessible home created mobility and/or communication problems, poor mental health, lack of dignity, increased social isolation and loneliness, and was associated with a four-fold increase in worklessness.[153] They found that people with disabilities were demoralised and frustrated by the housing system and that there is a chronic shortage, indeed a crisis, in availability of suitable homes (and this is a distinct and additional problem from the lack of resources in social care to support people living in those homes). Two-thirds of local authorities told the commission that they struggle to get developers to build more accessible housing, but only 3 per cent of them had taken action against developers on accessibility grounds. And it takes, on average, more than five months for people to get necessary adaptations to their housing, with some local authorities having wait times of more than a year (in January 2025, the government announced a very welcome £86 million boost to the Disabled Facilities Grant, so perhaps these wait times will start to shrink). Housing, planning and social care systems, including the National Planning Policy Framework, are in clear need of reform, but more money and more social housing are needed most, and first, to overcome the ways in which financial challenges, including poverty and trying to make ends meet on fixed disability benefits, compound the housing difficulties faced by those with disabilities.

Parity of esteem for disabilities

'Parity of esteem' is the idea that mental illness should receive the same resources within our health (and social care) system as physical illness, and that care and treatment for mental health should be as accessible and available as care for physical conditions. The idea has been around since the late 1990s and was enshrined in law in the 2012 Health and Social Care Act. It hasn't worked (yet): although mental health conditions account for at least 28 per cent of the total 'burden of disease', only 13 per cent of NHS spending is targeted to mental health. But at least the intention and the legislation are clear. As a society, we expect our NHS to care for everyone who needs it, supported by all of us through our taxes. However, we don't, these days, seem to have anything like the same public sentiment towards social care for people with physical or sensory disabilities, or to be demanding – with and for them – the parity of esteem that is needed here as well.

The Joseph Rowntree Foundation points out that from the early 1970s we *did* start to put in place a system of social security to cover the costs and overcome the obstacles of people with disabilities being able to earn a wage and live independently, but that we have seen these benefits be retrenched, through austerity, so far as to drive people into Victorian levels of destitution – deep income poverty that means people struggle to afford even the most basic of necessities.[154] The risk of deep poverty is 60 per cent higher in families where someone has a disability, and 100 per cent higher – twice as high – for single people with disabilities, compared to families with no household members with disabilities.

People with disabilities used to receive what was called the Disability Living Allowance (DLA) but that began to be phased out in 2013, for people over the age of sixteen, with claimants moved instead to a new benefit, Personal Independence Payment (PIP). The intentions behind PIP sounded worthy enough, and it was also anticipated that it would cut costs to society by 20 per cent (it hasn't, because more people need it; there has been an especially sharp rise in people needing support because of mental health problems). It is supposed to help with the extra costs of living with a chronic health condition or a disability and to be linked to actual, practical need rather than being handed out simply because someone has a particular diagnosis. Assessments of those needs, however, have been farmed out, as a target-driven process, to private companies. And the assessment process has repeatedly been shown to be of an appallingly low standard, with nearly 40 per cent of the in-person assessments performed by one provider found to be of an unacceptable standard, and 75 per cent of appeals against decisions being supported at tribunal, showing how often the initial decision was bad. Personal Independence Payments are also periodically reassessed for most beneficiaries.

Disability charities and advocates are united in expressing concerns about PIP, and the assessment process in particular, and there have been continuing scandals of deaths, including by suicide, of people deemed ineligible for PIP, or due to delays in making decisions and payments. This is under formal investigation by the Equality and Human Rights Commission as I write this. In fact, it may surprise you to learn that the Department for Work and Pensions, which conducts and commissions the assessment of claimants for Employment and Support Allowance, Universal Credit and PIP, has consistently argued that it has no 'statutory duty of care' towards claimants. It is high time that government legislated to ensure that they do. Whatever the motivations for PIP, we've ended up with more people who are chronically ill and/or have disabilities in increased hardship.

In summary, then, what is most needed to ensure that we are caring appropriately for people with disabilities is to ensure they have livelihoods and independence sufficient to optimise their wellbeing and their dignity. This should mean: all of the support for employment suggested by the House of Lords Committee; more scrutiny and enforcement of the Equality Act and other relevant legislation; more guidance for employers on the difference between positive action (which is lawful) and positive discrimination (which is not); a requirement of both public and private employers above a sensible size threshold to provide employment opportunities; more funding and provision of appropriate housing; and a dignified process to provide a proper income standard instead of, or to supplement, employment income. And this need for ensuring decent livelihoods is yet one more reason that I'll be looking at a state-funded basic income in Chapter 6, given its potential to benefit both informal and paid caregivers and smooth the receipt and the provision of care within families.

The Joseph Rowntree Foundation says it is 'becoming almost a cliché to observe we are in times where poorer Britons are having to choose between heating and eating'. They say that a significant number of people with disabilities will 'soon not even have that choice: as fuel bills rise, they will grow cold and they will go hungry. And the community will be punishing disability as if it were an indulgence – which will rather call into question whether it is a community at all.'[154]

I prefer to replace the word 'community' with 'society' in that last sentence; this is about us choosing whether or not to have the good society that cares for us all in our time of need, whether that is because of our infancy, our misfortune to have parents who can't look after us, or because of disability and/or neurodiversity. And while we might feel sure that we will never ourselves need extra care for any of those reasons, it would behove us to think very carefully indeed about what it means to have a caring society, as we are all, inevitably, going to get older.

Care for the elderly

'We will age, get sick and die. It probably won't be pretty, and we'll need care ourselves and/or have to give care to those we love. And all the while capitalism will punish us for both needing and giving care.'

Rob Delaney[155]

Benjamin Franklin is famed to have written that 'in this world, nothing can be said to be certain, except death and taxes'. But apart from being certain that we *will* die, how much do any of

ALL THE KINDS OF CARE WE NEED

us think about *how* we might die? Examine your own feelings about this, ask around among friends and family, and you'll find that most people hope that they will die peacefully, many of them preferring death to take place while they sleep, in their own home, in their own bed, with the people they love close by. Failing that, many of us say, we'd like to drop dead, from something sudden like a heart attack or a brain haemorrhage, gone before we really know we are going, perhaps before we even fall to the floor. Some people are very clear that they would prefer to be able to choose their own time and manner of departure, but although that is a legal option in more and more places in the world, it is generally available only to those who are terminally or chronically very ill. What people want least is to die with dementia, or to die in pain.

And what do most of us die of? In the UK, the leading cause of death across all age groups, accounting for 13 per cent of all deaths, is 'dementia and Alzheimer's disease'.[156] Lung cancer and chronic respiratory deaths together account for almost the same number of deaths among men as heart disease. Among women, lung cancer now kills more than breast cancer. These are not the deaths we're hoping for.

Almost half of British deaths happen in hospital, about 5 per cent in a hospice, and 44.5 per cent of deaths take place in people's 'usual place of residence' – for some that is what we would call their home, but for just over half of them it is a care home or nursing home. So only 1 in 5 of us dies at home, where most of us would wish to be.

Our end of life, then, for most of us, is a long way from our desired end. Pain and loss of identity are much more common than we want to acknowledge. And most of us don't go especially quickly – sudden deaths are rare – so as we age and become frail or ill, the vast majority of us will need to be cared for; we won't be able to take care of all of our own needs; someone will have to give us the care we need to be clean, and fed, and warm, and to manage our pain and our medicines and to lift us and move us around; to provide that care and, hopefully, to talk to us, soothe us and keep us company.

There is an awful lot of care being given to and received by older people in the UK. In 2023, more than half a million older people were receiving state-funded long-term care and about a quarter of a million received some short-term care (these won't all have been older people).[25] Close to a million people are in some kind of care setting – this includes older people in care and nursing homes, although that number will also include some non-elderly ill people.[157] And in 2023, local authorities, who are responsible for assessing social care needs and then providing the care needed, received about two million new requests for support; in 42 per cent of these cases, some kind of service was then provided.[158, 159]

Some of that care is being provided by paid caregivers, but about 2.5 million people are unpaid carers, looking after family members or friends, sometimes receiving a measly Carer's Allowance (£83.30 per week), but often not, and most of them (60 per cent) themselves in need of care, because they too have a long-term health condition or disability.[160] The charity Age UK estimates that two million older people have unmet needs for care and support.[161]

We have a truly broken system but one from which many of us avert our eyes, hoping (illogically) that we will neither need that care nor be called upon to arrange for and/or provide that care for someone else. But I've shown you already that your hope is not supported by the statistics, and the other important thing we all need to recognise is that this is an impending crisis on the grandest of scales: looking just at England, the number of people aged sixty-five years or older has increased by just over 50 per cent over the past four decades, and is predicted to grow by about a third again in the next four decades – meaning that we will end up with a population that contains more than ten million older people (and six million of these will be eighty years old or more), the vast majority of whom are going to need some kind of care, by the mid 2060s.[162] If you're reading this in your twenties, thirties or forties, imagine the pressures on the system by the time *you* might be needing some care. This is a global problem: the World Health Organization says that all countries face 'major challenges to ensure that their health and social systems are ready', with the world's population aged over sixty set to double between 2015 and 2050.[163]

This is also a gender problem. The majority of caregivers, paid or unpaid, are women. Women are disproportionately sacrificing their own careers and their own wellbeing to provide enough care so that governments can keep on *not* fixing the problem – it is women's work that enables our dysfunctional system to keep tottering on. In a report I contributed to, on the wellbeing of women in the North of England, we found that women in just three regions alone (the North East, the North West, and Yorkshire and the Humber) contribute £10 billion of unpaid care to the UK economy each and every year.[164] Imagine if this care was not being provided. How would we try to look after people instead? And this is also, of course, an inequality problem. In March 2023 the *Guardian* reported on the dismal experiences of people being 'cared for' in a care home in Southampton. The Care Quality Commission had condemned the home in 2022 as 'inadequate' after finding 'a mattress soaked with urine that had been left uncleaned for days, dirty bathrooms and broken tables. There weren't enough staff, none had completed their basic care certificate training, people were left unattended for too long, and there were unwitnessed falls. Staff tried to confine people to their chairs using tables . . .'.[165]

Meanwhile, the home's then-owners had 'been profiting handsomely. Over a two-year period, while care at the home was in no way up to standard, the two owners took more than £650,000 in dividends, loans and salary.' This is not unique, according to the *Guardian* – hundreds of care homes receiving the worst ratings from the Care Quality Commission were still receiving grants from central government and commissions for care from local authorities. And there were significantly higher numbers of state-funded residents, meaning more poor people, in these inadequate homes. Those who can afford to pay for their own care are more likely to be in the better-rated care homes. The newspaper concluded that the 'crisis in England's care homes bites deepest on the poorest'.[165]

An aside – but an important one – in 2024, the Care Quality Commission was found to be failing to do its job. The government reported that inspection levels were well below where they should have been, that inspectors lacked clinical expertise, and that assessments were inconsistent. The Homecare Association, which represents in-home carers, warned that more than a third of providers of in-home care hadn't been rated for at least four years and almost a quarter had never been rated.

Market failure

Although we also need to think about the culture of care – and I will come on to this – I want to first think about how we pay for it. In this chapter, I've already described problems with the for-profit system of care provision for little children and for children who need to be cared for by the state. By also allowing for a market in the provision of care for the elderly, the state has created another disastrously dysfunctional system. Instead of grasping the nettle of the investment needed to provide a proper level of care for those who need it, successive governments have tried to contain costs in the face of increasing need – a recipe for disaster. Susan Himmelweit, Emeritus Professor of Economics at the Open University, points out that care is 'a particularly bad candidate for privatisation and quality control improvement through competition'.[166] This is because care provision is necessarily labour-intensive, if care is to be good – and most person-based care cannot, and should not, be replaced with technology (although some technological support is of course to be welcomed). This means that the only way to realistically cut costs is to reduce staff numbers and/or pay staff (mostly women, often from ethnic minorities and often migrant) very low wages. The counterweight, in this particular market, to cost-cutting pressures should be consumer choice – bad care homes should fail because care clients take their care needs elsewhere.

But in a market where there are not enough care places everywhere they are needed, and when moving between residential homes, in particular, might be stressful and unwelcome to those in need of care and their families, and when the inspection system cannot be trusted to tell us which care providers are good and which are sub-standard – the market fails. Moreover, because government has never invested sufficiently in care, and has cut funding to the local authorities who are statutorily required to provide it, those who don't meet the extremely high threshold for having all of their care paid for by the state end up cross-subsidising care through higher fees. The current care system is failing both taxpayers *and* private payers. Economist Guy Standing, Professorial Research Associate at SOAS, the University of London, expresses proper outrage at the example of 'one foreign [investment] fund acquiring a chain of 450 mental care homes, loading the firms with debt while creaming off large profits, declaring "bankruptcy" and then selling out to another foreign private equity body'.[167]

As I write, there are warnings that the existing financial crisis in social care will be made worse by the increases in National Insurance contributions and the minimum wage that will start to bite in 2025.[168] While the NHS (and probably hospices) and local authorities are exempt from these, charitable and private providers of social care are not: truly a non-parity of esteem for social care. The Nuffield Trust estimates that increased costs to the care sector will wipe out the extra money it was given in the autumn 2024 budget – the government will give with one hand and take away with the other. Many providers will face 'tough decisions', the trust warned: going out of business or 'laying off experienced highly paid staff, reducing staff hours, or freezing pay for those earning above the minimum wage'.[169]

The blueprints for social care for older people

In social care we see the same patterns as we did in relation to health inequalities: we know what needs to be done; we have repeated reports that align in their recommendations. We just need transformative action.

In 1998 a Royal Commission on Long-Term Care of the Elderly made the recommendation that the UK government should meet the costs of personal care in the UK – in other words, non-medical care or social care. The commission argued that conditions like dementia should have parity with conditions like cancer, for which medical care is, of course, free. England and Wales rejected this, but Scotland accepted the point, setting themselves on a distinct course among the UK nations. For more than twenty years now, Scotland has been paying for all the personal and nursing care provided to people aged sixty-five and over in their own homes, and paying an allowance towards those same costs for people in nursing homes. Personal care provision was extended, in 2019, to people of any age who have been assessed as needing care.[170] North of the border, then, there is a decent universal care offering and the Scottish government has, since 2022, been planning for a full 'National Care Service'. Such a service would provide comprehensive, publicly funded, and integrated support – delivering personalised, high-quality care across health, social, and community services to ensure dignity, continuity, and equitable access for all older people.

The next big review, published in 2006, was commissioned from Sir Derek Wanless, by the health and care charity the King's Fund.[171] Wanless had previously led a report on the future of health care, for the New Labour government in 2002, which led to significant investment in the NHS and made the case for investment in health care underpinning economic progress, as well as being the right thing to do for public health. Apparently, Wanless had wanted to include social care in his initial 2002 review, but was warned off it by the Treasury. The *Wanless Social Care Review* took a twenty-year perspective and asked how much should be spent on social care over that period to 'secure comprehensive, high-quality care that reflects the preferences of the individuals receiving care'. It also had an explicit social justice remit. Wanless estimated that by 2026, a good level of care would be costing the UK £31.3 billion per year, 2 per cent of its GDP.

We are not, of course, spending at that projected level, we are almost £3 billion short, and we're not getting anything like the level of care Wanless thought that amount of spending would achieve, because underinvestment has allowed costs to spiral, and needs have also grown. The demand for adult social care has grown and is projected to continue increasing due to an ageing population, rising chronic health conditions, and increased longevity, which together place greater demand on support services and health and care systems.

How did Wanless think we should fund better social care? His review plumped for a partnership model which would provide people with a free-of-charge minimum guaranteed amount of care – two-thirds of a benchmark 'package of care'. People could then make contributions, matched by the state (up to the limit of the benchmark care package), with extra support for poor people through the benefits system. This, it was suggested, would produce the best value for money, force far fewer people to have to get rid of their assets so they can access state-provided care, and be the most sustainable funding model. Basically, Wanless recommended that society should spend more on social care to support the same improvement in outcomes (better average and more equitable outcomes) as it expects and funds via health care, and that services needed to be reconfigured to achieve that goal.

A comprehensive and thoughtful review, then, even if it was mostly focused on how to fund more of the existing social care provision, rather than thinking about how to transform the culture of caring. It was 'well received by government and other stakeholders', and government did get to work on producing a Green Paper on social care in 2009 and a White Paper in 2010, which was a plan to create a National Care Service in the next Parliament.

But in 2010, the Coalition of Conservatives and Liberal Democrats took over government – and promptly set up a *new* 'Commission on Funding of Care and Support', led by Sir

Andrew Dilnot, an economist and former director of the Institute for Fiscal Studies. The Dilnot commission opted for a different model of funding for social care, one which had been considered but not preferred by the Wanless review. It called for a means-tested system for people to pay for their care up to the limit of £35,000 per person; any care needed beyond that would be provided by the state. Once again, the suggested reforms seemed to be welcomed by government, with both the prime minister, David Cameron, and the Leader of the Opposition, Ed Miliband, calling for cross-party talks to discuss the recommendations. Once again, though, the government took no action. The next Conservative prime minister (2016–19), Theresa May, had a bash at yet another new funding model for social care when seeking re-election in 2017, proposing that the upper threshold for free care be raised from £23,250 to £100,000 of assets, including property. Four days after launching her manifesto and after its characterisation by the press and political opponents as a 'dementia tax', May made a U-turn. In his first speech as the subsequent prime minister, in 2019, Boris Johnson promised that his government would 'fix the crisis in social care once and for all with a clear plan we have prepared to give every older person the dignity and security they deserve'.[172]

They didn't, of course, and the Covid-19 pandemic exposed all the failings of our underfunded, under-prioritised, and broken social care system. In the early months of 2020, the virus swept through care homes – partly because elderly hospital patients were suddenly discharged to care homes without being tested for Covid or required to isolate for a few days on arrival; partly because hospitals had priority for protective equipment over social care settings. In 2022, the High Court judged that this early release policy had been unlawful, failing to take account of the risks to elderly care home residents – another reflection of the lack of priority given to their needs and wellbeing. Almost 20,000 older people living in care homes died with Covid-19 in the first half of 2020.

Déjà vu all over again

In the early new year of 2025, Keir Starmer's Labour government announced yet another review of social care, to be led by crossbench peer Dame Louise Casey, and to take place in two phases. The first, reporting in 2026, will apparently look at critical and immediate issues; the second is not expected until 2028 and will, according to government, 'make longer-term recommendations for the *transformation* of adult social care' (my italics). This may, or may not, create 'a new national care service able to meet the needs of older and disabled people into the twenty-first century', as government claims,[173] but by the time the review describes this to us, they will be about a year from a general election. This will take us to a full thirty years of one report after another, and zero progress.

Talking about a (cultural) revolution

Both the Wanless and the Dilnot reports on social care focused, as they were asked to do, on funding – on feasible strategies to pay now and in the future for social care at the level needed because of the demographic shifts in the age structure of the population that are already underway. Neither asked deep questions about our culture of care. They are solid, research-based, methodologically sound attempts to model different funding options under sensible assumptions; they also make sensible recommendations for raising the pay and training standards of care staff.

To a large degree, however, they miss the bigger picture. Neither report seriously addresses how deeply our society undervalues care – both the work of caring for others and people's need to be cared for. Two think tanks, the New Economics Foundation and the Women's Budget Group, went further in 2022, describing a plan for 'Universal Quality Social Care'. As well as pointing out that the government strategy for care at the time was completely inadequately funded, and providing a proposal to close this funding gap, they called for co-production to be at the centre of social care to 'transform provision in line with the wellbeing principle in the Care Act' and for reform of the Care Quality Commission and additional regulation of the workforce.[174]

But, as author Emily Kenway suggests in her book *Who Cares* – a powerful examination of the meaning and practice of caring in our society and a personal account of caring for her mother as she died of cancer – care (thinking about it, providing it and receiving it) is hard because it contradicts what capitalism, and neoliberal capitalism in particular, has taught us to value and to expect from life: independence, liberty and freedom.[175] These have been valorised, and dependence on others has been pathologised in the West. We may be in chicken-and-egg territory here, believing we have the economic system we have because of our culture, rather than the other way round, with our economic system shaping our culture. But either way, this is why care has been, and continues to be, provided by the marginalised – women and migrant workers, unpaid or low paid, overworked and disrespected. But as Kenway also makes clear, we are *not* free of the need to care and nor should we wish to be. This harks back to the philosophical grounding of an ethics of care that I described at the start of this chapter. Requiring and providing care are human, relational imperatives – to structure our society otherwise leads to all the dysfunctional, broken systems described in this chapter. It is because we don't *think* about these issues as a society ordinarily (as opposed to when they impinge on us personally) – because they most often affect those with less power – that we have come to the sorry situation we're in, facing the impending multiple catastrophes of not providing enough, high-quality care.

What is needed to ensure care in a good society – in addition to the formal Universal Care Service approaches exemplified and described by Wanless, Dilnot, the New Economics Foundation/Women's Budget Group and others – are two fundamental and radical changes; both are necessary, and neither is sufficient on its own. If we can't work out how to make these two changes happen, then future generations will be catastrophically failed by a system in complete collapse.

One of those changes would be universal basic income. I've raised this already and it has powerful potential for helping to solve the conundrums of care for a good, caring society. It would mean people could afford to be carers without facing poverty, and those needing care would have more genuine choice about how and where they receive it. For now, hold that thought; I'm going to discuss this more fully in Chapter 6 because it is a solution that is relevant to all the issues I'm concerned with in this book.

The other thing we need is to create networks for mutual care of all kinds.[176] This will include co-housing arrangements as well as more distributed, community-based networks, so that we can benefit from shared space, shared resources, shared care, through our individual contributions of money, time, expertise, experience, and love.

In York, where I live, the Quaker charity the Joseph Rowntree Housing Trust runs a retirement community that includes individual homes and a care home. Residents buy a home in the community and the fee covers care in the home and accommodation in the care home, should these be needed. Residents also are part of a community that includes a coffee shop and restaurant, gym and spa pool, hair salon and a minibus for social outings. There are on-site activities, including music, art, literature, bridge, theatre and concert outings (and even lectures; I have given one there myself).

The New Ground community in Barnet in North London is a senior women's co-housing community of purpose-built flats and shared spaces. The residents run the community under principles of mutual aid, with goals of active participation and social inclusion. Residents support one another in all the ways that can prevent the need for more intensive and costly kinds of care. Co-housing like this – where residents have private apartments or rooms alongside shared communal facilities – is relatively well established and increasingly popular in Denmark, Sweden and the Netherlands. In these countries, such models are supported by strong social policies, urban planning, and cultural acceptance of communal living, with Denmark and Sweden particularly noted for their mature co-housing communities that promote social interaction, independence, and mutual support among older adults. The Netherlands also has a growing number of elderly co-housing projects, often integrated into broader sustainable urban developments.

In contrast, co-housing for seniors in the USA remains comparatively niche but is rapidly spreading. The movement has gained momentum over the past decade, driven by ageing Baby Boomers seeking alternatives to traditional retirement housing that emphasise community, autonomy and affordability. The

'ElderSpirit' project in south-west Virginia, established in 2006, offers private homes with shared garden and common areas, meeting the needs of members for mutual support and community.[177] While still a small segment of the housing market, the pace of development is accelerating, with more projects emerging across cities and rural areas – some supported by innovative policy initiatives and grassroots organisations.

Non-residential care networks, where people are connected in existing communities, can also create rich networks of mutual support that can underpin childcare, support for parents who are struggling *before* their children need care, support for children and adults with disabilities and/or neurodiversity, and support for older people. Within such care networks, people can expect, over time, to be both givers and receivers, to balance independence with the needs to care and be cared for; for care to take place with compassion and skill, in structures that reinforce mutual respect and dignity.

Social innovator Hilary Cottam described examples of such care networks operating around the world in a 2021 report to the charity the Health Foundation, but also pointed out that what is needed for such models to flourish is a proper policy and regulatory framework. We need to regulate against profit-making in the care sector and support cooperatives and other forms of economic democracy to make this happen at scale and be sustainable.[178] Economist Susan Himmelweit calls for forms of deliberative democracy so that society – we the people – can decide what capabilities we want care to support and how we should fund it.[166] This could include these mutual support networks as well as more formal additional care for those with the highest needs – and remember that if we can care for one another well through networks of support, we will need less costly, intensive care provided by the state.

Another example shows how care networks can also benefit carers. The support network Somerset Carers asks on its website: 'Who cares for the carers? We do.' The service is for unpaid carers of all kinds in Somerset and provides an online hub to help carers find support, training, groups and activities, and online and in-person carer groups. They have 'village agents' – paid, trained community support workers who live in the cluster of localities they support, and connect carers to statutory and voluntary services. Somerset Carers is funded by the local authority and commissioned through a charity, the Community Council for Somerset. The local authority spends 38 per cent of its budget on adult social care and has recognised that investment in prevention and improved care in the community is likely to save it money in the long term and improve wellbeing. Case studies from the Local Government Association suggest that for every £1 invested in carers, there is a potential reduction in local authority costs of £5.90.[179]

The Women's Budget Group provides compelling analysis of the economic benefits of investment in a care economy, showing that investment in care produces more jobs, and therefore more revenue from income tax, than the same size of investment in construction.[166] And these savings are important, because government support will be needed for the kinds of housing and common grounds that will provide the spaces in which informal and formal care can be provided. In this context, think also about the pay differences between traditionally male roles in manufacturing compared to traditionally female caring roles, and how they reflect an outdated hierarchy of value, status judgement and reward.

Emily Kenway calls this web of care networks, co-housing, regulation, etc., a 'commons of care'. Somehow, we need to be able to make the cultural shift that creates this 'commons', ensuring that belonging to at least one rich network of mutual support becomes the norm rather than the exception.

I've often heard people say that when they get old, they are going to move into a big house with all their friends, and all look after one another. We cannot afford to wait until we need the care; it will be too late. If we fail to make the cultural shift towards a commons of care, we will be failing to build the essential components of a good society.

CHAPTER 3

Educating a Good Society

'If you are planning for a year, sow rice; if you are planning for a decade, plant trees; if you are planning for a lifetime, educate people.'

Chinese proverb

A tale of two readers

My daughter was an early reader and was reading well by the time she started school. I tell this story not to illustrate her early prowess, but because of what happened next. I was taken aside by the kindergarten teacher at her public primary school in Chicago, who said that when it was 'book time' my daughter was reading aloud to herself and thus disturbing the other children. They were not yet reading and so were looking quietly at the pictures. 'Sounding out' words is typical in the early stages of learning to read and, far from wanting my daughter to be quiet, a good teacher would have been pleased by her progress and encouraging her to make more, perhaps asking her to share the story out loud with her friends.

I had taught my daughter to read before she reached school age because she so obviously wanted to learn. She saw her older brother reading, she liked being read to, we were a very book-oriented household, and she was keen to become a reader.

Teaching her was easy; she took to it like a duck to water because she was ready and eager.

A year or two later, on holiday, my daughter made friends with a girl her age who was staying close by. The girls were both seven years old and enjoyed playing together in the garden and swimming, but when they set up a board game one evening, a game designed for children of five and upwards, there was a difficulty – the other girl couldn't read the game cards, although she said she wanted to learn how. It turned out she was attending a Steiner school, a system of education based on the teachings of Rudolf Steiner, an Austrian educationalist (among other things) who died in 1925. Steiner schools are an alternative education system, with schools across the world, often praised for their holistic approach, calm environments and emphasis on creativity, but they don't teach children to read until they are seven years old, even if a child wants to learn, because of a belief that children under the age of seven are not developmentally ready.

I don't think either of these girls was served well by their schools: both were bumping up against rules and one-size-fits-all policies that didn't suit their individual needs; neither were being encouraged to flourish at their own pace. It feels unlucky, perhaps even unfair to them, that their developmental needs were not well met by their well-intentioned schools. It made me think hard about how an educational system might serve, or indeed help create, a good society.

The value that I believe is relevant here, in addition to the ethics of care I described in the previous chapter, is that we should make progress towards a good society by seeking the common good that comes from maximising everyone's capabilities. The 'capabilities approach' of Nobel Prize-winning economist Amartya Sen and Martha Nussbaum, Professor of Law and Ethics at the University of Chicago, centres on developing the social, political and economic conditions that optimise each person's abilities, freedom to make choices about their life, and opportunities. The capabilities approach asks what people are actually able to do and to be. And the capabilities approach pushes policymakers to 'construct meaningful interventions that show respect for, and empower, real people, rather than simply reflecting the biases of intellectual elites'.[180] Professor Nussbaum lists, among the capabilities that a good society would provide: senses, imagination and thought, practical reason, and play. Which sounds like a good foundation – one that promotes human flourishing and wellbeing – for the kind of education system we might design if we were building one from the ground up.

Reflections of the rainbow

In Chapter 1, I introduced the rainbow diagram of the social determinants of health, which is found everywhere in public health. It turns out that everywhere you look in the field of child development and wellbeing there is a remarkably similar model.

Although it is presented as a circle rather than a rainbow, Bronfenbrenner's model similarly represents how different 'systems' interact to influence child development. The child is in the middle, just like the individuals at the centre of the rainbow diagram, and is affected by relationships with family, friends and teachers in what Urie Bronfenbrenner, government advisor for the Head Start programme in the US in the mid 1960s, called the 'microsystem', and these all interact with one another (the 'mesosystem'), and take place in the context of economic, political, educational and other so-called

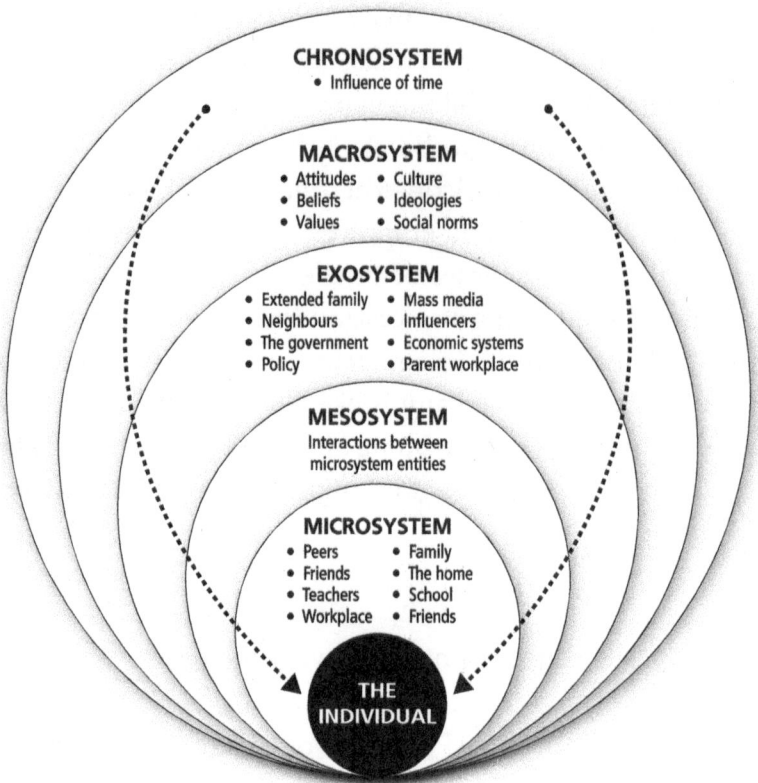

Bronfenbrenner's model of child development.[181]

'exosystems'. The whole lot sits within the 'macrosystem' of culture, laws and values. Bronfenbrenner also adds a time dimension to the model, which he perhaps unnecessarily labels the 'chronosystem' – which simply means how the child's experiences accumulate over their lifetime.

Why is this helpful when thinking about what an educational system for a good society should look like? I think it has an important lesson for us to keep very firmly in mind. Just as with the social determinants of health, it helps us to keep a focus on the upstream causes of good child development, showing us that we need to get the environment and the culture right for children, and can't expect schools or nurseries, or indeed parents, to do it all. All those layers need to be geared and synchronised towards growing children's capabilities and wellbeing.

The widest of playing fields

Education is a huge topic. From preschool to university, from vocational learning to private tutoring, and from questions about the national curriculum to methods of assessment, this is a topic that encompasses a wide range of complex and controversial questions. There are books on all of these subjects and more, reams of academic papers and shelves full of reports. And people have very strong feelings about all of this, including parents, teachers and governments.

I can't come even close to covering all aspects of education in this chapter, so I'm going to focus on two big issues: first, asking how well, or indeed whether, our current education system helps individual children to flourish; second, asking whether it creates a level playing field (because together these are necessary to ensure that everyone's capabilities are being maximised), and along the way looking at solutions for systemic problems, including how we might fund an education system that would do all that we want.

All roads lead to Finland

If we wanted to play 'fantasy education system' by picking the best elements from different systems around the world, we'd have a lot of options to choose from – different societies have made quite different choices; we needn't feel constrained to keep things the way they are if they're not actually serving the best interests of our children and/or our society.

And different countries achieve quite different levels of outcomes for children. Let's look at social mobility. One thing that everyone agrees on is that children should have equal opportunities to develop their capabilities and to flourish, but if we compare this in different countries, it is clear that some offer much higher potential for social mobility – a much more level playing field – than others.

Social mobility is a person's ability to move away from their social class of origin, to get to a different class or level of education or income than their parents. People can move up or down the social ladder, but it is upward social mobility that all politicians claim to want, a possibility for every child to realise ambition and aspiration. Leaving aside the highly relevant questions of whether or not any society can realise such an aspiration for every child, or indeed whether or not all children have, or should have, such ambitions, the Scandinavian countries stand out as doing particularly well. In the World Economic Forum's Social Mobility Index, Denmark, Norway, Finland and Sweden come top. The Land of Opportunity, the United States, ranks twenty-seventh; outclassed by more than half of the OECD nations, the UK comes in at twenty-first.[182] I've been making the same joke about this in lectures for more than fifteen years: if you want to live the American Dream, you had better move to Denmark. What are the Scandinavian countries getting right?

In almost all of the blueprints for a better education system that I have drawn on for this chapter, and indeed in a great many other reports and studies as well, Finland looms large. The story of how Finland overhauled its education system in the post-Second World War period, to drag itself up from dismal rankings to become a shining example of educational attainment and equality, is widely known. The government took stock, and they consulted widely (and we're talking years here, and three big commissions involving politicians of all stripes, teachers, unions and academics) and then they legislated, in 1968, to completely overhaul their system. Out went the two-tier system of grammar schools and 'civic schools' and in came comprehensive schooling for everyone. Out went an outdated curriculum and in came a child-centred, holistic approach. Over time, centralised control gave way to more authority and autonomy for individual schools and municipalities – teachers were entrusted with planning their own curriculum to meet the needs of their students rather than being restricted by a national curriculum. And they were trusted to do that because of the changes to teacher training, which created a highly skilled, well-paid, respected profession. The public discourse built public support, which in turn underpinned the political will to implement this transformative change. If we're going to play 'fantasy education system' then we don't really need to borrow features from a variety of systems across the world where they do things differently; we could just do what Finland did. Throughout the early 2000s, Finland took nearly all the top places in the OECD's international rankings – it still ranks high, although South-East Asian countries now take the top spots. Finland comes fourth in the UNICEF rankings of child wellbeing in rich countries.

Think about the education system we've got. We have a school year that some say was designed to suit the needs of families to have their children help with the harvest in the summer, but which now leads to some children (and guess which children?) falling behind over the long break. We have a school day that doesn't fit with anybody's working hours, making life stressful and expensive for too many families. We have a postcode lottery of provision for children with special educational needs and disabilities. We have an admissions system that, by design, favours parents who are rich enough to buy homes near desirable schools. We have an inspection system wholeheartedly opposed by the teaching profession. We have a system of university tuition fees that doesn't sufficiently fund universities and instead acts as a barrier to diversity and inclusion in higher education. There is much more, but in short, if you were to design an education system from first principles, to provide the best educational opportunities for everyone, it would emphatically not look like ours.

Time for school: a case in point

Let's start with one seemingly very simple issue that illustrates the need for a more carefully thought-through system to meet individual needs. At what age should children start school? Looking around the world, the UK is something of an outlier. In England, Wales and Scotland, children must start school by the time they reach 'compulsory school age', which is, loosely defined, the term following their fifth birthday. But children are entitled to start school in the September following their *fourth* birthday and starting at age four is compulsory in Northern Ireland, so almost all UK children are in school before they are five. Children start school at a later age in most countries: in about two-thirds, children start school at six, and 1 in 5 countries has a starting age of seven, so we're definitely in the minority.

Does it matter? The data that best allow us to compare overall educational attainment in different countries come from the Programme for International Student Assessment (PISA) run by the OECD. We're going to see a fair amount of data from PISA in this chapter so it's worth describing how they are collected.

PISA has tested the knowledge of fifteen-year-olds in randomly selected schools in eighty-one (at last count) different countries, every three years since 2000 (Covid delayed PISA testing by one year, so there was a four-year gap prior to the wave of testing in 2022). PISA tests include what they call mathematics literacy, reading literacy, and science literacy, and countries can be ranked by their scores on each of these, or across all three kinds of test. They sometimes throw in other tests as well: in 2022 PISA assessed 'creative thinking' and in 2025, as I'm writing, promises to assess foreign language skills. The PISA website suggests you can find out if you're smarter than a fifteen-year-old by playing around with questions from the PISA tests online, which I have to say is quite informative as to the kinds of things being taught in schools these days (spreadsheets! cosmology!).[183]

If we look at the 2022 PISA results, two of the European countries (Estonia and Denmark) whose children start school at age seven scored higher than the UK, but others scored a little bit lower (Sweden, Finland, Latvia, Poland) and two quite a lot lower (Romania and Bulgaria).[184] There doesn't seem to be much correlation between having a younger or older school starting age and average national educational attainment.

However, within a school system, a child's age relative to the other kids in their school year *is* correlated with how well they do, in school and even in later life. This is a sufficiently well-known phenomenon to have been tagged as the 'birthday effect', and the negative impact of being relatively young – and the youngest child in a school year can be almost a year younger than the oldest – has been widely researched.[185] Differences in attainment between the youngest and oldest children within a school year start early and persist throughout their school careers. Relatively older children do better on tests and are more likely to be picked for sports teams or given leadership roles. Relatively younger children are more likely to be diagnosed with learning difficulties, perhaps because their apparent struggles are actually just the result of being less cognitively and emotionally mature than their older classmates. The impact of being less mature, physically and psychologically, can undermine self-esteem, confidence and motivation. Once children are labelled – by teachers and by themselves – as more or less competent, they are set on virtuous or vicious cycles of reinforcement. Perhaps surprisingly, a lucky accident of birth month can drive lifelong success, with relatively older children more likely to end up both rich[186] and powerful.[187] That's an awful lot of advantage flowing from an accident of birth.

One single facet of our educational system can appear unproblematic until you scratch beneath the surface and see the inequities created by it. It is surely wrong to have a system that arbitrarily imposes a lifelong educational, mental health and economic disadvantage on some children, simply because of the month they are born, when we know that the system itself is causing the problem. What could be done to fix this problem? Can the system be tweaked, or do we need a radical shift to overcome it?

One model that seems as if it could be helpful, and that is already being used in many countries, is the multi-age classroom. When children start school, they join classrooms with a mix of ages, which gives the older children in that class a chance to be role models and to help the younger children, and the younger children to aspire to the capabilities of the older children, which is believed to help their cognitive and social development. The younger children will get their turn to be the older children after a year or two.

In New Zealand, three-quarters of children are taught in mixed-age classrooms in primary schools.[188] Proponents say that it helps teachers to think about children's individual needs, because they're not thinking about the average capabilities of a single age group, and that mixed-age groups give children opportunities to learn by teaching, and to problem-solve. This is thought to be good for both fast and slow learners. Think back to the two girls described at the start of this chapter – in a multi-age classroom, the early reader could be reading out loud to younger children or peers who are not yet reading and the child keen to learn to read could be taught when she was individually ready, and not at a fixed age. Obviously this is going to be easier in a system without a prescribed curriculum and standardised tests of attainment. Advocates also point out that children are regularly in mixed-age groupings outside the classroom – at home, during school breaks and in playgrounds or parks. As adults we almost all work and socialise in mixed-age settings, so this is not an entirely radical concept.

But what does the research tell us about mixed-age classrooms? Surprisingly, there doesn't seem to be as much of a leaning towards either positive or negative outcomes as advocates and critics state with certainty – not enough to be able to say with any confidence that mixed-age classrooms are either a brilliant idea or a terrible one. A comprehensive review from 2019 suggests that when mixed-age classrooms are adopted for educational reasons rather than, say, simply to deal with small school numbers (as in some rural schools), and when they are put in place with appropriate training and resources, they do have positive impacts in terms of learning outcomes.[189] But the same review points out that parents consistently don't like mixed-age classrooms, fearing that high-achieving children will be bored and insufficiently challenged, and that slower learners won't be able to keep up. Head teachers don't seem overly keen either, perceiving mixed-age groupings as more of a burden for teachers, although they do see benefits for children.[190] There doesn't seem to be much, if any, research asking children what they think, and very little consideration, if any, as to *which* children do better in these circumstances, so we don't really know whether children who are losers in the 'birthday effect' lottery do better in mixed-age classrooms.

On balance, mixed-age classrooms, with teacher training to enhance individualised approaches, look like a good building block for a redesigned system. And perhaps the upheaval necessary to implement this change in all schools is worth it if it might avoid the negative impacts of the current system on the 40 per cent of children who are considered summer-born (between April and August) and perhaps especially on the 1 in 7 or so children who are 11–12 months younger than their school peers, or indeed those born prematurely.

Mind control?

Many people my age will remember the lines from the 1979 Pink Floyd song 'Another Brick in the Wall', from the album *The Wall*, associating education with brainwashing and sarcastic authoritarian teachers. The video used imagery of uniform-clad children trudging along a school conveyor belt into a meat grinder that extrudes them as sausages. Not the most subtle of comments on rigidities in education. Visually it was quite shocking, and the lyrics were deeply transgressive, with teachers portrayed as forbidding bullies; apparently both the Inner London Education Authority and Prime Minister Margaret Thatcher hated the song.

The idea that schools are trying to shape children to a single mould and that the education system is too rigidly focused on achieving success on standardised tests of academic achievement is still at the heart of contentious debate around what our education system should be like. Indeed, the National Education Union, the biggest teaching union, refers to an 'exam factory culture' in our education system. Meanwhile, there is 'a growing consensus among social scientists and philosophers alike that a sense of life's meaning and purpose is a key aspect of flourishing'.[191]

The Children's Society, a Church of England-linked children's charity, has been asking children and young people (aged 10–17 years) about their lives, in annual surveys, for more than a decade. In 2024, they put these survey findings together with annual data from one of the UK's biggest household surveys (called 'Understanding Society'), and from the OECD's 2018 Programme for International Student Assessment (PISA). This 2024 *Good Childhood Report* found that UK children's happiness – with their lives as a whole, with their friends, their appearance, their school and their schoolwork – was lower than it had been a decade earlier. More children were unhappier with school (14.3 per cent of them) than with other aspects of their lives. Sadly, UK children had the lowest life satisfaction among fifteen-year-olds in twenty-seven European countries,* with just over a quarter reporting low life satisfaction; that compares to just 6.7 per cent in the Netherlands – a huge difference. Other top-scoring countries were Finland (10.8 per cent), and Denmark (11.3 per cent). But it wasn't just the usual (Scandinavian) suspects who did well; Romania (11.4 per cent) and Portugal (11.6 per cent) were up there too. The UK was also the country with the biggest gap in life satisfaction between its most disadvantaged and its most

---

* I should note that in the more recent PISA data from 2022, the UK crept up a place to twenty-sixth out of twenty-seven.

advantaged children; it had the second-highest level of bullying, and also scored low on school safety, sense of belonging in school, and long-term school absence. Not a pretty picture.[192]

What young people said they wanted from education varied, of course, but there were strong themes. Children want more mental health awareness, more support, and more acceptance of difference and diverse identities. One young person said: 'school does ruin your mental health. It basically makes every single child that doesn't fit into every single societal norm be ostracised.' Young people also wanted a wider choice of subjects, including practical things like learning to budget and to cook, and more work-related opportunities. Perhaps reflecting the high levels of anxiety among this cohort, they wanted more online school availability and more coursework-based assessment rather than tests and exams. Young people's concerns seemed to coalesce around two, equally heartbreaking, shortcomings of the system: the pain of feeling different and unsupported, and not being taught crucial life skills.[193]

Children seem to be a sensible lot. They know they can't learn well unless they feel safe and secure and looked after. And they know there is stuff they need to learn and opportunities they should be able to access beyond the academic curriculum. They often don't ask for much, but we seem to be letting them down nevertheless by not prioritising care, cooperation and consideration over tests and exams.[194]

We've seen how the 2018 PISA survey included in the 2024 Good Childhood Report found that UK children had the lowest life satisfaction and the biggest gap in life satisfaction between disadvantaged and advantaged children. UNICEF puts that same score for life satisfaction together with adolescent suicide rates as a combined measure of *mental wellbeing*, adds in levels of child overweight/obesity and mortality as a combined measure of *physical wellbeing*, and then puts together data from PISA 2018 maths and reading scores with what children say about how easy they find it to make friends and calls this *skills wellbeing*, and finally puts those mental, physical and skills wellbeing scores together as an index of *child wellbeing*. On those measures we come 27th among thirty-eight OECD rich countries for overall child wellbeing, 29th for mental wellbeing, 19th for physical wellbeing, and 26th for skills wellbeing. Really not good at all. The PISA educational data that UNICEF pick for this exercise is the proportion of children who meet what they define as basic standards: a basic level of proficiency in both reading and maths. As UNICEF points out, 'even in the best-performing country, Estonia, more than 1 in 5 children do not meet the basic proficiency standard', but in the UK, more than a third (37 per cent) of children failed to meet that basic standard in 2018 (twenty-one other rich countries did better).

Teachers want reform of the curriculum to be more 'engaging and inclusive' (to include teaching on anti-racism, more emphasis on the arts, and more time for physical education), to end tests in primary schools and to overhaul secondary school tests. Ahead of the 2024 general election, the National Education Union also called for the abolition of the system of schools inspection run by Ofsted.

Ofsted – the Office for Standards in Education, Children's Services and Skills, a government department charged with inspecting schools – was set up to improve standards and give parents a basis on which to choose schools. Up until autumn 2024, Ofsted inspected schools on an intermittent basis and gave them a single grade of Outstanding, Good, Requires Improvement, or Inadequate. After primary school headteacher Ruth Perry took her own life in 2023, when her school was downgraded from Outstanding to Inadequate, following what a coroner described as a 'rude and intimidating' inspection, there was widespread criticism of the harms caused by the inspection regime. Teachers are adamant that the Ofsted inspections are harmful. But does Ofsted actually raise standards, as intended? We don't really know if any benefits outweigh the harms. According to the National Audit Office, who looked at whether Ofsted offers good value for money, Ofsted had 'limited information on [its] impact'.[195] There were a few adaptations made in 2024: the same grades will continue to be used but, instead of getting a single grade, each school will get a 'report card' of separate grades for overall performance, quality of education, pupil behaviour and attitudes, staff development, leadership and management, and the effectiveness of safeguarding policies. This is definitely a minor tweak rather than an overhaul. It's difficult to imagine how the grade for overall performance won't have exactly the same meaning and impact for a school as the previous single overall grade, and, as I'm writing, the teaching profession continues to campaign to end Ofsted.

From the three Rs to the three Cs

Education researchers share teachers' concerns that the system focuses too much on attainment outcomes – performance on standardised tests and exams – and not enough on the well-rounded education and wellbeing of children and young people. Experts describe the need for an ethics of care, the importance of creating a sense of belonging and inclusion in schools (for parents as well as children), often summing this up in three Cs instead of the traditional three Rs of education (reading, writing and arithmetic). This is as much about meeting young people's mental health needs as broadening the curriculum to offer, for example, more play and more creative or practical subjects. The idea of moving away from the three Rs to the three Cs is all over research and reports on reforming the curriculum and teacher training. But the three Cs are rather various! I have seen:

- Care, consideration and cooperation
- Care, criticality and creativity
- Character, community and context
- Connect, construct and create
- Critical thinking, creativity, and collaboration
- Creation, connection and curiosity
- Creativity, challenge and communication
- Competence, creativity and care.

The three Cs might vary (although you can see there are themes among them), but there is a consistency among education experts that we need to re-orient the *culture* of our education system along these lines.[111, 119, 196–198] That means prioritising well-being ahead of results on standardised tests and exams. And it also means that we would need to design an evaluation regime for schools to align with how well schools are doing on the three Cs. Looking once more at Finland, assessment of school performance is largely a matter of schools reviewing themselves and making plans for self-improvement.[199] This might sound alarming (no objective tests?) but avoids all the problems that are created by teaching and learning 'for the test'. Finland's excellent educational results show that standardised testing doesn't have to be part of a high-attaining system.

All of this might feel obvious, and I'm sure that everyone concerned with education will say that they are aiming for (and achieve) a caring child-centred environment. It is clear, however, that schools are *not* always doing this sufficiently. As I was writing this chapter, a group of parents with children at an academy school in Hackney, London, rated as Outstanding by Ofsted, accused the school of 'causing serious harm to children's mental health, with teachers humiliating and "screaming" at pupils'.[200] One anecdote, one school, you might think. But then came news of an investigation being undertaken in three Essex schools, recently taken over by the same academy trust, while Hackney Council confirmed it has received more than 300 'separate accounts of alleged emotional harm . . . from parents, former students, teachers, local GPs and child psychologists'.[201] Progress in understanding child development, and indeed how to motivate anyone of any age, means that we know this isn't how to help children flourish, however challenging their behaviour in the classroom might be. We no longer tolerate a culture of shouting and humiliation in the workplace, and it has no place in a modern education system.

If children are made to feel unvalued or stigmatised in school, they cannot flourish. I'll come on to absenteeism later, but for now, leaving aside the children that are absent – because they cannot face school that day – how many are in school but not fully engaging or participating, feeling discouraged, sad, or stupid?

We don't know the numbers of children burdened by what education researchers call 'low attainment designation' – the stigmatisation of low-achieving students by teachers and other children – but Dr Laura Quick, of the Institute for Education at University College London, describes such children as suffering the triple pressures of being expected to perform academically, expected to assume responsibility for this performance and, on top of all that, being expected to maintain a positive mental attitude. In her words, they are being put in the 'impossible position where they feel shamed, blamed and stigmatised for their low attainment while expected to deny or overcome the distress this can cause them'. During her four years of intensive research with children experiencing this burden, one boy in primary school told Dr Quick:

> that poor work meant teachers were angry, shouted at you and would 'rip up your page, scrunch it up and put it in the recycling bin'. He said that children who don't learn 'properly . . . don't get the job' and their 'life is ruined', contrasting this with a student with good marks feeling 'powerful'.

Another child felt 'it might be easy for other people, but it might be just like "oh it's so hard" for me . . . I'm just so angry and sad at the same time, like, I'm angry because it's so hard'. This child remembered all his bad marks from previous years and said he felt 'very sad and disappointed' when his results were read aloud, and that his teacher should 'not shout, not shout out the scores . . . it makes me feel really sad, embarrassed . . . Like he shouts it out to the whole class.'[202]

Dr Quick raises the very real problem of our schools and our society 'uncritically conveying a model of [personal] value based on narrow individual academic achievement' that is less achievable for some children because of structural issues of deprivation, social class and (sometimes) ethnicity.[202] We tell children to aim high and at the same time make many of them feel they lack the capability or character to get there. They are trapped in 'a cruel and cynical fiction',[203] where 'the elite have earned their place at the top' whereas their own position is the result of their inadequacy, and is all that they deserve.[204] The children that Dr Quick spent time with, labelled as 'low attainers', nevertheless had other attributes – such as a commitment to being kind and supportive of other children – that we surely want schools to nurture and develop for the good of society. Creativity, care and character are among the Cs that we want.

What should we ask of schools?

It feels as if we have become trapped into having an educational system where school success (and therefore individual achievement) is assessed in extremely narrow terms – scores on standardised tests – and the assessments given such elevated importance that everything becomes subservient to the inspection regime, rather than the system of assessment being geared to produce holistic educational wellbeing and happy, confident children. We have reacted to historically poor achievement in basic subjects like maths and English and tried to provide a course correction by over-gearing the curriculum towards achieving progress in those skills at the expense of much else. Reading about Finland's assessment of schools makes me want to weep with frustration. Children's wellbeing and mental health come first in Finland, and the curriculum is designed with the primary purpose of engaging children's curiosity in the world around them, rather than trying to fill them with a set body of knowledge. Class time isn't (always) artificially split into distinct subjects and teachers have the autonomy to provide flexible, child-centred learning. Teachers can innovate and experiment and openly share their successes and challenges with other teachers, without risk to their professional standing; within trusting networks, they learn together and peer review one another's work. This is a system that supports the capabilities of both children and teachers.

School refusers . . . and schools refusing

Perhaps the most worrying problem in education right now – and one that highlights the need for the culture shift of the three Cs – is the crisis of school absence and what is known as school refusal in UK schools, especially acute since the Covid pandemic. The overall absence rate on any given school day increased in the UK from less than 5 per cent in the 2015/16 school year to more than 7 per cent in 2023/24. That doesn't sound very dramatic – although it is a 57 per cent increase – but when we dig a little deeper the scale of the problem becomes clear. 'Persistent absence' means that a child is absent for 10 per cent or more of the time they should be in school. This also doesn't sound too awful – those children are in school for 90 per cent of the time – but that level of absence translates to not being in school for at least four weeks of the school year, effectively missing a month of learning each year. In primary schools, 15 per cent of kids are persistently absent; in secondary schools it's 27 per cent. And lots of persistently absent kids are out of school for a lot more days. 'Severe persistence absence' is defined as missing half or more of school days and this has almost tripled since before the pandemic and continues to rise, although less severe absence might be settling back a little.

Persistent absence, severe or otherwise, means missing out on all the other non-scholastic benefits of being in school – relationships with peers and teachers; play, sports and other extra-curricular activities; perhaps a healthy hot lunch or breakfast club. Schools also play an important role in safeguarding children, detecting neglect and abuse, and keeping children from harm's way and being exposed to or taking part in criminal and gang-related activities.[205] School exclusions are often a starting point for children being exposed to grooming and exploitation. Teachers and other school staff need to be able to have their 'eyes on the child' to play this vital safeguarding role, and schools can be a safe environment for vulnerable young people.

The children most likely to be missing out on school are

those with special educational needs and disabilities (SEND) – a third of these children are persistently absent from school – and children with depression and anxiety, who are three times more likely to have missed more than three weeks of school than other children.[206] Common mental health conditions among children and young people are at unprecedented levels, as I described in earlier chapters, and have been spiralling upward since at least 2011, with the pandemic pushing levels of anxiety and depression even higher, to what can only be viewed as crisis levels.[207, 208] Remember that 1 in 5 children have mental health difficulties.[209] The figure is slightly higher in 17–19-year-olds (23 per cent) and it's 22 per cent in young people aged 20–25 years, many of whom will be trying to complete their education at university or in an apprenticeship or other training. Children with mental health conditions are four and a half times more likely to have been bullied at school (37 per cent compared to 8 per cent of children without mental health problems), and almost four times as likely to have been bullied online (11 per cent compared to 3 per cent). Not feeling safe in school was often given as a reason for persistent absence among children receiving free school meals and among vulnerable children supported by social services or youth offending teams.

At a recent event that included wealthy philanthropists, one told me that there wasn't a single family with teenagers among her acquaintance that wasn't coping with a child with mental health challenges. However, children with mental health conditions are more likely to be in poor families, who struggle to access the support they need or pay for private counselling, or to spare resources for them to engage with out-of-school activities, sports and social events with friends, which might help. These young people really need to be in school.

I'm staggered by these levels of absence from school. It's

hard to contemplate the levels of distress that cause this crisis of emotional avoidance of school. And hard to comprehend the emotional and other consequences for parents who are trying to cope with children who cannot leave the house, and for schools who are trying to provide the right support but don't have the resources, not to speak of the ultimate consequences for society. Prevention needs to be the focus, with investment in early support for children at risk of disengaging from school. Absence in the early years is predictive of persistent absence in later years, with all its knock-on costly effects (health problems, unemployment, crime) so early intervention is worth the investment. Key strategies called for in the Child of the North's 2024 *Evidence-based Plan for Improving School Attendance* include daily attendance monitoring; collaboration between schools, social services and healthcare providers; implementing targeted support plans; and also addressing underlying issues of family stress, mental health and poverty.[210] A rebalancing away from the exam factory culture to instead 'foster a sense of belonging and inclusivity' is also needed. The Child of the North report also calls for schools to create:

> a supportive culture through peer support systems, extracurricular activities, and a focus on mental health. Ensuring that children feel connected to their school community can improve attendance rates and reduce disengagement. There is a need to support schools to provide extracurricular activities as these play a crucial role in fostering belonging. Participation in enrichment programmes, peer support systems, and volunteer opportunities help students feel engaged and develop a sense of identity within the school. These activities are particularly beneficial for disadvantaged students, as they provide a platform for building self-worth and social connections.[210]

The problem of children missing out on school isn't only caused by children and young people refusing to go to school; it's also because of the high levels of school exclusions – schools suspending or permanently excluding children for misbehaviour in or out of school. School exclusions have been rising: 9,400 children were excluded during the 2022/23 school year – that is 241 children, nine whole class sizes, during every week of term.[211] Schools are not allowed to exclude children *because* of a disability or special educational need that they cannot meet, but nevertheless children with SEND are three times as likely as non-SEND children to be suspended – and, by the time they are 16–17 years old, three times as likely to be classified as 'Not in Employment, Education or Training' (known as NEET), with the lifelong consequences that we saw in Chapter 2. Children with mental health difficulties are ten times more likely to be excluded than average. Excluded children miss a lot of school while they wait, usually for months, to be found a place in another school or a Pupil Referral Unit. Most of them will never return to mainstream school, and their prospects are poor – in terms of educational attainment, becoming NEET or becoming involved in criminal activity. Black children, Gypsy, Roma and Irish Traveller children, and poor children are also excluded at high rates.

The government-commissioned Timpson review of school exclusion, published in 2019, reported that, as well as lacking funding and resources that would help them try to prevent exclusions, pressure on schools to meet attendance and exam performance was leading to avoidable exclusions.[212] Teachers report that student behaviour has deteriorated since the pandemic, as young people missed crucial social experiences during lockdowns. Resources, however, are also more stretched than ever, and the pressures related to exam performance have not gone away. This has created a tension between the drive to improve performance on academic tests and to manage children seen as disruptive or failing. One survey found that 77 per cent of school leaders strongly agreed that 'making sure my school does well in Ofsted inspections is one of my top priorities', and the school leaders the researchers interviewed 'felt incentivised to prioritise the interest of the school over the interest of particular groups of, usually more vulnerable, children'.[213]

Dr Simon Edwards at the University of Portsmouth has developed an intervention called 'narrative counselling' that has been successful in preventing exclusions by counselling and mentoring those young people (and their parents and teachers) who are at risk of exclusion due to behaviour, finding that mutual acknowledgement and understanding leads to improved behaviour.[214] This is exactly like the public health approach we saw in Chapter 1, moving away from the cliff edge and preventing problems before they become a crisis, with the initial investment of time and money paying off in terms of longer-term benefit. In this case, building relationships between teachers, children and their parents creates the engagement and connections with school that allow the young people to flourish. Though it may not provide the kind of short-term payoff in good exam results that a marketised school system demands, the potential lifelong impact of investing in this kind of prevention for young people is a benefit to society as a whole.

Getting the balance right

Of course, none of the foregoing is to say that having expectations of high standards in educational attainment, including in core subjects like reading, writing and maths, is wrong, or that we don't need a national curriculum, or external exams like GCSEs and A levels. The issue is about balance and not letting the focus on tests and exams dominate to the extent that it is stressful and alienating, leaves some children feeling like failures, and crowds out time for enrichment activities, such as play, or a wider curriculum including more of the arts and humanities that have been disproportionately cut from both schools and universities.

While I was writing this chapter my thoughts kept drifting back to when I first saw the Simón Bolívar Youth Orchestra, conducted by Gustavo Dudamel, playing with virtuosity and joyful exuberance at the 2007 London Proms. Both the orchestra and Dudamel himself are products of El Sistema, the orchestral classical music programme, which has transformed the lives and opportunities of some of Venezuela's poorest children. Since then, El Sistema has been established in some of the UK's poorest communities – called 'Big Noise' in Scotland and 'In Harmony' in England – with the same positive impact on individual lives. Richard Wilkinson attended a concert in West Everton, Liverpool, and was moved by the tears on the face of a grandmother of one of the child performers. When asked why she was crying, she said that she never thought that such an opportunity would come to a poor community like hers. Evaluation of the Scottish programme has found positive impacts on confidence, discipline, pride and aspiration, and better teamworking, better academic skills, healthier behaviours and a sense of belonging and fulfilment among participants. Surely programmes of this nature, in more of the arts, are needed for all children.

And quite apart from having opportunities for creative development, something is clearly awry if, even with the current emphasis on core subjects and testing, more than a third of our young people are failing to reach basic standards in maths and reading by age fifteen.

In the 2022 PISA rankings, the UK moved up to eleventh place among OECD countries; this was driven by an improved relative ranking in maths, while reading and science stayed about the same. That sounds quite positive, and the government at the time certainly saw this as a tick and a gold star for their educational policy, which had been very much focused on tests and standards (when he was Secretary of State for Education, Michael Gove delighted the Twittersphere by appearing to have told the Education Committee that all schools should be above average![215]).

There are, however, two caveats to this seemingly quite good ranking: first, the absolute scores for the UK on maths, reading and science were actually *lower* in 2022 than in 2018 (we moved up in the relative rankings because other countries had even bigger drops in their scores). And second caveat: in the UK, 1 in 3 schools and 1 in 4 pupils who should have taken part in PISA, because they were scientifically sampled to do so, refused to take part. Participating in PISA does involve significant effort for schools and students, including the burden of making logistical arrangements and setting aside time for the testing process itself. The UK not meeting the PISA threshold for taking part means that the scores are not properly representative of UK performance, and as higher-achieving students are more likely to have ended up included, the UK scores are probably higher than they should be, perhaps enough to mean that we really should be several places lower in the league table. And if we look at scores among the lowest-achieving students (the bottom 10 per cent), their maths, reading and science scores all dropped significantly between 2018 and 2022.

There are a couple more international scoring systems that

tell us about primary school rather than secondary school attainment. PIRLS, which stands for Progress in International Reading Literacy Study, measures reading; and TIMSS, which stands for Trends in International Mathematics and Science Study, looks at maths.[216]

In the most recent 2021 PIRLS results, England moved up in the rankings from eighth to fourth, although just as with PISA, actual scores were slightly lower than in 2016 – other countries seem to have taken more of a hit from the disruption to education caused by the Covid-19 pandemic. Sadly, English children's enjoyment of, and confidence in, reading has declined. In the most recent TIMSS, which was pre-Covid, England came eighth in maths but twenty-seventh for the gender gap in maths; and twelfth for science, but twenty-third for the gender gap in science. In both maths and sciences, boys scored higher.

Quite a complicated picture, then, certainly not a uniformly rosy one, and sometimes the statistics need to be interpreted with caution. In the most recent PIRLS, for example, England saw a reduction in its gender gap in reading, which sounds great, but this was because girls' scores declined, and not because boys improved.

The bottom line? The UK doesn't seem to do too badly in terms of average attainment in maths, reading and science, but not brilliantly. It feels as though we are paying much too high a price, from both a capabilities and an ethics perspective, when we look at lack of mental wellbeing and school absence. Overall, I'd give us a middling grade (C+ maybe) for how we're doing on attainment, on average, and a failing grade for our long tail of underachievement and widespread unhappiness. And this is why I'm a strong backer of the Cs being given at least as much priority as the Rs.

In 2024, the Labour government announced an independent

review to 'refresh the curriculum and statutory assessment system for 5–19-year-olds, to make sure they meet the needs of every child and young person'. The stated aim is to have a curriculum that balances 'ambition, relevance, flexibility and inclusivity' for all children and young people, with more emphasis on music, art, sport and drama, and vocational subjects. Some of the Cs (e.g. creativity, competence) seem to be in there with the three Rs, and the government is seeking views from parents, teachers and others in a consultation process, which is a welcome development. But the review is about the curriculum rather than the culture of the education system, despite the need for reform of both. Some educational experts talk about the need for a reorientation towards the rights of children, and the need for a rights-based approach that fully implements the United Nations Convention on the Rights of the Child.

This UN convention contains fifty-four articles, and the UK has been signed up to be legally bound by these since 1990. Perhaps the most relevant provisions of the convention in this context are Article 29, which states that education must develop every child's personality, talents and abilities to the full, and Article 31, which states the rights of children to be able to relax, play and take part in a wide range of cultural and artistic activities. Educational experts also call for stronger teacher and other staff training, especially for supporting children and young people with social and emotional mental health, special needs and disabilities, but also for more professional autonomy, including input into a system of assessment that promotes learning rather than cramming, and into a more balanced curriculum.

To end this discussion of curricula and culture, you might be surprised to find that employers seem just as keen on the three Cs as the three Rs. There is a long history, dating back at least to the 1970s, of employers complaining about the failure of schools to meet 'the needs of industry'. Independent academic Glenn Rikowski describes employers – throughout the 1970s, '80s and into the 1990s – being appalled at school leavers' technical skills, their basic numeracy and literacy, their work attitudes, social skills and even their appearance, despite the introduction of a national curriculum, work experience schemes and national vocational qualifications.[217] In reality, of course, labour markets and their needs vary widely across regions and industries and might be very different in the future. Automation and artificial intelligence (AI) are expected to transform labour markets, creating new jobs while making others obsolete. Technological developments will create new markets for highly specialised skills, but changing demographics will mean that we need more people in (what are now low-earning) caring roles. The International Baccalaureate Schools and Colleges Association surveyed business leaders about their views on education and found something of a split in what employers feel that education is for.[218] Two-thirds said education was there to create well-rounded human beings, but a third said its purpose was to develop efficient workers. Business leaders did agree, however, on the skills they were looking for. The top five skills that were desired by employers had very high endorsement and included communication skills (88 per cent), an inquiring mind (which we can label 'curiosity': 78 per cent), critical thinking (76 per cent), open-mindedness (72 per cent), and being principled (64 per cent). These soft skills were valued more highly than what young people *know*, their subject-specific knowledge.

A tale of two schools (Part One)

I saw a shining example of those soft skills being nurtured when, about a decade ago, I was invited to visit an independent school for girls to give a talk on my research. The girls were confident, well informed and curious. Their headteacher and the other staff knew them all by name and the girls were thriving academically and personally, with access to great resources and a wide range of courses, including seven different languages at A level. I was impressed, but also depressed. The school's fees are currently more than £43,000 per year for day girls, and almost £60,000 for full-time boarding. These young women came from backgrounds of privilege, social and cultural capital. No wonder they were so confident.

Uneven playing fields and class ceilings

In 2015, the BBC decided to mark the fiftieth anniversary of the *World at One* news and current affairs programme by asking a number of celebrities to say what Britain excels at. The then-prime minister, David Cameron, nominated British universities and science, the leader of the opposition, Ed Miliband, plumped for the NHS, and actor Jude Law picked British theatre. But acclaimed playwright and author Alan Bennett created controversy by his statement that what the British really excel at is hypocrisy. Among his targets was private education: 'A substantial minority of our children receive a better education than the rest because of the social situation of the parents,' he said, and 'then we wonder why things at the top do not change or society improve. But we know why. It's because we are hypocrites.'[219]

The economist Thomas Piketty makes the same point in his 2022 book, *A Brief History of Equality*. This was a book that I was finding uplifting – pointing as it does to the long progressive arc towards greater equality that has accompanied the construction of the modern world: the demise of slavery and colonialism, the continual expansion of human rights and the development of the welfare state – until I came to a section entitled 'Educational equality: always proclaimed, never realised'. In it, Piketty draws attention to the 'monumental gap between official statements regarding equality of opportunity and the reality of the educational inequalities that the disadvantaged classes face'.[220]

Governments, unfailingly, say they want every child to have an equal opportunity of a good education. This is the fundamental policy stance and educational priority of successive UK governments. The Labour government elected in July 2024 said it wanted to 'break down barriers to opportunity by reforming our childcare and education systems, to make sure there is *no class ceiling* on the ambitions of young people in Britain'.[221] When the Conservatives came to power in 2010, they promised (also my italics) '*fair access* to universities, the professions, and good jobs for young people from *all backgrounds*', saying that they would 'give many more children access to the kind of education that is currently only available to the well-off'. Prior to that, when New Labour were elected in 1997, it was on the promise of making education their number-one priority, 'developing the potential of *all our people*' (again, my italics). And so it goes on, back through the decades, with successive governments promising equal access to high-quality education and the creation of equal opportunities for social mobility through educational attainment. More than anything, it seems, governments want a level educational playing field.

And yet we have a very divided educational system – or rather, we have parallel systems that reinforce and exacerbate social divisions and inequality. One parallel system consists of private schools and some of these are so other-worldly in comparison to state schools in deprived areas that it's as if they exist in a parallel universe. The average annual fees for a private day school in 2024 are just over £15,000 per year, which is just about the equivalent of a year's entire household income in the lowest-earning fifth of households. Boarding schools come in at £39,000 and the most expensive schools, like Eton, Harrow and Westminster, cost in the region of £50,000–63,000 per year. If you don't know what one of those schools is like, do a bit of googling and check out the leafy estates, the impressive architecture, even the school menus. And perhaps notice particularly the descriptions of pastoral support. One top school describes the team of people devoted to this: house masters and assistant house masters, matrons, tutors, chaplains, doctors, psychologists and counsellors. It couldn't be further from the under-resourced and overburdened state system. Also of note on private school websites is what they have to say about their success in exam results, and sending kids to top universities – especially Oxford and Cambridge. All of this is what I was seeing in action during my visit to that independent girls' boarding school.

About 7 per cent of UK school children go to private schools, but about 30 per cent of Oxbridge students have come from one. Sociology professors Aaron Reeves and Sam Friedman, from the London School of Economics, studied more than 125,000 members of the British elite from the 1890s to the present day for their 2024 book, *Born to Rule*, and found that there has been no change over that time in the likelihood that someone born in the top 1 per cent makes it into (or rather stays within) the elite.[222] We have a Victorian system of hereditary privilege, one that is in part manufactured and fully maintained through the private school system.

Does it matter? If parents want schools with high educational attainment for their children – why shouldn't they pay for that? Well, it does matter, and for three good reasons. The first is that parents who choose private schools are not actually bearing the full cost of their choice. Both fee-paying parents, but more especially private schools, have benefited from tax schemes, and the schools from charitable status, which means, in effect, that the state has been heavily subsidising private education for many decades. From 2025, independent schools will pay the standard rate of 20 per cent VAT but (at the time of writing) will still retain their charitable status and concomitant tax benefits. Why should British taxpayers subsidise an education that not only doesn't benefit them but actually undermines the state sector? The state system would benefit from the support of parents committed to education, so that is a second good reason for thinking that private education is a societal problem. The third reason is that these parallel systems increase inequality and create social divisiveness, entitlement and elitism that are damaging to society – not just to poor children, but to everyone and on a large scale. They put a stranglehold on social mobility, meritocracy and social justice.

Private schools aren't the only obstacle to us having a unified education system for all. We also, bizarrely, have a patchwork of selective school systems, with 163 grammar schools dotted around England – a historical hangover amidst the vast majority of localities with fully comprehensive systems, admitting high-attaining children on the basis of an exam at age eleven. Rather than a universal move to comprehensive secondary schools, after a Labour government demanded change in 1965, local authorities were allowed to move at their own pace, with some now having dragged their feet for a full sixty years. In 1998, New Labour passed an Act to preclude any new selective systems, but still this dinosaur of a system lumbers on.

The reason this matters is the same as for private schools – selective schools damage the non-selective schools (and their students) in their vicinity. They create social and resource divisions – you won't find it hard to guess which groups of children are least likely to be admitted to selective schools, not least because their parents can't afford the private tuition many children receive to 'cram' them for the so-called 11+ exam. And you won't find it hard to guess which kinds of schools find it hardest to attract good teachers in selective school districts. But you might not know what damage the selective system does to many children: it creates overwhelming levels of stress for most children, parents and indeed teachers in the run-up to the exam, and those who fail are labelled, before they have even reached their teens, as 'low achievers'. A study from the National Foundation for Educational Research found that primary school teachers in a selective school system 'see children crumble when the results come out. They see themselves as failures, whatever we say. We do a lot of work on self-esteem, leading up to the 11-plus, and after. Talking them through the disappointment takes a huge amount of time.'[223]

Even within the state school system there is an uneven playing field, reinforced by a system of school choice that privileges affluence. As I said, only about 7 per cent of children go to private schools, although this varies by region – it's 25 per cent in London and 2 per cent in Wales. In England, parents who are not 'going private' make an ordered list of choices of schools. Researchers can look at these rankings to see what kinds of school parents prefer. They aren't perfect indicators of true preference because we know that some parents pick schools for which they think there will be less competition than the ones they actually want, but they are good enough to help us see patterns of preference. Because some schools are more popular than others, they are over-subscribed. Some children are therefore allocated to less preferred schools and we can look at where children go, as well as where their parents would like them to go.

Looking at the schools that parents pick for their preference lists, educational researchers Simon Burgess, Ellen Greaves and Anna Vignoles, from the universities of Bristol and Cambridge, showed that, overall, parental choice is most strongly related to school performance on tests and exams (these are the easiest metrics on which parents can compare schools); the level of deprivation or affluence of the area where the school is located; and whether the school is close to home. Most of the time, parents get their top-ranked school. But parent choice works much less well for lower-income families. Poorer families are less likely to live near high-achieving schools, and this shapes who goes where more than any difference in preferences for good schools among richer and poorer parents.[224] Poorer families don't want different things for their children and they are not failing to engage with the system, as some have suggested. In fact, comparing families eligible for free school meals to better-off families, there are no differences in the number of schools they put on the list, or the likelihood of putting the nearest school top of the list.[225] Both poor and rich parents seem to be equally willing to travel to a school that meets their preferences, but the way most allocation systems work is to give priority to children who live near a school. Living near a good school gives a family privileged access to that good school, and house prices around good schools go up. So, because richer families can afford to live close to good schools, the so-called 'choice' system is giving them an advantage.

It feels as if there is something of a clash between what parents are choosing via their school preferences (good exam results) and what teachers want (an end to 'exam factories'). Parents are preferentially selecting schools based on scores on the very tests that teachers would like to see abolished or overhauled and on the results of those Ofsted inspections, which teachers abhor but parents seem to like and trust.[195] But parents are doing their best with the system as it is, rife with inequalities, and the information they have access to. A state school system where parents getting what they want for their children – high-achieving schools – is dependent on their social class and income is antithetical to both social justice and to maximising every child's capabilities. We end up with children from poorer backgrounds being more likely to attend low-achieving schools – schools where fewer children achieve the benchmark of at least five grades of C or more (or 4+ in the new grading scheme) at GCSE level around age sixteen, with all the negative consequences of that for their life chances.

In 2022, the Institute for Fiscal Studies (IFS), as part of the Deaton Review of Inequalities, published a comprehensive, and comprehensively depressing, overview of educational inequality in the UK, really putting educational inequalities under the microscope. They found that children eligible for free school meals, which is a way of comparing poor children to others, do worse from start (school readiness) to finish (A-level results) in the education system, and that the gap between poor children and the rest hasn't changed in the last fifteen years. The IFS also looked across the whole income spectrum and found a gradient for educational attainment just as I showed for health in Chapter 1: at every step up the income gradient, children do better at school. This continues into adulthood, and there are inequalities in who goes on to get a degree or equivalent: almost half (49 per cent) of the most affluent fifth of children go on to get a degree, compared to only 17 per cent of those in the poorest fifth; among those who go to private schools, 71 per cent get a degree. The report concludes, damningly, that: 'Instead of being an engine for social mobility, the UK's education system allows inequalities at home to turn into differences in school achievement. This means that all too often, today's education inequalities become tomorrow's income inequalities.'[226]

The independent, charitable research centre the Education Policy Institute found that in the period pre- to post-pandemic the socioeconomic gap in educational attainment grew in all regions of England except London.[227] Poor students were found to be *nineteen months* behind non-poor students by the time they did their GCSEs, and if they have been persistently poor (i.e. eligible for free school meals for 80 per cent or more of the time they had been in school), a full *two years* behind. When the 2024 GCSE results came out (these were for children who had been in their first year of secondary school when the pandemic began, and who then experienced two years of lockdowns and disruptions to their schooling), the North East of England had the lowest level of top grades, while London had the highest.

I could go on for far too long describing inequalities in the system, but will finish with the inequities faced by the more than 1.5 million children in England with SEND. That's over 18 per cent of all children at any one time, and an astonishing 40 per cent of children are identified as having these needs at some point during their school years.[228] Parents, as well as teachers, can request an Education, Health and Care needs assessment to see if their child has SEND and, if they do, can request what is known as an Education, Health and Care plan (EHC plan).[229] These should be produced within twenty weeks, but fewer than half are completed within that time. In some places in the UK the waiting times are staggering: the average wait for young people for an assessment of attention deficit hyperactivity disorder (ADHD) is almost four years in one local authority in West Yorkshire.[230] And SEND provision is causing some local authorities to fear bankruptcy: in 2025 the *Guardian* found that the vast majority of English local authorities had SEND spending deficits, with at least twelve with deficits of £100–312 million.[231]

Poor children are less likely to get an EHC plan than non-poor children and are more likely to be categorised as having less well-defined conditions, such as the vague catch-alls of 'Speech, Language and Communication Needs', 'Moderate Learning Difficulties', and 'Social, Emotional and Mental Health Difficulties'. Affluent parents are better able to work their way through the complexities of getting their children diagnosed, getting an EHC plan, making sure that services are provided and putting in appeals when provision is denied, and better able to pay for legal and educational psychology support. The parental lottery (don't be born, or become, poor!) sits on top of the postcode lottery for diagnostic and treatment services. It's no good blaming local authorities or poor parents: the system is difficult to navigate and desperately underfunded. Everything that I've said so far about prevention being better than cure applies here. Although there are understandable concerns about the stigma of diagnosing and 'labelling' very young children, all the evidence points to the benefits that come from early intervention.

Time to talk and put our money where our mouth is

If we were to do what the Finns did, and start a national conversation to transform our education system to both reflect and create the ambition of a good society, we could put the idea of a unified and equitable education system, a National Education Service, on the agenda – for which journalist and education campaigner Melissa Benn provides a meticulously researched legislative policy blueprint in her book *Life Lessons: The case for a National Education Service*.[232] She calls for, among other details, the abolition of standard tests of all children in primary school, to be replaced with ongoing teacher assessment and sample-testing on a representative random group (this removes stress from kids and schools), and for Ofsted to be abolished and replaced with a local school support and improvement office. Government would need to repeal the relevant sections of legislation that set up academies and return powers to local authorities to open schools, manage admissions (removing the pressures on schools that have arisen from marketisation), and coordinate health, education and social care services for children. All state schools, including academies, free schools, and faith schools could be put on the same footing for funding and governance, and a new regional education authority could make sure that each local authority within it provided early years, primary and secondary, further and adult education, and career support. A revised broader national curriculum could bring in a baccalaureate model, currently much used in private schools, and which allows students to explore a wider range of subjects than A levels. Selective schools and private schools would be integrated into a fully comprehensive state system, just as the island of Guernsey has recently chosen to do, phasing out its 11+ exam and one remaining grammar school.

Note that Benn's proposed National Education Service isn't just about schools. It includes early childhood education (which I covered in the last chapter). I've already described the proven health and educational benefits of Sure Start centres, which often served as community hubs. Many experts support schools becoming more fully integrated into communities, serving as hubs for more purposes than just education, and serving the needs of parents and other adults as well, with benefits for school attendance and engagement. Schools could be a focal point for community cohesion if health and other social services and lifelong learning were on tap.

How could we fund such a National Education Service? In England, per-student funding from the state fell by 8 per cent, or £10 billion in real terms, over the decade from 2010. Who would have thought, though, that schools in the most *affluent* areas had a smaller cut and, between 2017 and 2022, bigger increases than those in the most deprived areas, who in turn had bigger cuts and then smaller rises?[233] Surely that should be the other way round? An extra payment to schools, called the Pupil Premium, was – and still is – supposed to target more spending to the most disadvantaged areas, but it isn't enough and doesn't anyway apply to 16–18-year-old students. There is a consistent call among experts for more money for secondary schools, hit the hardest by austerity, and for the reinstatement of something like the old Educational Maintenance Allowance, which was 'discontinued' in England in 2011, having helped disadvantaged young people to stay in education after the age of sixteen.

Benn is not short of ideas of how to fund all of this – from an all-age graduate tax to replace university tuition fees, setting up a national higher education endowment fund (to provide all school leavers with a three-year learning entitlement), to a 'Building Human Capital Fund' for long-term investment in state education (and especially the areas that have been most underfunded: early education, further and adult education) funded through a tax on capital transactions. This would be a tax paid by individuals or companies when they buy, sell or transfer assets like property, stocks or land. This type of tax aims to generate revenue for public services and can also discourage excessive speculation or short-term trading of assets. This could raise billions for improving pay and conditions, training and development for teachers and early years workers, repairing school buildings, supporting children with SEND, putting more money into deprived areas, and levelling out geographic inequalities – closing gaps in per-pupil payments between places, and between private and public schools. The additional VAT coming in from private schools from January 2025 is supposed to support the recruitment of more teachers into the state sector.

Not all the changes that experts envision cost money – a culture of care and kindness doesn't necessarily come with a price tag – but if we raised preschool and primary and secondary school funding by 9 per cent, further education by 14 per cent, and higher education by 18 per cent to take us back to pre-austerity levels, it would cost £9.77 billion a year, which is less than 1 per cent of tax receipts and other state income.

We should remember that this is *investment* that creates a good society, from which we all benefit, even if we don't have children ourselves, or want to go to university ourselves. We all benefit from a good education system that underpins the population's health and wellbeing, meets the needs of our economy, and leads to innovation. Remember that Nobel Prize-winning economist James Heckman at the University of Chicago, and his colleagues, estimate that investment in comprehensive, high-quality, birth-to-five early education gives a high return on investment. In fact, for every £1 spent, society should reap a reward of £13 in savings in areas as broad as health costs, reductions in crime, improvements in children's education and lifetime incomes, and mothers being able to work.[234]

At the other end of the educational journey is higher education, a sector that my own university's vice-chancellor, Professor Charlie Jeffery, along with many others, has described as a system in crisis. Universities aren't the only source of further and higher education, of course; there are degree apprenticeships, a vast range of online and lifelong learning and training opportunities and more, but universities are perhaps in a particularly bad place.

The way we fund universities doesn't work for many students, who are either put off from attending by high tuition fees, or end up with some of the highest levels of student debt in the world. As Professor Jeffery points out, the student loan repayment system now means, bizarrely, that 'nurses will end up paying more for their degrees than doctors, teachers more than bankers, and women more than men'.[235] This is partly due to changes in the value of maintenance loans, meaning that students from lower-income backgrounds now leave university with higher levels of debt: with more to repay, and accruing more interest, they end up paying more. University incomes no longer cover the costs of teaching and research, and the system has been propped up by the higher fees paid by international students, who are no longer choosing to come to the UK in the numbers they used to – partly due to Brexit and an increasingly restrictive student visa system (we are strangely cutting off the hands that feed the system). The higher education system is yet another fragmented and woefully underfunded system, seemingly disconnected from student need and national and regional economic strategy. But it isn't just a nice-to-have; a thriving university sector is vital to a good society. In 2021/22 it was estimated that it adds more than £70 billion per year of gross value added and £116 billion in terms of general economic output to the UK.[236]

In recent years, funding for the arts and humanities, and especially the creative arts, in higher education has been disproportionately affected, despite the fact that the creative industries deliver more than £115 billion in value to the UK every year and create jobs at three times the UK average.[237] Access to those jobs, however, is, and has always been, inequitable; the social mobility charity the Sutton Trust describes an elite pipeline from private education through elite universities and conservatoires to jobs in the creative industries.[238] Although only 7 per cent of children go to private schools, 43 per cent of top classical musicians and 35 per cent of top actors went to private schools; 58 per cent of classical musicians went to a specialist university or conservatoire, and 12 per cent to Oxford or Cambridge. With recent funding cuts, this situation can only get worse.

Meanwhile, our society faces a severe shortfall of people trained in sciences, technology, engineering and mathematics – the so-called STEM subjects – for the jobs in the current economy and the jobs that are likely to grow in the future. In the UK, however, we struggle to get sufficient numbers of students signing up for these subjects. It's no good prioritising STEM funding to universities if we aren't enthusing and educating school students earlier in the process to encourage them to enrol for STEM degrees. Arguably, we need to think about the subjects that we teach in schools and beyond as much more integrated than we currently do. The Turner Prize-nominated artist David Shrigley suggests rebranding STEM as STEAM – to include the arts – making the point that creativity is at the heart of problem-solving in any subject.[239] Here's yet another reason to be putting some of those three Cs on as high a pedestal as the three Rs.

Swimming upstream again, away from the cliff edge

I've described an education system characterised by built-in unfairness and inequities and hamstrung by a narrow vision of what education is for; a system that, as Professor Diane Reay from the University of Cambridge puts it, exacerbates rather than reduces the social distances between us.[240]

But even if we implemented all of the reforms and solutions described in this chapter (from mixed-age classrooms, to prioritising the three Cs, to abolishing Ofsted, to setting up a fully comprehensive, all-ages National Education Service) – all of which are common-sense, evidence-based responses to some of the problems stalking our educational system – they are not enough. The problems of poverty and inequality, and especially child poverty, which pervade the entire educational system cannot be fixed by that system alone.[194, 241, 242] And yet it is precisely those inequalities and vulnerabilities – deprivation, discrimination, diversity – that we seem, unrealistically, to expect an underfunded and overburdened school system and teaching profession to fix.

Reforming the education system will not address the million children in the UK who come to school hungry, or the quarter of all children who don't have a quiet place to study because they live in overcrowded accommodation or are without a secure home. And it won't help children living in poverty and destitution afford the uniforms, books, lunches, stationery, transport and school trips that they need in order to be able to attend, participate fully and avoid stigma.[243] There is a movement to 'poverty-proof' schools, but surely we should be concentrating on poverty-proofing society.

During evidence sessions in the UK Parliament, I've heard descriptions of children coming to school without shoes, of families disconnecting from energy supplies because they cannot pay bills, of parents unable to pay the bus fare to be able to take their child to a medical appointment. And I've heard a young person describe the impact of poverty on her own education: 'school is difficult . . . It isn't just hunger. The worry is still there. That feeling of worry never leaves . . . How you've not seen your mam eat. All going through your head in a chemistry lesson.'[244]

Are we surprised that a third of our young people leave school without basic skills and qualifications when a third of our children live in poverty? How short-sighted we are to expect an education system to fix these problems. Everyone involved in education knows this; it's why the National Education Union called for an end to child poverty as the second of its list of demands, just behind more funding for education, in the lead-up to the 2024 general election. And why experts consistently call for the auto-enrolment of children entitled to free school meals as well as the extension of these to all children. And it's why the recommendation distilled from health experts and public health research in Chapter 1, to ensure that everyone has a healthy standard of living, is *the most important* thing that could be done to ensure the wider distribution of better educational outcomes that will characterise our good society.

A tale of two schools (Part Two)

I want to end this chapter on a positive note because there is some reason to hope that more evidence might begin to make its way into educational policy. In late 2024, the UK Department for Education established a Science Advisory Council of a dozen academic experts to give it an independent pipeline of relevant research; only time will tell if the advice translates into tangible impact on the educational system.

It's also important to recognise all of the nurseries, schools, colleges and universities that do get things right for children and young people, supporting their development, capabilities and wellbeing. There are myriad good examples of what could be achieved everywhere – if the playing field were level. About the same time I visited the impressive private girls' school I described earlier, I was also asked to give a talk at a comprehensive school for girls in a deprived inner-city London borough, where the majority of girls come from ethnic minority backgrounds, most having English as a second language, and in a district with five times the national average being eligible for free school meals. The school might not have had the same resources, but they managed to provide a laptop to every girl who didn't have digital access at home. And I saw the same caring and connection shown by the headteacher and staff as I'd seen in a more privileged setting. The girls were fizzing with curiosity and doing brilliantly. This school also involves parents in courses ranging from English and digital skills to physical activity and vocational skills.

Rather than coming away impressed but saddened by the exclusivity I'd experienced when visiting private schools, I came away impressed and elated. The former First Lady of the United States, Michelle Obama, apparently felt the same when she visited the school, telling the girls: 'It is such a joy for me to visit this phenomenal school. For all of the brilliant, bold and beautiful young women here – I can't wait to see all that you will achieve in the future.'[245]

Let's make good practice like this a reality for all our children, and free schools from having to overcome the myriad challenges of economic inequality.

CHAPTER 4

Imprisoned by Injustice

> 'A nation should not be judged by how it treats its highest citizens, but its lowest ones.'
>
> Nelson Mandela

York Castle Museum is housed in the eighteenth-century former prison buildings that are part of York Castle. The current York Crown Court, which deals with the most serious crimes, such as murder, rape and assault, operates in the adjacent building; people have been imprisoned at this site for more than a thousand years. In fact, a large sign within the museum proclaims 'A THOUSAND YEARS OF JUSTICE', above illustrations of the Norman motte-and-bailey castle which still stands on the site, a public hanging, and views of the execution yard.

A thousand years of *injustice* might be a more appropriate label, given that the prison held hundreds of Quaker conscientious objectors from 1660 to 2019, and so many interned Austrian- and German-born Yorkshire residents (mostly pork butchers, confectioners and waiters) during the First World War that they had to be housed in tents pitched in the castle precincts.[246] The castle prison museum publicity materials invite visitors to 'experience a brutal and crooked prison'; the people whose stories are displayed throughout include a woman victim of domestic violence who'd murdered her husband after years of abuse; a Luddite protesting against the new machinery that was threatening jobs in the textile industry; and a corrupt and bullying turnkey, or keeper, who forced prisoners to buy food and drink from him at exorbitant prices.

A tourist website lists thirteen prison museums that can be visited in the UK. *Want to explore the darker side of social history?* it asks – adding that you can get an extra frisson of interest at Dartmoor Prison Museum as it is sometimes staffed by actual prisoners. It's an odd experience, visiting such places and being invited to contemplate the overcrowding, insanitary conditions, cruel punishment and miscarriages of justice, as if they were entirely confined to the past. We're perhaps as fascinated now by crime and punishment as we were when such crowds flocked to public hangings that roads were blocked, public disorder flourished, and penny ballad sheets were printed to mark each occasion. Visitors to York Castle Museum are invited to think about the overcrowding, violence, and hopelessness of prisoners in times past, but there is no information on display about prison conditions today, or anything to prompt people to reflect on contemporary issues.

Standing out for all the wrong reasons

What do you imagine a day in the life of an average prisoner to be like? In 2017, the *Metro* newspaper ran a feature describing exactly that, based on the experience of a former prisoner. He described a day of rigid timetabling and boredom, with an early start to a six-hour day of mundane work, which might be prison tasks such cleaning or laundry, or working in a prison industry, for about £10 per week (as most prisoners smoke, most of this was spent on tobacco). One of the jobs he described was

'CD scratching' – destroying unsold copies of albums. Work, he said, helped to pass the time, but he found it demeaning that prisoners were punished if they didn't work, comparing it to the forced labour of the past. In the middle of the day, prisoners were locked up for two hours, so that staff could have their lunch breaks. Then there was more work, until dinner, which was served in the cell. There wasn't a table to eat at, which he said was all right if you had the bottom bunk, as you could sit there and eat; but if you had the top bunk, it was easier to eat sitting on the toilet, with your dinner on your knees. The food, he said, was varied, but the quality was poor; he once asked a prison officer what he had been served – she said she wasn't sure, but she thought it looked as if someone had already eaten it.[247]

After that early dinner, prisoners are locked up for the night at about 6 p.m. Some prisoners take courses in prison, as well as or instead of work, and these are mostly programmes to address offending and basic English and maths classes.[248] Violence in prisons, including bullying, self-harm, assaults, and gang violence, is a daily threat and increasing. The overall impression of prison life is of boredom overlain by simmering threat.

This is a description of life in an adult men's prison, but we should remember that there are currently about 3,600 women also incarcerated. Imprisoning women sometimes involves their children being in prison as well; about two-thirds of women prisoners are mothers of dependent children.[249] Women who give birth in prison can keep their baby for the first eighteen months, and prisoners with children up to eighteen months old can ask to bring the child to a mother and baby unit, although there are only six prisons in the UK with these units.

Some children are in custody in secure children's centres for their own criminal behaviour. There were 170 children aged 12–17 years old in secure children's centres in England and Wales in 2025. Although the age of criminal responsibility is shockingly low – ten years of age (twelve years in Scotland) – it is a relief to note that no 10–11-year-olds have been imprisoned in England and Wales since 2010, and the numbers of imprisoned children are thankfully much lower than in the past.

These highly vulnerable children experience appalling conditions. In the autumn of 2023, the Chief Inspector of Prisons found secure children's centres to be even more violent than adult jails, and that some children were effectively in solitary confinement, locked up with 'barely any human contact'.[250] So although the numbers are small and declining over time – and in March 2025 the government announced an immediate end to the placement of girls, who disproportionately account for self-harm incidents, in young offender institutes – our historically low age of criminal responsibility contributes to the disturbing fact that we lock up more children than almost all Western European countries (the age of ten was established in the nineteenth century, reflecting the Victorian belief that children's moral and mental capacities were similar to adults' and that children were capable of understanding right and wrong from that age). In the most recent comparative study I could find, only the USA and Netherlands had higher rates; the UK's rate was four times that of Portugal, twenty-five times the rate of Belgium, and a hundred times that of Finland.[251]

Just how bad have conditions in the UK's adult prisons become? The answer can be measured not just in statistics about overcrowding and violence, but in the growing reluctance of our international partners to engage with our criminal justice system. In September 2023, a German court refused an extradition request from the UK 'in view of the state of the British prison system'. Westminster magistrates' court had asked that an Albanian man, who normally lived in the UK and who was accused of cocaine trafficking and money-laundering, be returned from Germany, where he had travelled to visit his sick fiancée. The accused's defence lawyer cited research on the overcrowding, staff shortages and violence in UK prisons and the German court sought reassurance from the UK, which it did not get, that the UK system was compliant with the minimum standards required by the European Convention on Human Rights. Reports from both His Majesty's Inspectorate of Prisons and human rights organisations have documented instances where prison conditions – such as inadequate mental health care, excessive use of force, poor general living conditions – have fallen below the standards required by the convention. As reported by the *Guardian*, a member of the Law Society of England and Wales declared this court case to be a 'severe rebuke' and 'an embarrassment'.[252] The Ministry of Justice responded to the report by saying that the government was committed to delivering a staggering (my word, not theirs) 20,000 new prison places.[252]

We have a LOT of people in prison in the UK. At the time of the extradition request to the German court, the official numbers stood at 87,685 prisoners in England and Wales alone, up 7.5 per cent from a year previously, and with numbers projected, by the Ministry of Justice, to reach 100,000 by the end of 2025. There are a further approximately 8,000 people in prison in Scotland, and around 2,000 in Northern Ireland, so we're above 90,000 in the UK – which is about 145 per 100,000 head of population. This is twice as high a rate as in Switzerland, Sweden and Denmark, almost three times as high as in Finland and Norway, and four times the rate of Japan and Iceland.

The UK's high rate of imprisonment stands in stark contrast to that of other Western European countries, including some, such as France and Croatia, that have seen numbers fall in recent years. We keep on imprisoning more and more people, in spite of the fact that we haven't got room for them. The Dutch have reduced their prison population by 40 per cent over the past two decades, while we hurtle in the opposite direction. That is a statistic that should wake us up: it shows just how possible it is to make a radical course correction. Part of the Dutch turnaround is a consequence of falling rates of serious crime; though this is part of a common international pattern, it is also to do with shorter sentences, alternatives to prison, and better support for mental health for those in the criminal justice system.[253] Experts have not been able to put their finger on any single cause of this reduction, instead describing the multifaceted nature of changes in policing and in the courts. The Dutch have been so successful in reducing prison numbers that they have been able to convert prisons into schools, hotels and apartments, and have had to address the issue of unemployment for former prison officers. Think of the positive impact on just a single aspect of having high imprisonment rates – prison overcrowding – if we did only *half* as well as the Dutch in reducing our prison population.

The Ministry of Justice has a Certified Normal Accommodation policy that sets standards for decent prisoner accommodation. A prison is considered overcrowded if it holds more prisoners than can be housed to this decent standard. In the summer of 2023, close to two-thirds of prisons in England and Wales were overcrowded.[254] In one prison, HMP Leeds, the occupancy rate was getting on for double what it should be, at 173 per cent. No wonder that, in 2020, the European Committee for the Prevention of Torture described our prisons as 'violent, unsafe and overcrowded'. Although His Majesty's Inspectorate of Prisons has found HMP Bristol, Woodhill and Wandsworth all to be 'unsafe', we continue to 'stuff them to the gunwhales', in one prison governor's pithy turn of phrase.[255] And our prisons are rife with self-harm, violence, drugs, weapons, assaults and deaths, including suicides, in part attributable to these indecent conditions.

All this makes the German court's dim view of our prisons less surprising.

Who cares?

In a good society, who should be in prison and who should not? What does it say about a society that it has a large prison population? Does it mean we are successfully dealing with crime and keeping people safe? Or does it mean that our society is inculcating high levels of crime, or punishing people too harshly?

These questions matter because, at a fundamental level, a good society can only be one in which people and property are safe. To live a good life, to have good community relationships and an active civic sphere, means each and every one of us having personal freedom from fear of encroachment on our bodies and our property. But achieving that safety isn't simply about locking more people up – it's about understanding what creates crime in the first place and responding in ways that actually reduce harm.

The psychological toll of living with crime and the fear of crime is profound and far-reaching. Beyond the trauma directly experienced by victims of serious crimes, there's the corrosive effect of chronic anxiety about safety that can reshape entire communities. In neighbourhoods where gunshots are commonplace, the sound of a car backfiring becomes a source of dread rather than a minor annoyance. This persistent state of hypervigilance changes how people live and think – limiting where they go, when they venture out, and how they interact with their neighbours.

Violence against women and girls

Violence against women and girls represents one of the starkest examples of how our society fails to protect its most vulnerable members. In the UK, according to the latest Femicide Census, more than 2,000 women have been killed by a current or former partner since 2009.[256] Domestic abuse affects an estimated 2.3 million adults each year in the UK.[257] Yet despite these devastating statistics, we continue to treat this violence as isolated incidents rather than recognising it as a systemic problem rooted in the same social determinants that drive other forms of harm.

The relationship between poverty, inequality, and violence against women is both clear and consistently overlooked in policy responses. Women in the most deprived areas experience domestic abuse at significantly higher rates than those in affluent communities. This isn't because poverty causes men to be violent – domestic abuse occurs across all social classes – but because economic deprivation creates conditions that trap women in dangerous situations and limit their options for escape. Women without independent income, secure housing, or family support networks find it nearly impossible to leave abusive relationships. The closure of women's refuges due to funding cuts, the shortage of social housing, and the inadequacy of benefits all combine to keep women locked in cycles of violence.

Meanwhile, the austerity measures of the past decade have systematically dismantled the very services that might prevent or treat violence or support survivors. Legal aid cuts mean many women cannot access the courts to obtain protection orders. Reduced funding for domestic violence services has created waiting lists for refuge spaces and support programmes. Youth services that might provide alternative models of masculinity for young men have been slashed. The message seems to be that we are willing to accept violence against women as an inevitable feature of society rather than invest in the structural changes needed to prevent it.

Barbed wire, electric fences and big dogs

In 2014 I got some sense of what it's like to live in a lawless and frightening society on a visit to Mexico. When I'm visiting a new country, I like to have a guidebook to learn about the history and culture of the place and to check out practical details. In a section of my guidebook to Mexico dealing with personal security and health, I was shocked to read the following: 'It is best to avoid the police in Mexico; they are rarely helpful and can make difficult situations worse . . . police corruption is rife . . . avoid driving at night . . . steer clear of isolated routes or beaches.'[258]

While there, our hosts chose to take us only to restaurants where we would not have to walk any distance from a car to the door. Money that was to be given to us to reimburse our travel expenses had to be taken out of the bank and handed over in a sequence of elaborate transactions to avoid a mugging or theft that might be triggered by the bank clerk alerting accomplices. There were plans for us to visit mountain villages near Popocatépetl, to witness the Day of the Dead traditions, but ultimately our hosts considered it was too dangerous to take us there.

It isn't, of course, tourists who are in the most danger. One of our hosts had been sent to school out of the country after her brother had been kidnapped. Academic colleagues told us how constrained their teenage children's lives were – they could only be ferried back and forth by their parents to socialise in one another's houses; it was too unsafe for them to be outdoors. We noticed how all the houses, in both rich and poor neighbourhoods, were surrounded by barbed wire, like mini fortresses. The omnipresent low-level sense of threat was a weight that became most obvious from the sense of relief felt when leaving the country.

A year later, in South Africa, the same sense of danger and risk was communicated by hosts who were horrified that we had walked in the capital city, Pretoria, at night. In Cape Town, there was the same shepherding from car to venue as in Mexico, to make sure that we weren't vulnerable to a mugging on the street. As well as barbed wire, we saw houses defended by electric fences, with signs threatening an armed response to any trespass, and guard dogs patrolling the gardens and driveways.

What Mexico and South Africa have in common is an extreme level of wealth and income inequality, as well as high levels of poverty and deprivation. According to the World Bank, South Africa is the most unequal country in the world, and Mexico is the second most unequal of the OECD countries, just behind Turkey. In an international survey of 148,000 people in 142 countries, the more unequal the country, the higher the reported crime, lack of confidence in the police, and fear of crime.

Those findings reflect what it felt like to me to be in Mexico and South Africa. In some communities in the UK residents similarly fear crime and are exposed to more violence and mistrust the police. This is the quotidian experience of many deprived areas, and it is not what we want in a good society.

The inequality–crime link is best explained by understanding the psychological and social impact of inequality: how it increases the importance of differences in status and anxieties related to class and status, drives the residential segregation of rich and poor, undermines social cohesion and generalised trust.[259] Violence is more common in unequal societies because the heightened importance of status makes it even more necessary to react when we feel looked down upon. Violence is most often triggered by disrespect, humiliation or loss of face. While some economists have tried to explain this relationship through purely rational economic calculations – suggesting people weigh the monetary benefits of crime against the risk of being caught – this narrow framework fails to account for the reality that most crime occurs between people of similar economic circumstances, ignores white-collar crime by the wealthy, and cannot explain the irrational or spontaneous nature of much violent crime.[260]

The problem that sits at the heart of this chapter is that there is a vicious circle connecting inequality and poverty to crime and imprisonment and back to deprivation, and that this impinges on everyone's wellbeing. And it's crucial to understand that rates of imprisonment are not simply a consequence of rates of crime – this is one of the most important but least understood aspects of how criminal justice systems actually work.

The relationship between crime and imprisonment is far more complex and politically driven than most people realise. Many crimes go unreported, particularly domestic violence, sexual assault, and fraud. Of those that are reported, conviction rates vary dramatically depending on the type of crime, the resources available to police and prosecutors, and the social characteristics of both victims and perpetrators. But even when convictions occur, imprisonment rates depend heavily on sentencing policies – and these are shaped by political attitudes, media coverage, and public opinion, rather than evidence about what actually reduces crime.

Remember the Dutch experience: the Netherlands deliberately reduced its prison population by 40 per cent between 2005 and 2017, not because crime rates fell dramatically, but because they chose rehabilitation over punishment, invested in mental health and drug treatments, and redesigned their sentencing guidelines. Their crime rates didn't soar – in fact, many types of crime continued to decline. This demonstrates that high imprisonment rates are a policy choice, not an inevitable response to crime levels.

Criminologists Alfred Blumstein and Allen Beck looked at changes in prison populations in the US over two decades, from 1980 to 1996, and found absolutely no effect (really – a proper zero in their table, not just a small number) of changing crime levels on changing rates of imprisonment. The explosion in American incarceration during this period was driven entirely by harsher sentencing policies, not rising crime.[261] Comparing crime rates across different countries is tricky (except for murders, which are reliably and accurately reported), but the UK doesn't have an especially high crime rate, and some kinds of crime are declining. Our exceptionally high imprisonment rates in the UK, however, do feed into that vicious circle, looping from poverty, inequality and deprivation to crime and back again.

A fantasy prison system made real

When it comes to prisons, there are examples of exemplary systems that get almost all aspects of criminal justice right, including preventing re-offending. Norway, Finland and Iceland, in particular, stand out as systems with a better regard for prisoners' wellbeing and their families' welfare (we should keep in mind the long-term adversity meted out to children whose parents are sent to jail), higher success in rehabilitation and reform, and far, far lower rates of imprisonment. Conversely, the US's system is one that seems to get everything wrong, with an excessively high imprisonment rate and some horrifyingly punitive prison regimes.

When I lived in the American mid-West, I used to drive through an area of beautiful countryside, where road signs warned drivers not to pick up hitchhikers because they might be dangerous escaped prisoners from a nearby federal prison. Such signs are common near US prisons. A favourite example of mine is a grammatically challenged sign from Texas that reads 'Hitchhikers may be escaping inmates', in which case, I think the poor hitchhikers deserve a lift.

Contrast this with a Norwegian prison located on an island, reached by a boat operated by the inmates, who spend their time working in the woods and fields. Apparently, if they choose to escape, they are asked to please let the prison know they have got away, so that nobody will have to worry that they might have drowned. Escapes are rare in the Nordic system of open prisons, which are characterised by a focus on rehabilitation, trust and reintegration rather than traditional punitive approaches. These systems are significantly more 'open' than conventional prisons, emphasising normalised environments that resemble everyday life. Many inmates are granted extensive freedom of movement within the prison, often living in semi-open or community-based settings. Some prisoners work or study outside the prison during the day, and return in the evening, with minimal restrictions. Fences, guards and strict controls are reduced or absent for lower-risk prisoners. The emphasis is on trust and responsibility. Prisoners often start in more secure facilities and, upon demonstrating responsibility, are transitioned into less restrictive environments where they have access to paid work, education, and social activities designed to prepare them for release.

Dutch criminologist Francis Pakes, who has spent his research career comparing prison systems, spent time as a 'quasi-prisoner' in an open prison in Iceland, where the inmates spend their time looking after animals, cooking meals, and moving freely around the prison estate. Pakes describes the normalised relationships between staff and prisoners – the latter able to access the internet, maintaining links with home and work.[262] Rather than representing yet another trauma in the lives of those who are sent to prison, the rehabilitative culture of the Nordic systems suggests there is a better way.

In a fascinating, watch-this-space research study to see if Nordic prison culture can work just as well elsewhere, the Scandinavian Prison Project has set up a single housing unit, 'Little Scandinavia', in a prison in the Pennsylvania Department of Corrections. It's a collaboration between the American, Norwegian, Swedish and Danish prison authorities, where prisoners are randomly chosen to be housed in the unit, and there is rigorous assessment of whether the successes of the Scandinavian approach can be transplanted to other contexts. The unit has single cells, along with shared, nicely furnished areas, with plants and a fish tank, looked after by both staff and inmates. The shared spaces include landscaped outdoor green areas and a well-equipped kitchen, where prisoners can prepare fresh food that they have ordered, with staff cooperation, through a local grocery store. Prisoners work or take training courses every day. There is a high ratio of staff to prisoners, and staff are specially trained, especially in communication skills.

It's impossible to watch the extended trailer for a documentary on Little Scandinavia on YouTube without feeling moved by the transformations experienced by both prisoners and staff, and inspired by the possibilities for positive change: the American prison staff visiting a Norwegian prison are incredulous at first, and then excited; one initially sceptical officer points out all the potential weapons in the prison kitchen used by prisoners, declaiming 'weapon, weapon, weapon' as he points to pans, kettle and knives. But, as he spends time with inmates, he starts to look more thoughtful, and by the conclusion of the short film he's a believer. And by the end of 2024 there had been no violent incidents involving those knives. The two-year research project ended in May 2024, and I'll be following the results and analyses.[263] The numbers will take a while to come through, although by mid 2025, nobody released from Little Scandinavia has yet been returned to prison.

I think it is helpful, as we think about reforming the criminal justice system, to look at the historical arc that led to the overturning of the death penalty, both in the UK and in some US states. That progress came about, not because of the groundswell of public opinion which sometimes underpins social change – like the civil rights movement in the United States – but more because of strong moral leadership. Laws were passed and the criminal justice system reformed, despite public opinion remaining in favour of the death penalty.

In the UK, it is only very recently that opinion polls have shown a majority against the death penalty, and there are still strident calls for its reinstatement whenever the public and the media are outraged by a particularly upsetting crime. The case against the death penalty has been reinforced by several cases where DNA evidence or proof of police manipulation of evidence have demonstrated the innocence of convicts on death row in the USA and long-imprisoned lifers in the UK, sometimes decades after their conviction. But at the time politicians were convinced to bring capital punishment to an end, they were driven more by morals and values than by evidence that the system sometimes got things wrong. Do we need to be making the case for the reform of the criminal justice system more on the grounds of justice and morality than on the grounds of economics, or re-offending numbers – using stories more than statistics? Or do we simply need more leaders willing to go with the courage of their own convictions, while they're in office as well as when out of it, to make the changes that will influence our societal culture to accept the reforms and welcome the better society that would follow? We deserve better in the UK. We deserve the better protection from crime and the good society we would get if we focused our criminal justice system on prevention and rehabilitation.

A long arc of progress?

We like to think that we are making progress as a society, that we are part of what Dr Martin Luther King famously labelled 'the arc of the moral universe' that 'bends towards justice'. We no longer hang people, or whip them down the public street, or call it 'petty treason', punishable by death, when a woman kills a man who has been violent to her. We may have a lot of people in prison (and too many of them are mothers of dependent children, people of colour, children, people with disabilities, those who are unwell, poor or illiterate – I'll come back to this) but surely we are making progress? Surely we imprison fewer people than we used to? And surely we are making society safer by incarcerating criminals who are a threat to our peace and domestic security?

Let's take those issues one at a time and start by looking at long-term trends in imprisonment. Prison populations, both actual numbers of people in prison and rates of imprisonment, have been rising in all the UK nations for more than a century. Through the first half of the twentieth century there were declining numbers and rates of imprisonment, but that began to change around 1940, and although there have been small decreases from time to time, with the exception of imprisoned children, long-term trends show an ever-increasing rate of incarceration – the long arc reaches ever upwards, not downwards.[264]

That first half of the twentieth century saw the culmination of a sequence of progressive campaigns and changes to the law that had begun in the nineteenth century. Over time, we decriminalise some behaviours (blasphemy, homosexuality, public drunkenness) and criminalise others (cyber-bullying, domestic abuse), but changes in sentencing policy, parole and early release have much the biggest influence on trends.

Does prison work?

We need to ask whether increasing rates of imprisonment are supported by any evidence of benefit – does prison do what it is supposed to do?

There are four justifications generally offered in support of the right of the state to deprive someone of their liberty. Imprisonment is arguably justifiable if it protects the public, keeping them safe by taking criminals out of the community; if it delivers retribution, punishing the criminal for their wrongdoing; if it deters crime; and if it rehabilitates the criminal – this being a benefit to the offender themselves as well as society.

The retribution argument is a moral argument, and not one that can be won or lost on straightforward evidentiary grounds. The moral permissibility of punishment is contested by philosophers – with differing schools of thought criticising each other's theorising – and non-philosophers alike. Our personal moral views on punishment are shaped by everything from abstract factors (such as religion) to concrete experiences (such as being a victim of crime), and also by cultural context. In contrast, the questions as to whether imprisonment protects the public, deters crime and rehabilitates those imprisoned are questions that can be answered with empirical evidence.

Have our streets, businesses, homes and persons been protected by putting more and more people in prison?

If prison works, then we should be seeing rapidly falling crime rates and a more secure public. Official statistics for England and Wales come from two sources: the Crime Survey for England and Wales, which asks representative samples of people about their experiences of crime using surveys, and crimes recorded by the police. These two sources have, over time, told inconsistent stories. The most recent numbers, published in March 2024, look at twenty-year trends in reported and recorded crimes.

In the self-reported data, it looks as if crime is generally declining. This is a big, robust survey, with more than 30,000 people responding in the most recent round, all asked about their experiences of theft, robbery, criminal damage, fraud, computer misuse, and violence with or without injury. The survey shows declines in all kinds of crime except fraud and computer misuse. But crimes recorded by the police began rising from 2014, and there have been significant recent rises in robbery and knife crime, as well as longer-term increases in stalking and sexual assault. The Office for National Statistics says it is confident that crime overall is falling, except for fraud, stalking and sexual assault (these latter crimes are still greatly under-reported, but were even more so in the past, so some of this rise will be due to more reporting). It doesn't, however, offer comment on the recent rises in robbery and knife crime.

A bit of a mixed picture then – and maybe high rates of imprisonment are keeping us safe – but this aggregate view obscures a crucial reality: crime is not distributed evenly across society. Only 5 per cent of people experience 60 per cent of all crimes for which there are victims.[265] This means that while the majority of the population lives relatively free from crime, a small minority – typically the most disadvantaged and vulnerable – bear a disproportionate burden of victimisation. These are often the same people living in deprived communities, struggling with poverty, physical and mental health issues, or domestic violence. They experience repeated victimisation – the same individuals are burgled multiple times, assaulted repeatedly, or become trapped in cycles of abusive relationships.

In 2013, *The Economist* reported that people and property seemed to be safer than ever across the rich, developed world, putting the trends down to changing demographics (most crimes are committed by young men and our populations are ageing), better policing, less drug use (this was before the opioid epidemic, most intense and widely documented in the United States, but emerging in other parts of the world), better security measures that included everything from burglar alarms and car immobilisers to bulletproof screens and marked money in banks, and steeply falling prices of the technological goods that used to be prime targets for theft.[266] The trends in imprisonment did not explain the crime patterns – crime was dropping in countries and states where prison numbers were falling, like the Netherlands, as well as in places where numbers were rising, like the UK. The *Economist* article concluded that 'most of what remains of the crime problem is really a recidivism issue'[266] – recidivism being a fancy word for re-offending.

The revolving door

Most people get out of prison in the end. Whole-life terms, with no possibility of release on parole, were only introduced in 1983 and have been issued only about a hundred times, with seventy-three prisoners currently serving whole-life terms in England and Wales. The average prison sentence is just over twenty months. The average length of sentences has been increasing steadily since 2000, when it was just fourteen months, even though the general public think that sentences are shorter than they used to be. Still, the majority (55 per cent) of all new custodial sentences in 2022 were short sentences of less than a year; in fact, 38 per cent were for less than six months. And most prisoners don't serve their full-term; for sentences up to seven years, prisoners typically serve half their sentence in prison and the other half released on probation. In England and Wales the percentage of first-time prisoners has been falling – at 8 per cent it's currently down by almost half since 2007; meanwhile the proportion of prisoners with a lot of convictions has risen: the average prisoner given a short sentence has already committed over fifty offences. What this all adds up to is that we're looking at a picture of increasing recidivism – of people rotating in and out of prison.

With short sentences there is no time in prison for effective programmes to address mental health or addictions – even if these programmes were fully available – and no time for any education or training that might help to turn lives around. But all the negative consequences of imprisonment for those convicted – relationship breakdown, job and housing loss, stigma, and so on – persist, as well as negative impacts on the system, adding to overcrowding and overwhelming services. No wonder, then, that about two-thirds (63 per cent) of those who receive sentences of less than six months re-offend within less than a year of release; that happens less often when people are given either a community order (56 per cent) or a suspended sentence (54 per cent).[267] Lives that were already deeply challenged are broken further by imprisonment. Rather than deterring crime, imprisonment entrenches and amplifies it.

Who is in and who is not

There are well-known and very stark inequalities in imprisonment – especially inequalities related to ethnicity and to social class, just like the health and educational inequalities that we saw in earlier chapters – but the scale of the inequalities in imprisonment is so marked that it is worth looking at the numbers even if we know the story they are going to tell.

Racial/ethnic bias and discrimination is apparent in every part of the criminal justice system, from policing, through to the court system, and post-release support. At the most recent census, 82 per cent of the general population of England and Wales was White, 9 per cent Asian, 4 per cent Black, 3 per cent Mixed and 2 per cent 'Other ethnic'.

In 2020, 18 per cent of police stop-and-search incidents involved Black people (almost all young men), as did 12 per cent of remands in prison; 13 per cent of the prison population was Black. Black prisoners were more likely to serve their full sentence, in part because of discriminatory treatment within prison leading to behaviour preventing their early release. Black prisoners are less likely than White prisoners to report 'positive experiences, including feeling respected by staff . . . and having enough cleaning facilities'. A third of imprisoned children are

Black. I want to repeat that: not 4 per cent as it should be if the prison population reflected the general population, but 32 per cent, an eight-fold excess. People of Asian ethnicity are slightly under-represented in the prison population, but they too experience biased policing: 14 per cent of stop and searches involved people of Asian ethnicity.[268]

These differences should not be taken as evidence of bias, says the Ministry of Justice report within which they are reported, because the comparisons between ethnic groups have not been adjusted for 'other characteristics of ethnic groups (such as average income, geography, offence mix or offender history)'. A Cardiff University study showed that, in 2021, you were ten times more likely to be sent to prison from the most deprived local authorities in England than the least deprived.[269] The same Ministry of Justice report also showed stark regional differences: you're two times more likely to be imprisoned if you live in the North West than in the South West, and rates are also high in the North East, London, and Yorkshire and the Humber. Among young offenders, over half were eligible for free school meals, which is a marker for poverty (in the population at large only 14 per cent of children are eligible).[268]

About a third of prisoners have learning and other disabilities, and around half have a neurodivergent condition, such as autism or ADHD, according to government data.[270] Without additional support, these prisoners find it extremely challenging to engage with education or any other programmes while they are inside, meaning that life after prison is even harder for them than it should be. Illiteracy isn't confined to those prisoners with diagnosed disabilities; more than half of prisoners have difficulties with reading and writing. According to a joint review from His Majesty's Inspectorate of Prisons, and Ofsted, prisons are not giving the right priority to improving prisoners' reading skills.²⁷¹ Finally, more than half of prisoners are experiencing mental health problems. These are probably undercounts, but 45 per cent have anxiety or depression and 8 per cent have a diagnosis of psychosis; 60 per cent have a traumatic brain injury, affecting mental health and cognitive and emotional functioning.²⁷²

We are giving short, disruptive sentences to people who already have limited resources and little support. Our prisons are full of people living with trauma and mental health conditions, especially those individuals with drug and alcohol addictions, those who have been through the care system as children and/or experienced abuse or maltreatment, people with learning difficulties and those lacking basic literacy and functional skills. What makes this feel almost medieval is that we are locking up those who are unwell, have disabilities, the traumatised and the poor, when the data tell us that we have the lowest chance of preventing re-offending (and therefore keeping ourselves and our property safe) by putting these people in prison.

The evidence shows that the reduction in re-offending associated with community sentences is actually greatest for those people with larger numbers of previous offences, younger offenders aged 18–20 years, and people with mental health conditions, including serious psychiatric problems.²⁷³ In other words, we're doing exactly the opposite of what we should be doing for a good society.

Remember who is not in prison

In her 2021 book, *Prisons Make Us Safer: And 20 other myths about mass incarceration*, the American journalist Victoria Law points out that:

incarceration . . . happens *after* harm has occurred . . . We must also remember that incarceration addresses only certain types of harm. People who sell drugs on the street risk arrest and imprisonment. But the same rarely applies to wealthy people like the Sackler family, who earned billions from OxyContin, the addictive painkiller launched in 1996 that spawned today's opioid crisis. Likewise, board members and corporate executives responsible for oil spills and other environmental disasters or for precipitating economic crises rarely face handcuffs and jail time.[274]

Arguably, if we want to keep our societies free from harm we would do well to focus more of our attention on what American public health academic Professor Nicholas Freudenberg calls the 'lethal but legal' business practices in the alcohol, car, gun, food and beverage, pharmaceutical and tobacco industries[275] – to which we should now add corporate polluters and all industries with harmful environmental health impacts.

Some kinds of corporate crime inflict huge damage on society but don't result in much at all in the way of convictions. Legal scholar William K. Black has coined the term 'control fraud' to describe what happens when 'those who control a seemingly legitimate entity use it as a "weapon" to defraud' – accounting being the weapon of choice in the financial sector.[276] He describes how accounting control fraud caused the savings and loan fiasco of the 1980s (which may ultimately have cost the US taxpayer $124 billion[277]), the Enron energy company scandal (employees lost billions of dollars of pension benefits), and the 2008 global financial crisis (which cost the US alone $21 trillion in lost production and over ten million job losses). Sometimes one or two top executives are jailed for crimes such as these. The Enron boss, Jeffrey Skilling, served twelve years, but only one

US banker went to jail over the global financial crisis. In the UK, at the time of writing, no person or corporation has yet been held criminally accountable for the seventy-two deaths caused by the 2017 Grenfell Tower fire, although the central reason for the spread of the fire was that the cladding on the building's exterior did not comply with building regulations and had been fitted because somebody had ignored those regulations for financial gain.

White-collar crime affects all of us, although we won't always be labelling the damage as a crime when reckless and destabilising economic policies (think Truss, think Trump) cause our mortgage or energy bills to rise, or when there isn't enough money for public services because of government diverting money to cronies, as in the PPE scandal during the Covid pandemic.

And to go back, briefly, to the question of whether or not imprisonment is justifiable because criminals – those who violate societal norms by breaking laws – deserve to be punished: we should notice that when this is debated by moral philosophers, they generally make their arguments based on assumptions that both the law and the criminal justice system are fair and just. All the evidence laid out so far in this chapter suggests that, in the UK, those assumptions are very far from the real state of affairs – there are injustices in who and what kinds of crimes are punished, and how the system fails those within it. The problems extend well beyond prisons themselves: the Crown Prosecution Service struggles with chronic underfunding and staff shortages, leading to cases being dropped and delayed; legal aid cuts have created a two-tier justice system where access to proper representation depends on wealth; court backlogs mean victims and defendants wait years for resolution; and conviction rates for serious crimes, like rape and domestic violence, remain shamefully low. Even if the system were fair and just, we could still debate whether or not imprisonment is a legitimate act of a state, but when every part of the criminal justice apparatus – from police investigation through prosecution to sentencing and imprisonment – is so far from those ideals and looks more like a (failed) system for social control of the most vulnerable and marginalised in society, surely comprehensive reform should be the primary, and urgent, goal?

Hawks vs doves

Who gets imprisoned isn't only about who has committed crimes – it's fundamentally shaped by the political choices successive governments make about how to respond to crime. The long-term trends in imprisonment in the UK show a pretty steady increase from the 1940s to the present day. Unlike what we saw in relation to health inequalities in Chapter 1, it doesn't seem to matter which of the two main political parties is in power. They have both pretty much consistently adopted policies and passed laws that have increased rates of imprisonment through sending more people to jail rather than using alternatives to custody, sending people away for longer, and under-resourcing the prison system so that it has no hope of reducing recidivism. And even though some leading politicians have ended up expressing regret for their policy choices, nobody has seemed able to halt the inexorable rise in imprisonment.

Criminologists Colin Hay, Stephen Farrall and Naomi Burke, examining Acts of Parliament passed in the 1980s, argue that an ideological trend towards punitiveness began with Margaret Thatcher's political rhetoric; according to Thatcher, the country wanted 'less tax and more law and order', and she was in favour of capital punishment.[278] Despite her wish to appear as a staunch defender of law and order, her home secretaries varied between being progressive on crime (Willie Whitelaw and Douglas Hurd) and punitive (David Waddington and Leon Brittan), and most criminal law passed during her premiership was – perhaps surprisingly – in line with a pre-existing liberal approach that tended towards limiting the use of custody, rather than falling into line with the Thatcherite rhetoric. The White Paper *Crime, Justice and Protecting the Public*, published in early 1990 during Waddington's time as Home Secretary, stated that prison 'can be an expensive way of making bad people worse'.[279] But by later the same year, during John Major's Conservative government, public worries about crime, or at least politicians' belief in public worries about crime, began to reinforce Thatcher's ideology and lawmaking took a notably punitive shift.

This shift was made emphatically visible when hawkish Michael Howard became Home Secretary in 1993, taking over from the more dove-like Ken Clarke. At the 1993 Conservative Party Conference, Howard loudly proclaimed that 'prison works', signalling a tougher stance, and that the government would 'no longer judge the success of our system of justice by a fall in our prison population'. He followed this up two years later with another speech to party conference: 'If you don't want the time, don't do the crime. No half-time sentences for full-time crimes.' The Criminal Justice and Public Order Act, passed in November 1994, increased the powers of the courts to imprison young offenders, increased police powers of stop and search, allowed juries to infer guilt from an accused's silence, and increased maximum penalties for a range of offences; this was followed by a steep rise in rates of imprisonment.

The evidence of 130 men

What basis did Michael Howard have for believing that 'prison works'? In large part, he seems, like economist Gary Becker, to have had faith that people make rational choices, and was relying on the belief that potential criminals make rational choices *not* to offend when sentences get longer – they don't mind doing the time if sentences are short but will sensibly avoid stiffer sentences. Howard referred, at the time and thereafter, to a study by Dr Ros Burnett of the Centre for Criminology at the University of Oxford. Dr Burnett had monitored 130 men, imprisoned for property crimes, for two years after their release from prison, and asked them what they thought had affected their re-offending or ability to go straight. As Dr Burnett and her colleague, Dr Shadd Maruna from the University of Cambridge, have since written, Howard's interpretation of their study, that 'avoidance of imprisonment was the most frequently mentioned reason for not wanting to reoffend' was 'a selective reading . . . to say the least'.[280] In fact, 62 per cent had already re-offended within the two-year follow up. When the researchers went back to see what had happened more than ten years after the men's release, they managed to trace the records of all but one: 82 per cent of the men had further convictions for serious crimes and 63 per cent had been back to prison. The average man in the group had had *six* more convictions and spent more than twenty-seven months in further imprisonment. Prison evidentially hadn't worked for them.

Burnett and Maruna also report that, while an offender's hope for the future – their belief that they could change their lives around and avoid re-offending – was indeed correlated with their ability to stay out of trouble, the predictive value of this sense of agency withered in the face of social problems such as homelessness, bereavement and extreme poverty. If 'prison works' at all, it seems that it can only work within a system of supportive rehabilitation and resettlement. As Burnett and Maruna concluded: 'The notion that Britain's "decent but austere" prisons can scare inhabitants straight through sheer deterrence, and also somehow become hotbeds for hope and developing self-efficacy seems a far-fetched fantasy.'[280]

A crusade against crime

So what of New Labour? Far from any return to liberal and progressive approaches to crime and punishment that might have been expected, in 1997 Tony Blair's government was keen to be seen to be 'tough on crime and tough on the causes of crime', and the drift towards a more punitive system continued, including the introduction in 2003 of indeterminate sentences of Imprisonment for Public Protection (IPPs) by the then-Home Secretary David Blunkett. (About 7,000 IPPs were handed down, many for fairly low-level crimes, before being abolished in 2012; the change, however, did not apply retrospectively and close to 3,000 prisoners are still in custody, most of them far beyond their minimum term of sentence.)

One stand-out policy enacted under New Labour was the introduction in April 1998 of the notorious Antisocial Behaviour Orders (ASBOs). Intended to address nuisance neighbours, juvenile delinquency and the kinds of street crime that can cause so much misery in predominantly deprived areas, ASBOs were supposed to deter crime, but because violating an ASBO could lead to imprisonment of up to five years, that, along with other 'tough on crime' increases in maximum penalties introduced with the same legislation, pushed imprisonment rates and prison numbers ever further upwards.

The ASBO approach has since morphed into a range of Behavioural Control Orders, designed to tackle a wide range of offences from domestic abuse to stalking. The law reform and human rights charity Justice, in a report produced by a working group of academics and criminal justice practitioners, sees this as an 'unchecked explosion' of punitive law-making that has resulted in the imposition of such absurd orders as banning someone from swearing, preventing a pensioner from wearing a bikini in her garden, and restricting a family with an autistic child from closing the door too loudly. Meanwhile orders designed to protect women and girls are under-used and others disproportionately impact the homeless and destitute, who are actually more likely to be victims of antisocial crime than perpetrators.[281]

Hawks turn to doves (when they're not in office)

Perhaps the most striking stories of political action in relation to crime and punishment after the Conservatives returned to power (first in Coalition with the Liberal Democrats) in 2010 were the reversals of their thinking among prominent politicians who had been in power as prison numbers rose and more punitive legislation was passed.

Former New Labour Home Secretary David Blunkett concluded 'I got it wrong' as he campaigned for the reversal of IPPs in 2014. And former Conservative prime minister John Major now essentially disagrees with his former Home Secretary Michael Howard that 'prison works': in 2023 he declared that 'we over-use prison and undervalue alternative sentences'. Over time, Ken Clarke, who served twice as Home Secretary, became more and more dove-like; in 2010 he described the 'bang 'em up' prison culture of the preceding twenty years as Victorian, and political debate on law and order 'reduced to a competition over whether government has spent more public money and locked up more people than its predecessor' – pointing out that it costs more to keep someone in prison for a year than it does to send them to Eton.[282]

A turning tide?

Keir Starmer's Labour government was elected in July 2024 with a landslide majority. As a former Director of Public Prosecutions and head of the Crown Prosecution Service, Starmer has more hands-on experience of the criminal justice system than any previous prime minister. The new government rapidly committed itself to the previous Conservative government's promise to create 20,000 new prison places – so it didn't appear to be interested in radically reducing rates of imprisonment. At the same time, James Timpson, a prominent prison reformer, was given a baronetcy, installed in the House of Lords, and made Minister of State for Prisons, Probation and Reducing Reoffending.

James Timpson was, until this appointment, chief executive of Timpson, the well-known shoe repair and key-cutting business, with 1,300 shops and kiosks throughout the UK and Ireland. The business is known for its long-standing commitment to recruiting and training ex-offenders to work in its shops, which began under James Timpson's father, John Timpson – running pre-release training schemes in several prisons. Twelve per cent of Timpson employees are former inmates and three-quarters of them stay with the business long term, bucking all the trends of re-offending. James Timpson's track record of advocacy for former prisoners doesn't stop there; he has chaired an employer's forum for reducing re-offending, founded a network of advisory boards that link prisons to employers, and chaired the Prison Reform Trust until his ministerial appointment. He has said publicly that only a third of people in prison should be there.

Prisons hit the headlines almost as soon as the new Labour government took office, with Keir Starmer declaring that there were 'too many prisoners and not enough prisons' and that the prison situation was 'worse than [he] thought'.[283] Overcrowding was so dangerously high in the summer of 2024 that the government quickly introduced an early release scheme for those in prison for non-violent and less serious crimes, letting people out after serving 40 per cent, rather than the previous 50 per cent, of their sentences. This led to the biggest fall in prison numbers in a single week since the system began recording numbers of releases in 2012. In the week ending 13 September 2024, prison numbers dropped by 2.5 per cent, with 2,188 fewer people in prison than the week before.

The long-term trend, however, is continuously upward. Prison numbers rose by more than 7,000 just while I was writing this book, and the Starmer government has very much continued in the UK tradition of wanting to look tough on crime.

Getting it wrong

The only conclusion to come to, after looking at these twists and turns in ideologies, actions and outcomes, is that no government in the past half century has managed to strike the right balance of being able to keep the public safe and free from the negative consequences of crime while rehabilitating criminals.

And this is emphatically NOT because the empirical research or the expert opinions are divided. There is a strong consensus among academic criminologists, whether they are scholars of law, psychology, sociology or economics, that prison doesn't work, particularly with respect to short sentences. The Parliamentary Office of Science and Technology (POST), drawing on scientific information and research briefs, said that there is:

> a growing consensus that short prison sentences have limited effectiveness in reducing reoffending, or in achieving other goals such as rehabilitation, *compared to community orders and suspended sentence orders* [my italics]. They may also have wider undesirable impacts on the prison service and for offenders particularly for women and young offenders.[284]

What seems to be happening is that, while in government, politicians feel they cannot be seen to be soft on crime. John Major described it thus, in 2023:

> It is not so easy . . . to plead for people who have committed crimes, and are responsible for their own misfortune . . . Nor, very often, is it politically comfortable for 'active' politicians to plead for convicted criminals. In the rough and tumble of politics, compassion and consideration can too easily be derided as 'soft' or 'weak' – terms which can define as well as defame.[285]

Politicians fear the media as much as the electorate and so the zeal for harsher criminal justice continues, for the most part politically unopposed.

It seems as if politicians are truly stuck – between the evidence on the one hand and public opinion on the other. It's hard to make a case for spending on improving prisons and prisoner welfare when money is needed urgently for health care, education, social care and more – and the payoffs for tackling the prisons problem may take time to manifest. The evidence, however, isn't going away: prison isn't a good solution for most of the people who are sent there; it doesn't work (and this is true of short sentences in particular) in terms of keeping us and our property safe because it fails to rehabilitate criminals and prevent re-offending; it is hugely costly and riddled with injustice and inequities.

If you sat down to design an effective criminal justice system from first principles, based on the evidence we have from the system we've got, you'd surely design something that looked very different indeed. And yet this feels like an impossible task if there is no widespread public support for reform.

From victim to offender: how childhood shapes criminality

It is also difficult to see where our modern understanding of the psychology and epidemiology of trauma fits into our contemporary criminal justice system. We have such good evidence now of the links between adverse childhood experiences, often abbreviated to ACEs, and later criminal activity. ACEs first came to attention when an American study linked them to chronic health problems in middle age, including heart disease, depression and chronic obstructive pulmonary disease.[286] Childhood maltreatment (including physical, psychological and sexual abuse), physical neglect, and household dysfunction (including parental substance abuse, family breakdown, and mental illness), as well as witnessing domestic violence, are strongly predictive of children and young people getting involved in crime. These adverse childhood experiences also increase the likelihood of children having learning delays, inadequate coping skills, difficulty regulating their emotions, and problems relating to other people, as well as a wide range of mental and physical health problems.[287]

Low self-control is a corollary of adverse childhood experiences,[288] so questions of agency and responsibility become salient when we think about how the criminal justice system should treat people who, as very small children, suffered in ways that shaped their ability to learn, cope, relate, and foresee the consequences of their actions or a more positive trajectory for their lives. There is what is known as a dose–response relationship between ACEs and delinquency: the more adverse experiences children are exposed to, the greater the likelihood of serious, violent and chronic crime, convictions and imprisonment.[289]

In the UK, the Children's Commissioner has a statutory remit to bring the interests of children and young people to policymakers, and special responsibility for children in care, children receiving social services and those in the youth justice system. The commissioner reports on what are termed 'vulnerabilities': these overlap with ACEs and include children in households where a parent is experiencing domestic abuse, severe mental health problems or substance addiction; children suffering from educational disadvantage; those outside mainstream education; children in gangs, in poverty, or known to children's services; those with caring responsibilities; and children with SEND. As well as reporting statistics related to these vulnerabilities, such as an estimate that 2.3 million children in England are at risk (of poor outcomes) because of a vulnerable family background, in her 2019 report *Childhood Vulnerability in Numbers*, the Children's Commissioner told the story of a hypothetical child called Ben.[290] At age two, Ben is living in a hostel with parents who have mental health conditions, and is already experiencing developmental delays. At age five he is falling behind at school and struggling to regulate his emotions; by age twelve he has been expelled and is having difficulties with his parents; by fourteen he is in a gang and running drugs in county lines. He is then taken into a series of care homes, far away from family and friends. By sixteen he is in custody for assault; he has no qualifications or skills, no prospects or hope, but he is already a father – the intimation being that Ben's story will be one stage in an intergenerational cycle of adversity.

Adverse childhood experiences don't, of course, happen at random to children – there are ethnic and poverty-related differences in exposure. UK children born to poor parents are nine times more likely to experience ACEs than children in non-poor families.[291] Around 7 per cent of White British children were exposed to three or more adverse childhood experiences in a nationally representative study of children born around the millennium, compared to almost 20 per cent of Black Caribbean children, and more than a quarter of children from Pakistani, Bangladeshi or Black African families.[292] In the USA, Black and Hispanic children are much more likely to have experienced two or more kinds of ACEs.[293]

So we're seeing pathways to delinquency and crime that are set in motion in the very early lives of (innocent) children, which impact disproportionately on poor children and children from ethnic minorities. These are heartbreaking injustices, but such stories don't always land on sympathetic ears. Instead, crime is almost always viewed as a context-free choice, and the only people we don't hold fully responsible for their crimes are the very young (and we sometimes make exceptions even for them) and those who do not have the mental capacity to distinguish between right and wrong.

Vulnerability in the prison system

Data from Wales suggest that those who have suffered four or more adverse childhood experiences are twenty times more likely to have been imprisoned. A survey of men in a Welsh prison in 2018 found that 8 out of 10 (84 per cent) had experienced at least one ACE, almost half of them (46 per cent) had experienced four or more, and prisoners in that latter group were four times more likely to have spent time in a young offender institution than those with no adverse childhood experiences.[294] In a demonstration of the intergenerational grip of those experiences, the same group of men were asked about their own children and, among the fathers with over four ACEs, their children were six times more likely to have also experienced that many ACEs.[295]

The ACEs perspective and other trauma-informed approaches are starting to infiltrate the criminal justice system, with staff training for police and prison officers widely rolled out. Early evaluations suggest that professionals are starting to feel capable and confident in using these approaches. The Economic and Social Research Council, the public funding body for the social sciences, has funded the Vulnerability & Policing Futures Research Centre, which I am part of, that aims to reshape how the police and other organisations work together to reduce harm among vulnerable people. One project is looking at how the police use 'Out of Court Resolutions' to divert people from the criminal justice system, and how these could be better applied to vulnerable groups.

Another focuses on young people of colour in an inner city to better understand their perceptions of policing and safety in their community, and to develop, with them, a community plan for change. It is too early, though, to say much about the wider and longer-term impacts of these shifts in culture in the criminal justice system, and, as prison numbers keep on climbing, very difficult to see that this understanding is significantly affecting sentencing.

And instead of talking about these issues with any nuance, politicians and political parties on both the left and the right continue to compete with one another to look tough on crime.

A public health approach to criminal justice

In 2009 I attended an international conference on early intervention in Nottingham. I was there to speak on a panel about the impact of economic inequality on children's life chances, and I can't say that I had great expectations that the conference would be anything more than the usual academic talking shop. However, it was woken up by the energetic performance of Karyn McCluskey, now chief executive of Community Justice Scotland, who was at the time leading the Scottish Violence Reduction Unit, a groundbreaking initiative that treats violence as a public health problem. What energised the conference was her passionate call for resources for tackling knife crime – such as more police officers – to be spent instead on more health visitors.

Starting out in Glasgow, which then had the highest murder rate in Europe, plus an entrenched culture of violence and what is now often termed 'toxic masculinity', the Scottish Violence Reduction Unit had been set up at the instigation of the Chief

Constable of Scotland's biggest police authority, Strathclyde, in the recognition that the criminal justice system alone couldn't tackle the problem, and taking on board the World Health Organization's 2002 declaration that violence was 'a public health concern':

> Despite the fact that violence has always been present, the world does not have to accept it as an inevitable part of the human condition . . . Violence can be prevented and its impact reduced, in the same way that public health efforts have prevented and reduced pregnancy-related complications, workplace injuries, infectious diseases, and illness resulting from contaminated food and water in many parts of the world. The factors that contribute to violent responses – whether they are factors of attitude and behaviour or related to larger social, economic, political and cultural conditions – can be changed.[296]

A public health approach to violence (or indeed any crime) means understanding the epidemiology of it – where are crimes happening and who are the perpetrators and victims – understanding the social determinants of crime, and focusing on prevention by tackling the root causes. The Scottish Violence Reduction Unit has developed multiple programmes using this public health approach, including importing an evidence-based programme from America (called 'Focused Deterrence') in which gang members are challenged by the community to understand the impact of what they are doing to themselves, their families and others.[297] An independent evaluation of this programme found that it had led to reductions in violent crime among participants, as well as in knife and weapon carrying and gang-fighting.[298]

The Scottish unit also launched a 'Navigator' programme in

hospitals to support people who have suffered from any kind of violence; a social enterprise giving employment to people with a history of offending or at risk of committing crime; and volunteering opportunities for ex-offenders at the Edinburgh Tattoo and the Commonwealth Games (held in Glasgow in 2014). There is an intervention in schools to help students safely and effectively challenge bullying, and other forms of abuse, that is based on evidence from a similar set-up in the USA; a project that involves doctors in school-based violence prevention; support for migrants coming into Scotland; and training to help people who work with the public to recognise and intervene when they encounter people at risk of, or suffering, domestic abuse.

All these initiatives are helping – crime has reduced in Scotland from a peak in the early 2000s – and the approach is spreading. London now also has a Violence Reduction Unit, modelled on the Scottish experience. But if we think back to the cliff analogy of public health that I introduced in Chapter 1, a lot of these initiatives are like the net halfway down the cliff (the Navigator scheme for people hospitalised for violence, for example), or the fence at the top of the cliff (like the education programmes in schools); they still don't really touch the root causes of the causes of our high levels of imprisonment: the poverty, deprivation and inequality that underpin all the shocking statistics we've seen in this chapter. If we're going to tackle the root causes of imprisonment, we need all of the fundamental action on inequality and poverty that I've discussed in relation to health, educational and care inequalities in previous chapters. We need to reduce poverty, increase employment rates, raise educational attainment, focus on people's livelihoods and give every child the best start in life. All the important evidence-based programmes and schemes being implemented in violence reduction units need to sit on top of these foundational changes.

Just as with health, education and social care, a radical shift to addressing the causes of the causes will take time to filter through and prevent crimes being committed, and people committing crime coming into contact with the criminal justice system. But unlike those other sectors of society, the prison problem is also amenable to some quicker fixes. The criminal justice system is government-controlled, and policymakers could mandate changes to the system that would have profound and immediate impact, just as we saw with the Labour government's early release scheme in the summer of 2024. For example, the government could pass legislation that raises the age of criminal responsibility, or mandate the use of alternatives to prison for more crimes, or shorten prison sentences for specific crimes. Allocating adequate budgets for prison staffing, prison education and training, healthcare and post-prison support would very quickly affect recidivism rates.

Let's turn to what could be done now, with regard to imprisonment rather than crime, while more deep-seated changes are given a chance to shift the medium- and long-term future.

Blueprints for reducing imprisonment

In 1990 rioting broke out in Strangeways prison in Manchester, triggered by long-standing issues of overcrowding, poor conditions, inadequate health care, and staff shortages. Prisoners protested against these inhumane conditions, leading to a major uprising that lasted nearly three weeks and spread to other prisons across the UK, highlighting systemic problems. This was a significant story at the time, drawing widespread media attention and prompting public debate about prison conditions, reform needs, and the treatment of inmates.

The riots left two men dead and 194 injured and the government commissioned a report on prison conditions from Lord Justice Woolf, published in 1991 and hailed as a progressive blueprint for prison reform.[299] Reading it now, I can see why it gained such acclaim – it made twelve main recommendations and 204 detailed proposals that were undeniably sensible: better cooperation across different parts of the system, improved leadership, decent sanitation, an end to overcrowding, and so on. If implemented comprehensively, these changes could have prevented many of the problems that still exist, or have worsened, today.

Yet I find myself agreeing with critics like criminologist Dr David Scott of the Open University, who argues that the report wasn't actually that innovative and failed to question the fundamental legitimacy of imprisoning people at all, or adopt a human rights perspective on prisons.[300] What strikes me most is how the Woolf Report exemplifies the way official discourse co-opts progressive language while avoiding the deeper questions. Its main aim seems to have been to 'restore the authority, legitimacy and stability of the prison service', and prevent future riots, rather than genuinely transform how we think about punishment and rehabilitation.[300] The report offered reform within the existing framework rather than challenging whether that framework itself was fit for purpose.

One recommendation alone – 'a division of prison establishments into small and more manageable and secure units' – could have had a profound impact on the physical and social infrastructure of the prison estate and the wellbeing of prisoners. But within three years of the publication of the Woolf Report, the tide had swung away from reform, towards longer sentences and competition among politicians to look tough, and in the 25-years-on review in 2015, the Prison Reform Trust saw the report as looking 'increasingly prescient as a warning to our own time'.[301]

There is a strong consensus among academics and reform groups that by changing three things we can reshape how we use imprisonment to support a good society: the prison culture and what happens to people inside prison and when they leave; sentencing; and the infrastructure of the prison estate (by this I mean physical structures and staffing).[302, 303]

The prison gates open

In 1895, the Reverend William Morrison described a woman released from prison as 'the most hopeless creature in the world'.[304] A century and a half later, prisoners get an £89.52 cash payment (plus money from their prison savings if they have been working) and a travel warrant on release. Although they are supposed to have twelve weeks of accommodation arranged for them, many don't. At the end of December 2023, England's chief prisons inspector, Charlie Taylor, in an interview with the *Independent*, said that it was 'not rare' for prisoners to be released with tents and sleeping bags 'because they know they're going to be homeless', while women at HMP Styal were leaving their belongings in the property store, 'because it's the safest place to keep it and they knew they were coming back anyway'.[305] Scotland's lead inspector of prisons from 2018 to 2024, Wendy Sinclair-Gieben, described a young woman released to accommodation in a bed and breakfast where she wasn't allowed to stay during the day, with no money and no employment, who slipped straight back into crime and drugs and was soon back in prison.[305] And even worse than being released without adequate money or accommodation are the failures to equip prisoners for release by treating mental health and addiction problems and providing them with training, skills and proper links into employment. As well as proper provision for post-release housing, employment and services, how do we ensure that people are ready to benefit from them? The answer lies in establishing what has become known as a 'rehabilitative culture'.[306]

So what is this 'rehabilitative culture' that evidence suggests should underpin the whole of the criminal justice system, and prisons in particular? In the words of a world-leading expert, Dr Ruth Mann, who was a pioneer in its practice and developing its evidence base, a rehabilitative culture is 'a culture with a purpose; that is, to support people in turning away from crime and toward a different life'.[307] Relationships and interactions between prisoners and staff are key – staff coach prisoners to problem-solve for example, encourage them to engage in rehabilitation (e.g. training and treatment) and treat them with humanity and decency: they are expected to model the culture they want to encourage. A rehabilitative culture is also designed to give hope, use fair processes, encourage a shift away from a criminal identity to a more positive sense of self, and build prisoners' social capital.

An example of the kind of small but important deployment of fair processes is the use of door-sticker notices asking prisoners to not cover up the observation panel in the door, because it isn't there to spy on people but so that staff can check that prisoners are okay. This is an example of what is known as procedural justice – making sure that processes and procedures are fair and reasonable and explained properly – which research has shown can enhance trust, cooperation and positive behaviours.

Other seemingly small changes, such as making sure that prisons are quieter and darker at night, can have a big impact, as sleep disruption increases mental health difficulties and aggression. Encouraging a prisoner to focus on their identity as a parent or a provider can help shift them towards a positive, rather than a criminal, identity, and to feel capable of being concerned and caring towards others. Training prisoners with the cognitive skills to re-evaluate their criminal thinking and consider the long-term consequences of their actions more than short-term outcomes is easier when the prison culture is fostering positive, helpful social interactions and relationships. This is not dissimilar to the narrative therapeutic approach we met in Chapter 3 aimed at preventing behaviour difficulties leading to school exclusion. Many prisons now offer Parkruns, which operate just as they do on the outside – people can run, walk, jog or watch a 5k course once a week, gaining physical and social benefits and giving them a chance to develop a practice which they can then continue in the same predictable context after release. All of these examples are little things, but they can add up to a lot more than the sum of their parts.

Research shows that a rehabilitative culture is our best chance of creating safe prison environments (for both residents and staff) and better experiences for prisoners and prison staff, as well as our best chance of preparing people for a non-criminal life once their sentences end, and thus making society safer and a better place for all of us. The rehabilitative culture framework has incorporated research evidence from psychology, psychiatry, criminology, sociology and more; for example, an understanding of adverse childhood experiences and trauma underpins the interpersonal humanity and decency which can transform relationships and interactions. But this isn't an ivory tower theory with no relation to the real world, unlike Becker's theory of crime. The evidence base and delineation of rehabilitative culture has been generated within the prison service itself, hand in glove with researchers who have been able to evaluate its positive impact. The rehabilitative culture framework isn't fuzzy or soft; it's based on hard evidence of what works and requires hard work from everyone involved. And it's the best possibility we have for reforming a dysfunctional system that works for no one.

Sentencing: stopping short

There will always be a need for prisons to house people convicted of serious and violent crime. However, given all the research evidence of the harm caused to people and their families and communities by short sentences, the negative impact of this population on prison culture and costs, and the lack of evidence of a deterrent basis, sentencing needs radical reform.

The Labour government elected in 2024 committed itself to a comprehensive re-evaluation of sentencing, with the aim of avoiding the kinds of emergency releases to reduce overcrowding that it had to implement soon after taking office, but also with a stated aim of encouraging 'offenders to turn their backs on a life of crime, cutting crime by reducing re-offending' and expanding non-custodial punishments. Subsequently, an Independent Review of Sentencing was commissioned, chaired by former prime minister Theresa May's justice secretary, David Gauke, who had been outspoken on the need to move away from short sentences and his belief that this would be a balanced, considered and evidence-based approach: 'there is a very strong case to abolish sentences of six months or less altogether, with some closely defined exceptions, and put in their place, a robust community order regime'.[308]

The review was encouraged to use evidence and to look at

what other countries are doing, and to have an explicit focus on short sentences and how sentencing should be adapted for vulnerable groups, such as young adults and women. Published in May 2025, the report recognised that short prison sentences are ineffective compared to community alternatives, and proposed limiting short sentences to exceptional circumstances, as well as expanding suspended and deferred sentencing as practical ways to reduce ineffective custodial terms.[309] The review also emphasised the need to expand community alternatives, backed by proper funding for probation services, women's centres, intensive supervision courts, and treatment costs. It also proposed to limit the use of recall to prison, which so often creates a 'revolving door' effect. However, the review did not entirely please prison reform campaigners – mainly due to its failure to address the impact of longer sentences for serious offences.

There is a good case to be made for imposing a complete ban on sentences of six months or less, and what is called a 'presumption against' – a discouragement from – imposing sentences of between six months and a year, meaning that these could only be used in exceptional or particular circumstances. Scotland has had a presumption against sentences under one year since 2019; however, it has been pointed out that this has been less successful than hoped because what was meant by exceptional circumstances was not well defined, so too much was left to the discretion of judges. There were also unintended consequences of some people seemingly being given longer sentences because short sentences were less available.

Helen Mills, head of programmes at the Centre for Crime and Justice Studies, points out that reforming short sentences alone doesn't have a big impact on prison numbers or costs: a large number of short sentences avoided translates into a fairly small reduction in prison places needed (i.e. four people receiving three-month sentences will occupy one prison place per year), and more resources will need to be in place for managing the community sentence alternatives.[310] Action on reducing the length of longer sentences has a bigger impact on prison numbers – and thus on costs, staffing and overcrowding – than banning short sentences. Nevertheless, the two strategies can work together, and there is a human rights case to be made for the ban on short sentences, due to their disproportionately disruptive impact on people's lives, even if it is not a hugely effective strategy for bringing prison numbers down.

In August 2025, the UK government committed to introducing legislation before the end of the year to abolish most short prison sentences, toughen up community punishments and introduce a new system for inmates to earn early release through good behaviour.[311]

Transforming the prison estate

It seems to me that, rather than committing to building new prisons to create a net increase in available numbers, the investment should be in replacing prison infrastructure that is not fit for purpose in anybody's conception of a minimally decent society, let alone a good one.

In late 2023, there were still five prisons in England that had cells without toilets, despite the fact that this state of affairs was supposed to have ended in 1996. According to the director of campaigns at the Howard League for Penal Reform:

> In our overburdened and under-resourced prison system . . . it is common to see dirt, vermin, broken furniture, faulty equipment and the poor hygiene that comes with people

being forced to share cramped, poorly ventilated cells designed for one [and] slopping out [the practice of having to use a bucket instead of a toilet] is one of the grimmest practices that you will find.[312]

Sharing cells designed for one and not having access to a toilet violate the so-called Nelson Mandela Rules, which were first adopted by the United Nations in 1955 and formally called the Standard Minimum Rules for the Treatment of Prisoners. These were revised in 2015, setting out 122 rules, the first of which is that 'all prisoners shall be treated with the respect due to their inherent dignity and value as human beings'. I felt deep shame, reading these rules, recognising how far we are in the UK from achieving even that single rule with our outdated, dysfunctional prisons.

An important recommendation from the Woolf Report, described earlier, was that prisons should be divided into small and more manageable and secure units. If these were distributed more evenly across the country, then another important recommendation – for improving prospects for prisoners to maintain links with family and community, through visits and home leave – would be facilitated. Smaller prison units are much more conducive to establishing the bedrock of a rehabilitative culture, allowing for the development of more personal and trusting relationships between prisoners and staff. Housing prisoners in smaller units, with sufficient and fit-for-purpose space for work and education facilities, increases the possibility that prisoners can be engaged in purposeful, busy routines – rather than being confined to their cells during the daytime, as happens far too often at the moment, or engaged in the mundane purposeless routine of the typical prison day that I described earlier.

Prison accommodation ought to reflect the kinds of standards that a good society would implement across all public infrastructure like schools, hospitals and care homes, because this is how we respect people's 'inherent dignity and value as human beings' in compliance with the first Mandela Rule. If the state is accommodating people, for any reason, it should only ever be in well-ventilated, properly maintained, hygienic and clean facilities, warm in winter and cool in summer, with an expectation that staff and prisoners will work together to maintain the spaces in which they live and work with some mutual pride. We should not be building new prisons to simply add to the numbers of prisoners that can be accommodated; we should be building new prisons to replace our hopelessly outdated and uncivilised infrastructure.

Digital infrastructure is also crucial for a well-functioning system – healthcare and education systems need to talk to prison systems so that treatment and training for people in prison can be facilitated, and prisoners also need digital access and capabilities to keep up with the world outside and be able to take courses, apply for housing and jobs, and maintain family ties. Potential security risks of giving prisoners more access to digital communications are all manageable through technological controls, and the benefits to prisoners and in cost-savings surely outweigh the risks. Imagine how much money could be saved just if prisoners could take part, online, in education and training offered in the community, rather than it having to be provided face-to-face inside.

UK prisons have a chronic staffing problem, due to stagnation in pay and stressful conditions, with severe shortages and a high turnover rate meaning that expertise and experience is constantly leaking out of the system. As pointed out in Nelson Mandela Rule 74: '. . . it is on their [prison personnel] integrity, humanity, professional capacity and personal suitability for the work that the proper administration of prisons depends'. Better pay, more training and more supportive supervision and management are just as important as new buildings for transforming the prison system and creating a rehabilitative culture. Earlier, I described Nordic prison culture in which prison officers play a crucial and active role in engaging prisoners in rehabilitative activity. In Chapter 3 we saw how Finland transformed its education system in part through raising the status of teachers through better pay and professional standards. We could do just the same to improve recruitment and retention of excellent prison officers. Developing a rehabilitative culture improves conditions for both prisoners *and* staff.

Intersecting inequalities

Finally, everywhere in the criminal justice system, structural racism looms large. We can't reform our prisons without confronting this. The Conservative government-commissioned Lammy Review, published in 2017, pointed out that the criminal justice system bucks the trends of better representation of people from minoritised ethnic communities in sectors where they have been under-represented, such as higher education, the professions, and in politics.[313] The review put the cost of their disproportionate involvement in the criminal justice system at £309 million a year – we could do a lot with that saved resource. Crucially, this independent review of race and ethnicity in the prison system recognised that race and ethnicity intersect with poverty, inequality and deprivation, as well as health, education and social care inequalities – and that these intersectional inequalities need to be tackled outside the criminal justice system. What it focused on instead are the discrimination, prejudice and inequalities *within* the system (as well as the shocking lack of relevant data on ethnicity), making recommendations for improvement that are tractable within the system and its institutions. The Lammy Review covers disproportions in arrests, in pleas and plea bargains, in sentences, in relationships with staff, and in unmet health and social needs within prisons. Many of its recommendations focused on openness and transparency of process, underpinned by robust data and data analysis, as well as greater diversity of representation within the judiciary – all still need to be addressed. But perhaps the key recommendation was that all agencies within the system should either provide an evidence-based explanation for ethnic disparities or reform themselves to tackle them.

Breaking the cycle

In a nutshell, government should adopt, as a foundational purpose, a comprehensive framework for a rehabilitative culture across the criminal justice system, as well as enacting all the recommendations of the Lammy Review to tackle ethnic inequalities, holding all agencies within the criminal justice system openly accountable for both *explaining* ethnic inequalities and *reforming* them. Government should also radically refocus the system to remove or drastically reduce prison sentences of less than one year with realignment of resources to non-custodial alternatives; it should reverse its commitments to build extra prison places and instead commit to creating safe, hygienic, well-ventilated, warm accommodation in smaller units with closer connections to community to house a smaller number of prisoners. And finally, the prison system should move to follow the model of patient participation in health care; to embed meaningful prisoner, prisoner family, and prison staff participation in both the strategy and operations of the system.

Over recent decades, instead of the coordinated cooperation across government and between national and local bodies as called for by Woolf, we have seen probation services disastrously privatised in 2014 (a failed move which had to be reversed in 2019), resettlement services outsourced, and parts of the criminal justice budget devolved to locally elected police and crime commissioners. There is better coordination between health and prison services than in the past, but coordination with drug and alcohol services, and housing and employment services, is still limited. And rather than giving prison governors increased autonomy, as Woolf recommended, governments have seemed fond of issuing edicts which seem driven more by an attempt to appeal to a reactionary public than by intelligent strategy – dictating 'lights out' times in secure children's centres, for example, and a ban on sending books to prisoners in 2013, which was found to be unlawful and lifted in 2015.

The most recent government strategy, as I write in late 2025, remains the 2021 Prisons Strategy White Paper, set out by the Conservative government under Boris Johnson. According to the Prison Reform Trust, few of its ambitions were new; most had been 'articulated repeatedly' and not delivered on, creating an endless cycle of announcement and inactivity. As the trust went on to say: 'Repeating grand ambitions without pausing to understand why they have so often not been delivered in the past is a recipe for further disappointment.'[303]

PART TWO

How to Build a Good Society

CHAPTER 5

Time for New Economic Thinking

'It is easier to imagine an end to the world than an end to capitalism.'

Mark Fisher

At a political event in Leeds a few years ago, I met Linda. She was speaking about the enduring devastation caused to her former mining community in South Yorkshire by the economic calculus of the pit closure programme of the 1980s. As she talked about the impact on her father, a miner, she began to cry. Tears rolled down her cheeks as she described the pain of his, and her, experiences, still resonant thirty years on.

When the coal mines were closing in the 1980s, economists were promising that market forces would bring new prosperity. From then on, the UK did indeed have fairly steady growth in GDP. Except for the punctuations of the 1991 recession, the global financial crisis of 2008 and the Covid-19 pandemic, the UK economy was actually growing, averaging roughly 2–3 per cent growth each year, although this long-term growth remained below historical averages. But Linda's experience told a very different story. Her father never worked again. Her husband drives ninety minutes each way to an Amazon warehouse where he earns less in real terms than either his or Linda's father had in the 1970s. Her son graduated with £50,000 in student debt for a degree that couldn't secure him a job locally. What happened to the coal-producing areas of the UK has been described as the 'economic vandalism' of neoliberalism, compounded by subsequent austerity policies.[314] This was not the economic revival and prosperity the country had been promised.

Linda would look around at her community – the shuttered high-street shops, the rising food bank use, the increasing mental health problems in her family and among her neighbours – and see only broken promises. When Linda's husband was diagnosed with depression, the waiting list for NHS mental health services stretched to months. The private therapy that they couldn't afford would have added to the UK's GDP; their struggles to cope without it did not. When Linda spent twenty hours every week caring for her elderly mother, that labour registered nowhere in productivity calculations. When their local park was sold to developers for flats that had stood empty ever since, GDP rose but the community stagnated.

Linda and her family weren't alone. Similar stories have played out in the UK, in communities from Glasgow to Plymouth, across the decades. People are working harder than ever, yet so many are falling behind, as we've seen throughout this book. This isn't because the economy isn't growing – officially, it has in fact expanded over recent decades. But that growth has been captured almost entirely by those at the top. While GDP figures and stock market indices climb steadily upward, median wages have stagnated, housing has become unaffordable for entire generations, and public services have been starved of investment. The wealth created by our collective productivity has flowed disproportionately to shareholders and executives, while workers see their living standards decline despite longer hours and higher qualifications. We have a fundamental disconnect between economic theory and lived reality, because the measures we use to judge economic success – GDP growth, productivity gains, corporate profits – tell us nothing about whether that success is shared or whether it's improving people's lives.

How did we come to this – an economic system that has created fundamental and enduring inequalities and deprivation, across and within regions, alongside ecological collapse? And what kind of radical rethinking of economics can turn that around and set us on a path towards a good society?

'It is easier to imagine an end to the world than an end to capitalism,' wrote Mark Fisher, echoing a sentiment attributed to both Fredric Jameson and Slavoj Žižek.[315] But as Linda and too many others have discovered, we urgently need the economic alternatives, which many are already developing, to break through into mainstream politics and policy-making. From community wealth-building initiatives to cooperative enterprises, from universal basic income trials to wellbeing budgets, there are countless examples of different ways of organising our economy that prioritise people and planet over profit. The problem isn't a lack of imagination or innovation – it's that these alternatives remain marginalised, dismissed by mainstream politicians and media as unrealistic or unaffordable, while the economic thinking that has dominated policy-making for generations continues to fail too many people and our planet. It's time for these proven alternatives to move from the margins to the centre of political debate.

A shed full of broken tools

The 2008 global financial crisis should have been a turning point. When governments had to step in to save markets that were supposed to regulate themselves, when publicly funded central banks had to bail out private banks, it exposed the fundamental contradictions in neoliberal thinking. Yet, remarkably, we returned to business as usual. Even Nobel Prize-winning economists like Paul Krugman and Joseph Stiglitz, who warned against austerity and urged investment instead, were largely ignored.

The problem isn't that people don't recognise neoliberalism's failures – most do. The challenge is that we're still living with the systems and institutions it created. Our measures of success are still GDP growth and corporate profits rather than well-being or sustainability. Our political institutions are still structured around the assumption that markets know best. Our tax systems still reward wealth extraction over productive investment. As anthropologist David Graeber put it:

> Economic theory as it exists increasingly resembles a shed full of broken tools . . . The problem of how to determine the optimal distribution of work and resources to create high levels of economic growth is simply not the same problem we are now facing: i.e., how to deal with increasing technological productivity, decreasing real demand for labor, and the effective management of care work, without also destroying the Earth. This demands a different science.[316]

The question isn't whether neoliberalism works – it's how we dismantle the systems it built and replace them with something better.

Everything except what makes life worthwhile

Gross Domestic Product is a measure of the monetary value of all goods and services produced in a country over a specific period of time. But it's not simply a common way to measure the *size* of an economy; it is also, with rare exceptions, used to measure the *success* of the economy: growth in GDP is what politicians and economists are talking about when they refer to economic growth, and economic growth is, again with rare exceptions, the lodestar to which politics and policy are set.

Unthinking and uncritical pursuit of growth in GDP creates big two roadblocks on the road to building a good society, which means that we really need alternative goals, different ways of thinking about success, and a radical shake-up of our economic thinking. The first problem is that GDP measures some good stuff – sure – but it also includes some really bad stuff and leaves out some really important stuff. The second problem is that we can't just keep on and on growing when we live on a planet with finite resources, and when our exploitation of those resources is putting our planet into crisis mode.

Let's start with the first problem. GDP includes what is known as 'the real economy' – the production and consumption of actual stuff – and the financial services and systems that sit alongside. But it ignores many of the things that we might want to support and grow in a good society, such as unpaid, voluntary production of goods and services within households, like when family members care for children or the elderly. It doesn't value health or wellbeing for themselves – but, perversely, for instance, a high burden of smoking-related illness generates high levels of consumption of health care, which is a plus for GDP. Care isn't counted in GDP, but if we have lots of children needing child protective services or going through the family courts that's also a plus. In education, if we have to pay for a lot of remedial tuition and educational psychologists – that's good for GDP, as is training people to be productive in the economy. But developing well-rounded happy young people counts for nothing. Build a new prison? Good for GDP. Divert prisoners into voluntary work as an alternative to custody? Nowhere near as uplifting for GDP.

This is something that I've been writing about over the past decade, along with many colleagues,[317–319] as have countless scholars across the world (truly I'm standing on the shoulders of giants here). Books and articles abound on the problems of economic growth[320–325] and yet, as I mention above, politicians and mainstream economists still rarely talk about GDP except in terms of the 'need' for growth, and they certainly don't dwell on its downsides.

Robert F. Kennedy famously once said that a country's Gross National Product measures everything 'except that which makes life worthwhile'. The full quote is worth including here:

> The gross national product does not allow for the health of our children, the quality of their education or the joy of their play. It does not include the beauty of our poetry or the strength of our marriages, the intelligence of our public debate or the integrity of our public officials. It measures neither our wit nor our courage, neither our wisdom nor our learning, neither our compassion nor our devotion to our country; it measures everything, in short, except that which makes life worthwhile.[326]

And even the architect of GNP and GDP, economist and statistician Simon Kuznets, warned against mistaking growth in GDP for growth in wellbeing. The United Nations requires countries to report GDP in their national accounts and so we keep on putting GDP above any other measure of development or progress. This has happened even within the context of the seventeen UN Sustainable Development Goals for 2030, in which Goal 8 (Decent Work and Economic Growth) can be seen as in conflict with Goal 10 (Reduced Inequalities) and all of the goals relating to environmental issues, such as Goal 12 (Responsible Consumption and Production), Goal 13 (Climate Action), Goal 14 (Life Below Water) and Goal 15 (Life on Land).[327]

Proponents of alternative economics are fond of pointing out the ridiculous paradoxes inherent in the GDP metric – natural disasters, crime, and traffic jams add to GDP because they trigger market transactions, just as care, population health and volunteering do not, despite their benefits to society.[320] And yet we all go on uncritically listening to news items related to reports of GDP growth, without questioning what they really imply. These days we sometimes, and perhaps increasingly, hear politicians, policymakers and others talking about 'inclusive growth' or 'sustainable growth' – signs of more progressive economic thinking knocking at the door of orthodoxy – but so far none of the world's biggest economies are throwing the door open and letting the new ideas in.

Walking a different path

One small Himalayan country has, famously and as I mentioned earlier, adopted Gross National Happiness – GNH – as its goal rather than GDP. I visited Bhutan in 2013 as part of an international expert group commissioned with coming up with a 'new development paradigm' and saw the concept of Gross National Happiness being pursued in multiple ways, including bans on tobacco and plastic bags; conservation of forests; sustainable energy; and respect for traditional cultures.

Bhutan is not a perfect country by any means (the first person I spoke to there, a taxi driver, told me emphatically that *he* wasn't happy), but it has measured a significant increase in its 'happiness' or wellbeing between 2010 and 2022.[328] What Bhutan means by happiness is much broader than what we usually think of when we hear the word, and much more like wellbeing at the societal level. The Bhutanese measure nine domains of wellbeing: psychological wellbeing; health; time use and balance; education; cultural diversity and resilience; good governance; community vitality; ecological diversity and resilience; and living standards.

In Chapter 1, I introduced the Wellbeing Economy Governments – Iceland, Scotland, New Zealand, Wales, Finland and Canada – who are working towards building wellbeing

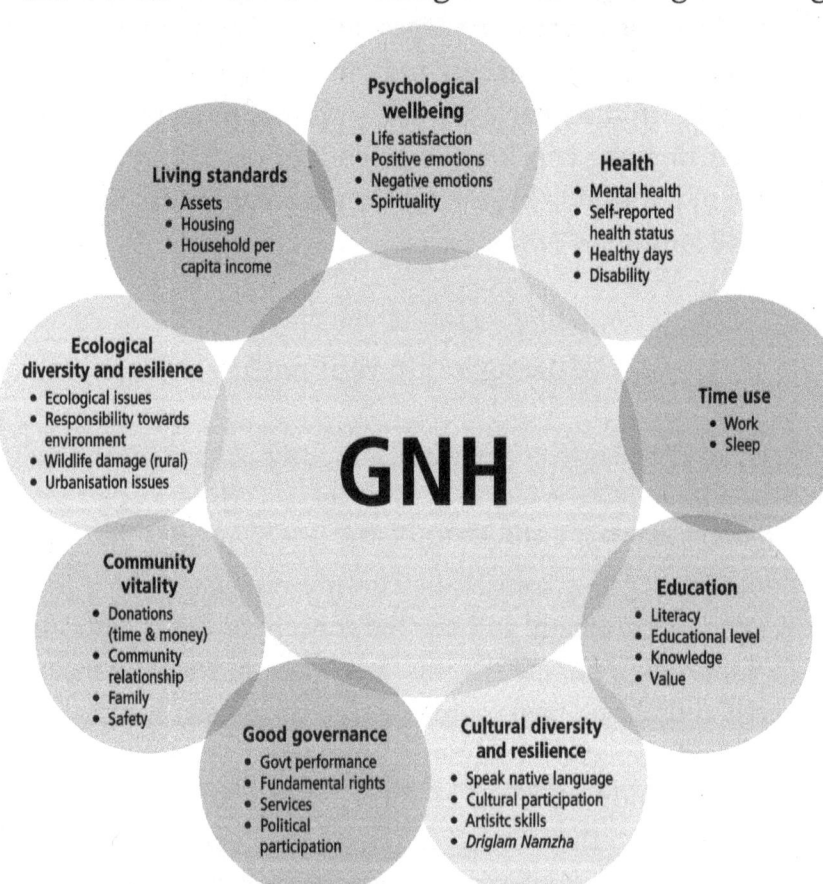

The 9 domains and 33 indicators of GNH (Gross National Happiness).[329]

economies, with an emphasis on the same kind of growth of good things as Bhutan.[330] In 2019, New Zealand adopted a Wellbeing Budget to change the way its economic success was prioritised and measured. The aim was to focus on five priority areas instead of just growth in GDP: climate and environment, productive work, Māori and Pacific opportunities, child wellbeing, and mental and physical health. The budget included $1.9 billion for mental health and more money for schools and hospitals, as well as climate-related projects, and investments less siloed within government departments and made with longer time horizons. Although a change of government has led to the Wellbeing Budget label being dropped, wellbeing objectives seem to have remained central to New Zealand government strategy. In Chapter 1, I also described Wales's Wellbeing of Future Generations Act (2015), its positive influence on environmental policies and how focusing on future generations might be one of the most effective ways to get people to support the sorts of solutions we need to build a good society, even when they don't have children and grandchildren themselves. And I pointed to the research that shows we do care about future generations.

We are starting to see examples of alternative economic ambition, but so far none of the world's biggest economies, none of the G7, have embraced any alternative to GDP.

When in Rome

In 1972, a network of around a hundred notable scientists, economists, business leaders and former politicians, known collectively as the Club of Rome, came together in order 'to define comprehensive solutions to the complex, interconnected challenges of our world'. The meeting led to a book, *The Limits to Growth*, in which they attempted to model what would happen if the world blundered on as it was doing. The book became an immediate, if unlikely, bestseller.

Based on a global statistical model of predicted changes in population, agricultural production, industrial outputs, non-renewable resource depletion, land availability and pollution, *Limits to Growth* suggested that our planet would be unable to sustain economic and population growth much beyond the year 2100. The authors of the report concluded that: 'The challenge of overshoot from decision delay is real, but easily solvable if human society decided to act.' Although *Limits to Growth* was promptly criticised for having reduced the complexities of the world down to a few tractable parameters, the Club of Rome's definition of 'the massive and untidy mix of intertwining and interrelated difficulties and problems that form the predicament in which humanity finds itself' was a step change in how researchers, policymakers and, indeed, politicians came to view global technical, economic and socio-demographic systems.[331]

Limits to Growth used a computer model called World3, created by scientists at the Massachusetts Institute of Technology to capture the dynamics of human activity and its consequences for our planet. By today's computing standards it was quite limited, but it was good enough to be used to model four predictive scenarios of what might happen. The scenarios were labelled: 'Business as Usual (BAU)' – what happens if we do nothing; 'Business as Usual 2 (BAU2)' – this one assumed we'd find or create more resources and do more recycling; 'Comprehensive Technology (CT)' – we would innovate to deal with resource limitations but not change our priorities; and 'Stabilised World (SW)' – we would shift our priorities away from material consumption and economic growth towards human wellbeing, environmental management and technological efficiencies. The BAU and BAU2 scenarios led to the collapse of world societal and economic systems by 2100; the CT scenario led not to collapse but to serious decline. Only the SW scenario led to a stabilised population with higher human welfare.

Since *Limits to Growth* was published, the world has ticked along and data have, of course, accumulated to show the extent to which the model predicted the reality of the situation we find ourselves in today. Perhaps surprisingly, given the limitations and simplicities and underlying assumptions of the World3 model, it has been spot on, tracking real-world data, on everything from population growth to mortality, pollution to industrial output, and ecological footprints, for almost fifty years.[332, 333] And the year 2100 is now easily within the lifetime of my grandchildren, aged at present between two and twelve years old. What on earth are we waiting for?

Ignoring the human in the room

Besides the growth delusion, another big problem of mainstream economic thinking is how such thinking has sidelined humanity. By this I mean how it has focused on a single aspect of our psychology and motivation for our behaviour to the exclusion of everything else. Mainstream economic theory has traditionally worked on the basis that human behaviour can largely be explained in terms of inherent self-interest – a tendency to maximise gain for ourselves. Economists in the nineteenth century coined the term '*Homo economicus*', or economic man, for this conceptualisation of humans as rational and self-interested. This related to the assertions of John Stuart

Mill and Adam Smith that humans will want to do the least amount of work for the most amount of gain and that we cannot rely on the benevolence of others but must look out for ourselves. Obviously, this is a simplistic presentation of our utilitarian tendencies, but it underpins claims like those promulgated in the contrarian economics bestseller *Freakonomics* – that our behaviour is shaped by our conscious and subconscious self-interest, what that book's subtitle describes as 'the hidden side of everything'.[334] Humans, however, are nowhere near that simple.

Chimpanzees are, though. In behavioural experiments they perform exactly as economic theory suggests that humans do behave, acting as self-interested so-called 'rational maximisers' when they play a version of what is known as 'the Ultimatum Game'. In the game participants are paired and a known sum of money is given to one, the 'proposer', who must then divide it as they please with the 'responder'.[335] The responder accepts or rejects the offer. If rejected, neither gets anything; if accepted, they both keep the share of money offered.

Economic theory suggests that responders should accept any offer, however small, because there isn't going to be a next time and something is better than nothing. And proposers should offer the smallest possible amount, just enough to get the responder to accept it, however derisory. When chimpanzees are playing the game (with raisins rather than cash!), they behave exactly as the theory predicts: they will take what they are offered and are not sensitive to fairness. Humans, on the other hand, reassuringly, are very sensitive to norms of cooperation and fairness when playing the same game. Human 'proposers' most often offer half the money rather than the smallest amount they think they can get away with, and human 'responders' tend to reject anything below 20 per cent, even though that means they get nothing. *Homo economicus* we most definitely are not. And in one of the more fascinating scientific papers I've read recently, it appears that even apes will act in the interests of others (prosocially) in the Ultimatum Game, rejecting unfair offers if the 'responder' has access to alternative offers.[336]

The problem with the view of humankind that has been the basis of much economic theory is that it tends to ignore our psychological and social tendencies, some of which – kindness, cooperation, fairness – are the better angels of our human nature. Instead, neoliberalism foregrounds self-interest, selfishness, individualism and materialism. In this view, our interactions and relationships are imbued with a transactional, commercial, anti-egalitarian hue which bears no relation to our actual innate altruism.[337, 338] The fact that traditional economics has got this so wrong, has taken us down a path of not recognising some vitally important aspects of our very nature, is really troubling, especially given the dominance of economic thinking in our policy-making. The French sociologist Pierre Bourdieu used the term 'symbolic violence' to describe how those with economic and political power can impose their preferred ideology on the rest of us by disguising their power, and how they manage to get us to take for granted that their ideology is the way the world *is*.[339]

The neoliberal homage to *Homo economicus* is, in these terms, a discourse of symbolic violence that keeps us all in our place, and prevents us from thinking that a different ideology is preferable, or indeed possible. If we want to create the good society, we must believe in our better nature and our capability for collaboration, cooperation, mutual trust and empathy.

The New Economics

Luckily, responding to the failures of neoliberalism and of orthodox economic thinking that led to the economic crisis of 2008, there have been some quakes and tremors within economics. One movement has been led by economists and other academics who founded the Institute for New Economic Thinking (INET) in 2010, bankrolled by a large gift from American investor George Soros. Devoted to 'developing and sharing the ideas that can repair our broken economy and create a more equal, prosperous, and just society', INET embraces what is called 'heterodox economics', in opposition to the neoliberal tenets of free-market fundamentalism, fiscal austerity, financialization, and private over public institutions. INET funds economic research and task forces on a wide range of economic issues. There are six winners of the Nobel Prize in Economic Sciences on the INET advisory group, so the heterodox might be on its way to replacing the orthodox, at least in the rarefied atmosphere of academic economics. Down in the trenches, however, not so much.

On this side of the pond, neo-Keynesian and other economists formed the Progressive Economy Forum in 2018, to advance policies addressing environmental breakdown and inequality. Meanwhile, economics students – starting at Manchester in 2014 and spreading to Cambridge, the London School of Economics, and others – demanded pluralism in their curricula, moving beyond narrow mathematical models to explore alternative economic thinking through the international Rethinking Economics network.

There are other groupings and other movements and other flavours of 'heterodox economics' and 'new economic thinking' – but what are they all about, and is there any coherence in their thinking that can help us create the good society within planetary boundaries?

Into the Doughnut

Let's start with one example. You may well have heard of 'doughnut economics', developed by economist Kate Raworth and popularised in her internationally bestselling 2017 book, *Doughnut Economics: Seven ways to think like a 21st-century economist*.[340] Doughnut economics is a great blueprint for creating a good society. It sets out the concept of a 'safe and just space for humanity', sitting between the ecological ceilings of what the planet can stand and the social foundations of our human needs. It's a clever evolution of what is known as the 'planetary boundaries' model, adding in the concept of the foundations needed for human wellbeing.

The planetary boundaries model comes from scientists at the Stockholm Resilience Centre and is a framework for tracking environmental challenges. The nine boundaries are thresholds that we must not pass if we want to keep Earth stable and within what the centre's scientists call the 'safe operating space for humanity'.[341]

When it was published in 2009, three of the model's boundaries had already been crossed: climate change, biosphere integrity, and nitrogen flows.[341] When they analysed new data in 2015, the same group of scientists found that we had also crossed the boundaries of safe land-system change and phosphorus flows.[342] By 2023 we had crossed six of their nine boundaries, including freshwater use and novel entities (which means plastics and other chemical pollutants), as shown in the Doughnut 3.0 model for 2025.[343]

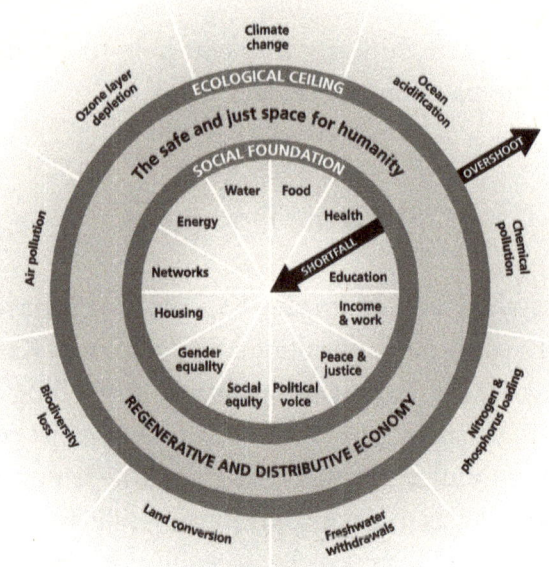

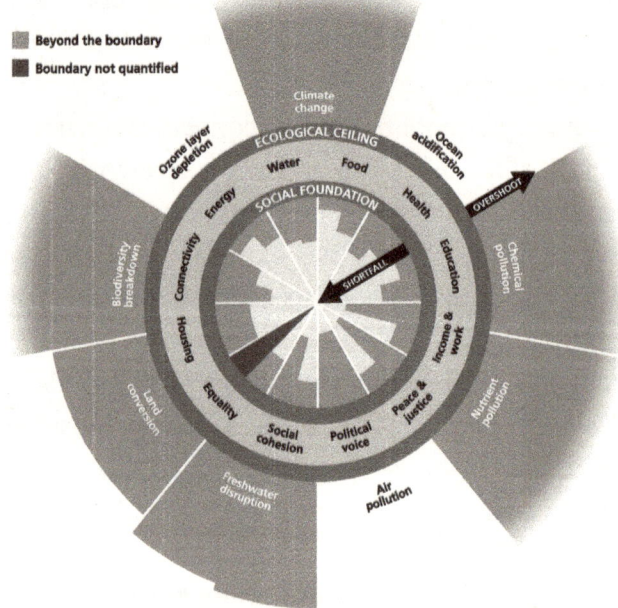

Kate Raworth's original Doughnut of social and planetary boundaries (top), and version 3.0 (bottom) showing where we stood in terms of planetary boundary transgressions and social foundation shortfalls in 2025.[340]

TIME FOR NEW ECONOMIC THINKING

Not everyone loves the planetary boundaries framework, just as not everyone loved the *Limits to Growth* modelling. But quibble as one might about the details, and whether or not global models are complex and nuanced enough to allow us to understand how things are changing on a more local basis, models like the Doughnut and planetary boundaries are powerful heuristics. They allow scientists to communicate with policymakers, politicians and the public – which ought to lead to change, right? Sadly not, though, and we now have evidence that the world is crossing numerous so-called tipping points, where we won't be able to row back from catastrophic outcomes; these include the melting of polar ice sheets, the burning and cutting down of forests, thawing permafrost, and dying coral reefs.

The subtitle of *Doughnut Economics* points to its seven-point framework for breaking away from traditional economic thinking. Kate Raworth and her colleagues have set up what they call the Doughnut Economics Action Lab (DEAL) to create and implement regenerative and distributive economies in cities and regions, in business and enterprise, and through engagement with government and policymakers.

The Doughnut Economic Action Lab has worked with more than eighty city and regional governments to help them put the ideas into practice. In the UK, this includes Glasgow and Cornwall, and in Europe: Amsterdam, Barcelona and Grenoble. In Sweden, the small town of Tomelilla used doughnut economics to design and build a new primary school. They used participatory processes to involve the community; planned for energy and food production to be built into the school design; are using local materials for sustainable construction, incorporating nature playgrounds, harvesting rainwater, and making sure that teachers and children can cycle to school; and have thought hard about how a school could be used by the whole community.

That's small scale, but the Brussels Capital Region in Belgium is large scale. Here they have used doughnut economics to map their existing policy goals against Earth's safe operating limits (the above-mentioned 'planetary boundaries') and the social foundations; from this they have developed a new regional economic transition strategy, to 'transform Brussels' economy into one that is decarbonized, regenerative, circular, social, democratic and digital',[344] while local businesses use the DEAL business toolkit: one food manufacturing company, for example, switched to using organic and regeneratively farmed ingredients. Amsterdam was the first big city to apply doughnut economics to its economic and social policy, including using it to develop the UNESCO World Heritage site Fort Pampus (a small island which used to guard the city harbour) to run entirely on sustainable energy.

A coherent New Economics

I'm on the advisory board for a project called Global Assessment for a New Economics (GANE), established at the University of York after the Covid-19 pandemic, to try and synthesise new economics knowledge, in the hope that pulling it all together might be helpful for policymakers, perhaps particularly in the need to think about future pandemics, but also in response to the climate, nature and inequality crises. The GANE project is a useful one because it involves looking at key texts on new economic approaches, suggested by international experts, to come up with key principles.[345] Doughnut economics is just one example of new economic thinking – but what, if anything, connects them all? What are all these new economic thinkers thinking?

There are a couple significant ways in which the new economic thinking is different to the old. The GANE project calls these 'holistic principles', and they are: an embracing of complexity, and an overarching aim of wellbeing.

Just as the Bhutanese meaning of happiness is something more complex than a jolly emotion, wellbeing here is not the so-called *wellbeing* movement of yoga, clean-eating, and stress reduction, or the adjacent wellbeing industry devoted to selling us scented candles, celebrity-endorsed vibrators, or expensive, scientifically unsupported supplements. This is wellbeing at both an individual level, which means having good physical and mental health, good relationships, and a sense of purpose and agency; and at the societal level, which means our collective capacity to participate in society and how well it serves us. The good society by another name.

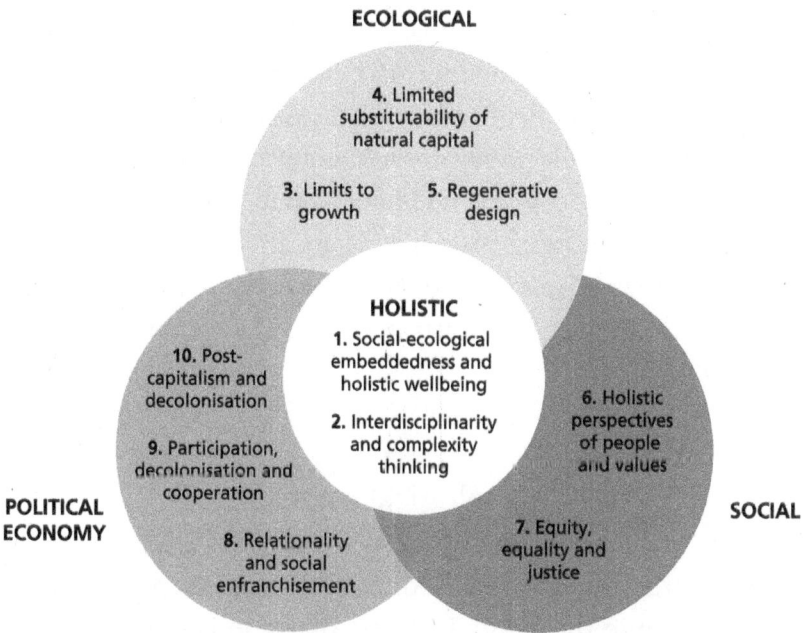

Ten principles for transforming economics.[346]

The New Economics Foundation, another powerhouse of new economic thinking, came up with the widely adopted and evidence-based 'Five Ways to Wellbeing' framework in 2008: *connect* (with other people); *be active*; *take notice* (be mindful and curious); *keep learning*; and *give* (time or care or money or whatever).[347]

The connections between human and planetary wellbeing within the frameworks of both Bhutan's Gross National Happiness and the Wellbeing Economy Governments are typical of new economic thinking, and their conceptualisation of wellbeing also exemplifies the other holistic principle – the need to acknowledge and grapple with complexity and to stop viewing the world through the narrow (blinkered) vision of neoliberalism. Our economies and societies are complicated, and they sit within the complex entanglements of our natural world. We need to think about all of those things together, instead of as separate systems. And that means we need non-economists alongside economists contributing to economic policy-making. As Professor of Economics Ha-Joon Chang says, good economic policy doesn't require good economists.[348] We need anthropologists and philosophers, environmental scientists and social scientists, historians and geographers, and even, dare I say it, epidemiologists. The economy is too important to leave to the economists; we all need a seat at the policy-making table.

The ecological principles

The GANE project identified three ecological principles in new economic thinking. The first of these is that there are limits to growth, exemplified by the planetary boundaries model – fundamental limits to the natural resources and balances of Earth's systems, at least insofar as having a planet fit for humanity.

A second, related, principle is that Earth has 'natural capital' which can't be replaced with anything else. Capital, of course, means assets that have value or provide a benefit. In traditional economics, capital is wealth and physical assets like land and factories, or intangible assets like intellectual property. Economists use the term 'human capital' to cover our personal skills, knowledge and experience, and social scientists talk about 'social capital' when they're referring to the social relationships and networks that give us mutual support for collective efficacy. Natural capital is the value and assets that nature provides, including clean air, water, soil, minerals, plants, and animals. Some natural capital gives us tangible benefits, like food; some is intangible, like the benefits of green spaces for mental health. This is using the basic economic principle of capital in new ways, to set a value on what nature gives us and also, importantly, recognising that nature is the foundation of all our other capitals. The idea is that this will help us properly count the costs of *not* looking after nature, and push us towards conserving and protecting it, thus ensuring the sustainability of natural resources.

Not everyone loves the idea of natural capital, or the so-called ecosystem services that get counted in it. Some of the naysayers simply don't like the idea of putting dollar signs on nature; some are contesting how natural capital should best be measured in any system of accounting. The UK government had a Natural Capital Committee advising it intermittently from 2012, feeding into environmental strategy, but it was dissolved in 2020. Defenders say that valuing nature in monetary terms is progress and enables new economic thinkers to speak to policymakers in language that they understand: that natural capital is a means of advocating for nature.

Once we've grasped the principles of limits to growth and natural capital, then we can start to design economies that respect planetary boundaries and preserve, protect or enrich natural resources – this is the third ecological principle. There are many designations for these sorts of innovative designs, including circular economies, regenerative economies, sharing economies, flourishing economies, and so forth. Circular economies aim to reduce, reuse, recycle and recover. A nice case study of a circular economy is the use of timber instead of bricks or concrete as the main structural material to reduce carbon emissions in construction. Good examples are projects in Amsterdam and Barcelona that produce high-quality wooden housing with reduced carbon footprints. (There is a collection of circular economy case studies online.[349])

A recent academic paper described 'regenerative good growth' as centred on all the renewable capitals (natural, social, human, cultural and sustainable physical capital) and the need to find storylines that will appeal to people concerned by the climate emergency, with the aim of getting individuals, businesses and policymakers to adopt new practices.[350] This is about getting the broad public support needed for change, rather than provoking protest.

The social principles

GANE also identified two things that characterise new economic thinking about people and values. First, human beings are viewed not as self-interested *Homo economicus* but more realistically as having a variety of motivations, and second is the recognition that our relationships with one another shape our values and our behaviour, as does our relationship to the environment. Brazilian environmentalist Fe Cortez proposes the term *Homo integralis*, in opposition to *Homo economicus*, to suggest that humanity can live in balance with nature.[351]

However, it's not so much new terms that we need as a fundamental shift away from thinking of ourselves as individualistic, competitive and out for ourselves. And this means a shift towards community ownership of resources for shared prosperity, rather than their exploitation by a small number of individuals for private profit, and deliberative democratic decision-making in our institutions. An illustration of the former is when communities come together to manage natural resources like land, forests, wildlife and water for local benefit. This is exactly what the first woman ever to win the Nobel Prize in Economic Sciences, Elinor Ostrom, meant by the governance of 'the commons' – showing how indigenous, traditional and contemporary communities managed their resources in sustainable ways.[352, 353]

A great example of this is the community conservancies in Namibia, formed since the 1990s and covering more than 14 per cent of the country. These formalise community management of communal land with rights over wildlife, giving incomes to communities whose livelihoods were previously based on hunting and tourism, and leading to a recovery of populations of black rhinos and lions.[354] Somewhat closer to home, projects in Belgium and Denmark are helping to protect biodiversity in privately owned forests through a 'reverse auction': forest owners offer to implement conservation measures on their land and these are bid on by the government to help them meet their sustainability goals.[355] This brings small privately owned forest areas into a wider patchwork of ecosystems, connecting up habitats and protecting biodiversity.[356] Too often, of course, the opposite is happening.

Professor Guy Standing, in two important books, *Plunder of the Commons*[357] and *The Blue Commons*,[358] describes the 'enclosure' of our national 'commons', such as the selling off of our state-owned utilities and social housing, and the privatisation of the 'blue commons' – our oceans and seas – with profits from fishing, marine-mining and offshore wind farms sequestered away to elites instead of being a shared public good. He suggests that what is needed is a 'Charter of the Commons with a Commons Capital Fund', from which 'Common Dividends' could be paid to help local communities rebuild sustainable economies.

New economic thinking also turns away from the single-minded pursuit of growth and efficiency to place equality, equity and social justice as priorities. What a transformation that would be. And yet all of the evidence gathered together in this book suggests that prioritising equality and equity in the provision of services, and reducing economic inequality within societies, reaps enormous benefits in both wellbeing and economic terms. Many flavours of new economic thinking, such as feminist economics, indigenous economics, caring economics, emphasise more equal distribution and call for more value to be placed on non-economic contributions to society. This is one of the big 'turnarounds' called for by the Transformational Economics Commission (which I will come on to).

The GANE review emphasises that equality is right *at the heart of all* new economic thinking. Tackling inequality is one of the most important ways we can move back from the metaphorical cliff edge, preventing the problems that cost society so dearly to try to manage and correct (poor health, low educational attainment, need of social care, high rates of imprisonment, etc.), and improving the population's capabilities, resilience and productivity in the long term. Inequality reduction needs to be reframed as good stewardship of our resources and our futures.

The political economy principles

Political economy simply means the way the economy is governed and impacted by institutions, laws and policy. New economic thinking as it relates to political economy puts our social needs and the common good back into economics, from where it was dethroned by neoliberalism. So this isn't something new age, utopian or woolly; it's just a shift away from a very warped and narrow view of what society should be like, and for whom the economy and all our institutions are in service. It's about the economy in service to the 99 per cent of us, for want of a better phrase. This is definitely about the return of a bigger role for the state in securing the good society. It's about universal services that serve our needs and enhance our wellbeing. The GANE reviewers dared to use the word 'love' in their description of one of the political economy principles of new economic thinking. The actual label for the principle was 'embrace pluralistic social and relational approaches that support social enfranchisement, social needs, and the common good'[345] – but getting some love into economics captures it nicely.

New economic thinking wants to get away from the dominance of mathematical models and quantitative analyses of economic issues – not to put them aside entirely but to put them in their place and for them to be more attuned to the complexity of the systems they are about, but also to complement them with people's thoughts, deliberations, contributions and experiences. If we want to think about how to value something, whether it is access to nature or a healthcare system, then we need to take into account the values and preferences of everyone who has an interest. So new economic thinking tends to value active citizenship (voting, volunteering, collaborating in community projects); participatory democracy (things like citizens' assemblies and people coming together to choose how to spend public funds); and economic democracy (things like worker-owned cooperatives and trade unions). If we really were all in it together, that would be a 'new political economy'.

The last of the 10 GANE principles (all shown in the diagram above) was for new economic thinking to be imbued with a desire to decolonise economic perspectives and move beyond capitalism. I draw your attention back to the quote at the start of this chapter: about imagining the end of capitalism. Well, all the new economic thinkers are imagining it, in diverse ways, and all are seeing different possibilities for us beyond the traditional relationship between capital and labour.[359] Some of those possibilities that the GANE researchers draw attention to are 'economic practices based on new technologies and a reduced need for labour, including new currencies that embed social and ecological values, communal ownership, new forms of cooperatives, and online networking spaces to promote non-profit forms of work and address labour mobility, empower disadvantaged individuals and support capabilities' – as well as moving beyond traditional models of development to embrace cultural diversity, democracy and reciprocity, and respect for nature.[345]

Updating a classic

While the new economic thinkers plan a better future in a good society, the world continues to turn. As a member of the Transformational Economics Commission, set up by the Club of Rome, I've been part of an initiative called Earth4All, which has developed a sophisticated computer simulation – think of it as a kind of 'flight simulator' for the global economy and environment.[360]

This model works like a giant calculator that processes hundreds of interconnected variables – population growth, economic output, energy use, climate change, inequality levels, and many others – to project what might happen to human wellbeing between now and 2100. Just as meteorologists use computer models to forecast weather by feeding in data about temperature, pressure, and wind patterns, we feed in economic, social and environmental data to see how different policy choices might play out over decades.

The model updates the 'Limits to Growth' model, dating back to 1972, that I outlined earlier, and we can test different scenarios by adjusting the policy 'dials' – for example, cranking up efforts to tackle global poverty, reduce inequality, empower women, create sustainable food systems, or shift to renewable energy. The data model then shows us the likely consequences of these choices, calculating forward year by year to 2100.

I'm going to focus on the blueprint for tackling inequality, here, as this is described by the Transformational Economics Commission as being 'as close to a silver bullet as we might find'.[360]

The first scenario we tested is called 'Too Little, Too Late'. We programmed the data model to assume that countries make only minor improvements in poverty levels and climate action, but do nothing serious about entrenched inequality. The model then churns through all the calculations and spits out a troubling prediction: declining population and economic growth, rising social tensions, falling trust in government, environmental degradation and biodiversity loss. By the century's end – as early as 2050 – it shows persistent global poverty, worsening inequality in rich countries, and a high likelihood of societal collapse, meaning the breakdown of governance and democracy, the rise of autocrats and populists, corruption, conflict, and our inability to adapt to environmental crisis.

Is this starting to sound at all familiar?

The Earth4All inequality turnaround would require us to pull three big levers: *progressive taxation* on income and wealth for both individuals and businesses; *strengthening workers' rights and trade unions*; and putting in place *social safety nets, innovation safety nets*, and *enterprise safety nets* to share prosperity and provide security during times of change.

These levers would help us get towards a situation where the richest 10 per cent within any society collectively have no more income than the total share of income earned by the poorest 40 per cent in society.[361] To put this in concrete terms: imagine if the richest 10 per cent of people in a country earned, say, 30 per cent of all the income in that country. The goal would be for the poorest 40 per cent of people to also earn 30 per cent of all income between them. This comparison of the top 10 per cent to the bottom 40 per cent is captured in something called the Palma Index. When these two groups have equal shares – when the top 10 per cent collectively earn the same as the bottom 40 per cent collectively – the Palma Index equals 1.

Reaching a Palma Index of 1 would mean we'd achieved a much more equal society than we see anywhere today. For comparison, the UK currently has a Palma Index of around 1.5, meaning the top 10 per cent earn about 50 per cent more than the bottom 40 per cent combined. You can see that this Earth4All goal is far more ambitious for tackling inequality than UN Sustainable Development Goal 10 (Reduced Inequalities), which merely aims to reduce the gap in economic growth between the bottom 40 per cent and the average, rather than the top.

Progressive taxation means a higher tax rate for those with more income or more wealth, and to achieve that in the UK, or indeed any country, we'll need to have a tighter regulation of international tax havens and financial loopholes that allow businesses to make money in one country and pay their taxes in a lower-tax state. The OECD countries agreed to impose a minimal international tax rate on business and 140 countries have signed up, which is great, but that minimum tax is set at 15 per cent on profits, which simply isn't high enough. It's a good start, though. Within countries, governments need to make the case – in terms of doing the right thing for the environment, to invoke the support of the majority of the population who favour protecting the environment over economic growth – for progressively taxing income and especially wealth. I'll be returning to wealth taxes in some detail in the next chapter.

Workers' rights and strong trade unions are vital to ensure that workers get an increasing share of national income. Extending democratic power to workers will also be especially helpful in constraining inequality. Workers on renumeration boards are unlikely to be in favour of massive salaries and bonuses for the top brass at the expense of their own incomes and investment in the company. This will be especially helpful in those sectors that are going to need to make the biggest transitions to environmental sustainability: energy, food, transport and heavy industry. Worker support for transformational change will be needed. The Common Sense Policy Group led from the University of Northumbria suggest a Green New Deal with a fully costed 'quadruple lock' that would protect the interests of workers in carbon-intensive industries.[362] The quadruple lock involves a transition job guarantee, strategic investment in the localities most affected by reducing our reliance on fossil fuels, an education and skills guarantee, and an enterprise safety net.

What does the commission mean by *social safety nets*, *innovation safety nets*, and *enterprise safety nets*? They mean bold policies like citizens' funds that pay out universal basic dividends. This can redistribute wealth that is generated through common resources (fossil fuels, rare minerals, land, or even social data such as open-source algorithms or social media data) more fairly to support the transition to zero-carbon and to incentivise creativity, innovation and entrepreneurship. One way of paying out

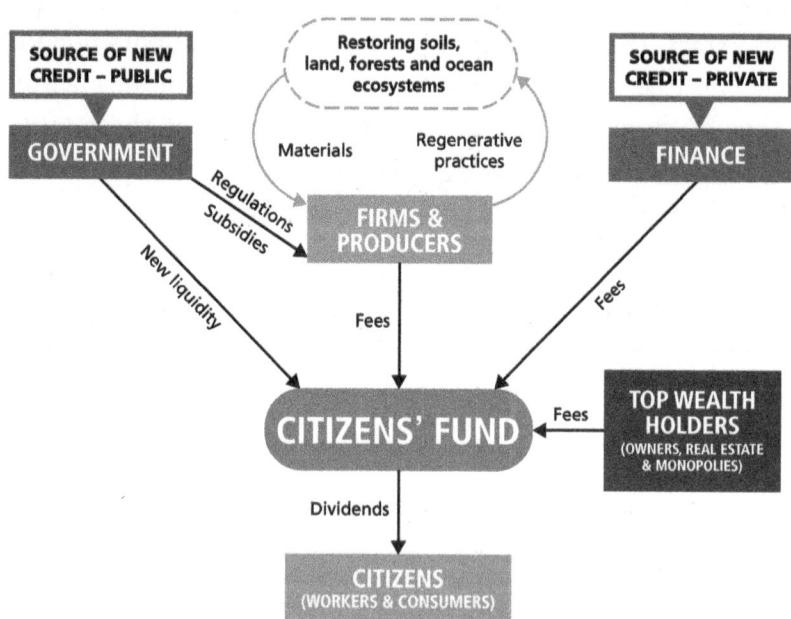

A fairer trickle down of wealth via a citizens' fund to all citizens.[360]

from a citizens' fund would be via a universal basic income. Along with wealth taxes, universal basic income will be the big story in the next chapter.

The good economy for the Good Society

> 'Current economic theory is less a science than an ideology peculiar to a certain period of history, which may well be nearing an end.'[363]

Spoken just after the global financial crisis, those are the words of mathematician David Orrell. SOAS Professor of Economics Ha-Joon Chang suggests a higher count of things neoliberal economics gets wrong in his *23 Things They Don't Tell You About Capitalism*.[348] The flood of writing on new economic thinking is becoming wide and deep and yet . . . the great French philosopher Michel Foucault claimed that politics, which arranges our society for us, is a branch of economics because that is the mentality which has imbued all of our established institutions with their rationale for policy-making.

Another philosopher, Professor Michael Sandel, says that 'without quite realizing it, without ever deciding to do so, we drifted from having a market economy to being a market society'.[364] He means that we have created a society in which the values of the market dominate everything, including our relationships with one another.

We need to stop drifting towards environmental and social disaster. The evidence shows us a better path – we just need to choose to take it.

CHAPTER 6

The Building Blocks: Evidence and Equality

'It is time to return to . . . core values, time to get back to basics . . .'
John Major

I've had the 1960s much on my mind recently. I went to see the recent Bob Dylan biopic, *A Complete Unknown,* and came away feeling deeply nostalgic for a time I am sadly too young to remember. The overwhelming sense that came through the film of what that decade felt like – matched by the remembrance of people I talk to who did experience the 1960s as young adults – was a strong sense of hope for a radical transformation of society and how the times really were a-changin'. I'm not ignoring the social divisions and upheavals of the 1960s, but the civil rights movement in the United States and progress in other areas of human rights, the anti-war and anti-nuclear protests, and the rise of counterculture, gave many young people, in particular, belief that they were on the verge of creating a better society. Political activism and sexual liberation went hand in hand, promising a world with both greater social justice and more personal freedom; the future looked shiny and bright.

No generation since has experienced that same widespread

optimism. Our sense of the future has always been bleaker. And when I say 'our' here I am not meaning the tiny minority who have done so well out of the shifting tides of neoliberal capitalism; I mean the 99 per cent, the vast majority of us, the 'we' who are the stories behind all the statistics in this book.

I have nothing like the same sense of nostalgia for 'my' youthful decade, the Eighties, as I do for the 1960s that I missed out on. I didn't do so badly, personally. Born in 1965, I was educated in the first comprehensive intake of a former grammar school, and was lucky enough to go to Cambridge University with a maintenance grant and no tuition fees. As soon as I arrived in the autumn term of 1984, I bought a student guide to Cambridge. On its cover were young people in ballgowns and black tie, in punts on the river, with the caption 'Drifting down the Eighties'. Inside were recommendations for cocktail bars and college food ('food at New Hall is imaginative, which makes you wish it was boring'), lists of student societies (lots of drama, music and arts, but also tiddlywinks and freemasonry) and 'comic' advice to students from earlier editions ('the frigid Miss retains her dignity and her own company', 1956). On politics, the guide suggested that Cambridge was not a hotbed of political activism: the Cambridge Union Society (a private members' society) was moribund, petty and self-important, almost entirely in the hands of the political right; the Cambridge Students' Union, more centre than left, had doubtful purpose amidst widespread apathy.

Yet elsewhere in the UK, miners were striking in protest against Margaret Thatcher's plans to close most coal pits, young people were rioting in Wolverhampton, anti-nuclear campaigners were being evicted from Greenham Common women's peace camp, the Bishop of Durham was attacking the government's social policies, and Band Aid was formed to raise money for famine relief in Ethiopia. As I headed to university, more than three million of my compatriots were unemployed, and school leavers were being fobbed off with endless youth training schemes that more often than not led nowhere. Towns and cities where the economy had grounded on the rocky shores of receding manufacturing became as moribund as the Cambridge Union was reputed to be. Drifting down the Eighties indeed . . . There was no comfort in peace and love and rock 'n' roll for our generation, or those who came later.

As the Eighties progressed, poverty and inequality rates began an inexorable climb. We could buy into the neoliberal promise of individual responsibility and set about making something of ourselves by competing in our marketised, small-state world, but there was little or no counter-cultural vision that we could align with, no solidarity in a collective imagining of a good society.

We all see the word 'vision' bandied about a lot these days – there are corporate visions, and personal envisioning – but my nostalgia for the decade I didn't experience is for a shared societal dream. My sense from talking to people who lived through and bought into that Sixties vision was that it slipped away from them with gradual disillusionment. As Joni Mitchell captured in one of her most famous songs from 1970 – which I heard piped tinnily through a supermarket the other day – we often don't appreciate what we have (paradise) until we've lost it, until progress has destroyed something beautiful and irreplaceable (burying it beneath a parking lot!).

When I first began to plan this book in my head, I thought I'd simply be describing our inadequate public health, education, social care, criminal justice and so forth, dusting off the blueprints for change and having a go at governments for ignoring them. I didn't really think I'd be doing the vision thing. But more than ever, we *need* a vision of a good society. Throughout this book I've drawn in the values and ethics of moral and political philosophers, and the analyses and evidence of all kinds of researchers, mostly social scientists, who have something to contribute to such a vision. The synthesis is mine, but the components are the work of thousands. I want to put nostalgia aside and set out a vision for a better society, and my hope is that this book might contribute to discussion and deliberation to find a way forward.

I began with the ideas so central to public health and so relevant to the big social problems we need to solve: the need to focus on the causes of the causes and the need to focus on prevention rather than cure. And these two perspectives lead to the conclusion that solving poverty and inequality is critical for the creation of the good society. I've found lots of other good interventions and solutions along the way, but dealing with poverty and inequality is the fundamental task.

Weaving the social fabric

And so, I'm going to end by describing the two fundamental solutions to poverty and inequality that I think are big enough to really deliver a transformed and better society – big enough to excite and encourage a movement for change. You might not like them, and that's fair enough, but we can't afford to nibble at the edges of the climate crisis, or the crisis in care, or the other big problems we're facing; we need wholesale change – we need to go the whole way. And alongside these we need new methods and institutions that could get all of our voices, and all the good evidence, into policy-making processes. Think of these solutions, combined with the methods and institutions, as the basic warp and weft of how we might weave a new social fabric for a good society.

I started this chapter with a quote from former Conservative prime minister John Major, who in 1993 called for a return to core values and for the country to get back to basics. I like those words, although his core values were (rather cosily) neighbourliness, decency and courtesy – rather than ethics of care, and the kinds of 'capabilities approach' proposed by Amartya Sen that we saw in Chapter 3 or social and environmental justice. And getting back to basics meant things like self-discipline, respect for the law, free trade and traditional teaching, whereas my basics are ensuring economic security for everyone by ending poverty and reducing inequality. But we can all get our visions out for debate, see where we want to go and make a roadmap. This chapter is me putting my suggestions on the table.

Back to basics

The good society should be built upon a universal basic income. It isn't so long ago that the idea of a basic income (often abbreviated to UBI, although not all basic income schemes are universal) was a very fringe idea indeed. I can remember giving public lectures in the early 2010s and sometimes being asked by audience members why I wasn't talking about 'UBI', but it felt so far left-field back then, so utopian and impractical – how could any society possibly afford such a thing? – that it took longer than it should have done for me to give it serious attention.

A basic income is paid by government to citizens: the kind of basic income I am talking about here is *universal*, paid to everyone (with add-ons for additional needs, like disabilities), and *unconditional* – you get it whether you are in paid employment or not, whether you are studying or caring for children or others, or volunteering, or in business for yourself. A basic income is the most fundamental way in which government can express its commitment to the economic security and well-being of its citizens.

A basic income might seem less far-fetched to you if you realise that we already have one, of a kind, for a particular age group: the state pension and pension credit schemes. During the Covid-19 pandemic, the government furlough payments of 80 per cent of people's usual salary up to £2,500 a month were a kind of temporary basic income. Until 2013, Child Benefit was also a universal basic income for a particular age group, paid to the guardians of each child under the age of eighteen, regardless of their parents' financial status. The fact that Child Benefit is no longer universal has had the stupid (perhaps unintended) consequence of putting a higher marginal tax rate on families and penalising lone parents. That's just one (typical) example of the tortuous complexities and perverse incentives that characterise our current system of welfare and social security, still a patchwork of poorly understood and difficult to access entitlements, despite what we were promised with Universal Credit. Too many people miss out on the benefits they are entitled to, and too many are harmed by the humiliations and stresses of means-testing and labyrinthine bureaucracy.

Basic income, on the other hand, is paid to individuals, in their own right, on a regular basis and as cash – unlike some existing benefits, such as Housing Benefit paid directly to landlords, or fee waivers or food vouchers. This means that basic income supports people's dignity and autonomy, in contrast to the current social security system, which people experience as stigmatising and demeaning, as well as difficult to navigate.

Let's pause for a minute. While this might seem obvious to many readers, particularly in countries with established welfare states, the idea that government should guarantee the economic security of its citizens remains contested. In the United States, for instance, there's ongoing debate about the proper role of government versus individual responsibility. But for those of us who do believe that ensuring economic security is what makes a modern civilised society different from the days when we didn't have a social security safety net – when the poor and those unable to work were left to fend for themselves or maintained in the debasement of the workhouse – then why not do it in a respectful way that supports people's autonomy and self-esteem and could solve the issues of poverty and inequality, almost at a stroke (well, two)?

I've been studying basic income with colleagues in the Common Sense Policy Group over the past few years, and it is the most efficient scheme imaginable for government to help solve poverty, reduce inequality, give people security of mind and assets, enhance civic participation and people's engagement with society, and promote population wellbeing.[365] I've helped to develop the model of impact, shown below, that traces how reducing poverty and inequality and giving people economic security through basic income not only increases health and wellbeing, but also gives people more ability to provide care for one another, reduces crime, and promotes educational attainment, entrepreneurship and productivity. These outcomes lead to reduced public spending on fixing problems and an increase in tax yields, with medium- to long-term cost neutrality at worst and most likely savings to society. This is why basic income is both efficient and effective.

The main objection to universal basic income that is most often raised is the worry that people won't work if they are

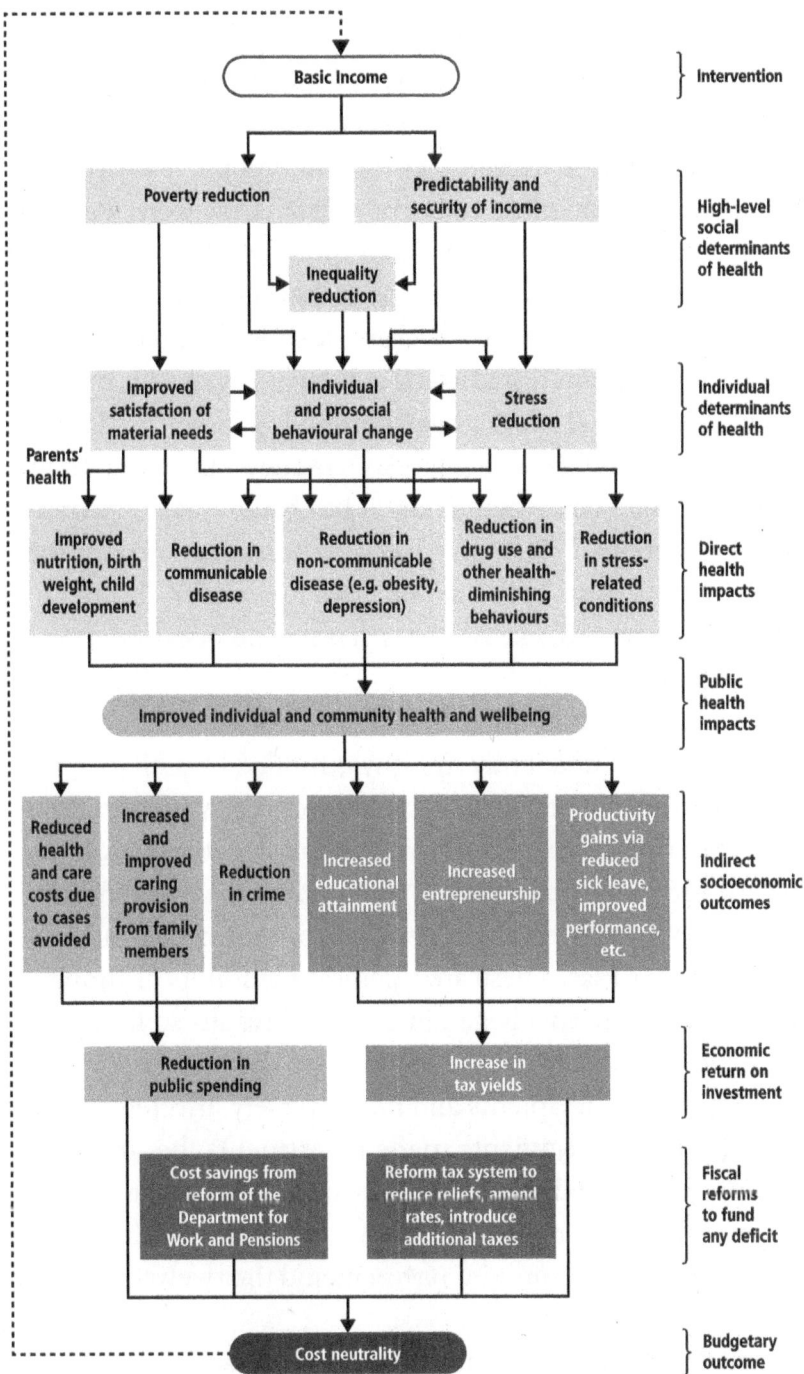

The overall logic of the case for basic income.[365]

getting an income from the state. None of the evidence from trials or implementation of basic income elsewhere in the world suggest that this is actually a problem. People want the additional income and sense of purpose that come from work, but a basic income would allow them more freedom and flexibility in their work choices throughout their lives. Two large UBI programmes and one big experiment show that basic income can be implemented without a negative impact on productivity. The state of Alaska has been giving citizens an annual payment of around $1,800 (in today's money) since 1982, funded by state-owned oil revenues, and it has had no negative impact on employment.[366] Iran also has a nationwide unconditional basic income, also based on oil revenue, which has been in place since 2011 and, like Alaska, it has had no negative effect on employment.

The biggest (non-universal) basic income research experiment to date is underway in Kenya, funded by a charity, with more than 20,000 people in rural villages receiving payments – some as a one-off lump sum of $500, some getting $22.50 each month for a two-year period, and others the same monthly payment but for twelve years, with a commitment to a further ten years after that. These are significant amounts of money in rural Kenya. The trial began in 2018, and results so far are preliminary, but already researchers can see that the basic income has empowered recipients and not adversely affected employment.[367] In fact, recipients made investments, became more entrepreneurial, and earned more income. The two-year limited income guarantee has, so far, been less effective, although still positive, than the lump sum payment and the twelve-year guaranteed income.

Smaller trials of basic incomes and cash transfers have taken place, successfully, in North and South America, Europe, Africa

THE BUILDING BLOCKS: EVIDENCE AND EQUALITY

and Asia, and provide evidence of improvements in population health and wellbeing, as well as education, employment, people's ability to provide care for one another, entrepreneurship, and involvement in society.[366, 368–371] A basic income can do some very heavy work in building a good society, acting on the causes of the causes, away from the cliff edge of crises. It would go some way to solving multiple problems, by tackling their wider determinants and preventing the need for more expensive solutions. In Chapter 1, I introduced the evidence that a healthy livelihood, having enough money to meet basic material and psychosocial needs, is fundamental to improving population health and reducing health inequalities. A basic income can support healthy livelihoods for everyone, with the added benefits over existing social security schemes of predictability and dignity.

Dutch historian and author Rutger Bregman claims that 'a universal basic income would be the best way to give everyone the opportunity to do more unpaid but incredibly important work, such as caring for children and the elderly'.[372] And as economist Guy Standing and others have pointed out, a basic income enhances the capabilities and freedoms of those with care needs (indeed, everyone's) as well, avoiding the paternalism that characterises our current system of care provision.[167] A universal basic income optimises our capacities for self-care, gets us away from the moral hazards of means-testing – which everyone agrees is an abhorrent fundamental feature of our current care system – and empowers each and every one of us to balance our involvement in the labour and care economies. Additional income supplements to a universal basic income, even at a Minimum Income Standard, would obviously be needed for those with additional needs, but with a universal basic income, parents could balance work and childcare, family members could look after adults, the elderly and children who are ill or have disabilities, and older people would be able to provide for their needs without being dependent on having worked enough to have earned sufficient state and/or private pension income.

Basic income supports our instincts to want to care for each other, across generations, and across our social networks. It can't solve the care problem by itself, but it could underpin all of the other solutions and reduce what we will need to spend on the National Care, Education and Children's Services that we should also create and fund.

The poverty-reducing impact of a basic income would be an important foundation for reducing educational inequalities and low attainment from early childhood onwards. Basic income can also smooth young people's transition from education into adulthood. Currently there is quite widespread support for financial initiatives to support young people, such as the proposal by the Resolution Foundation for a citizen's inheritance – a lump sum of money to be given to every young adult at the age of twenty-five to improve their sense of security and hope for the future.[373] As proposed, this money could only be spent on certain things: young people could invest in education, a pension or a home, for example. Arguably, a lump sum at age twenty-five would come too late for many young people, and the conditionality is less attractive than the respect for autonomy that is baked into basic income. As mentioned earlier, the Welsh government is piloting a targeted unconditional basic income scheme for all young people leaving the care sector, giving them £1,600 (taxable) every month for a period of two years from their eighteenth birthday. This is a bold and courageous social policy born out of the government's interest in testing a basic income and their recognition of the unique and significant challenges that care leavers face. An evaluation, led by a Cardiff University research team of which I am part, is looking at the impact of this basic income on the young people's health, wellbeing and more, and is due to be completed in 2027. I set out some early insights in Chapter 2, but to reiterate, recipients have described having opportunities and choices. As one young person said:

> I know a lot of us care leavers have a lot of worries about financial security . . . You know, we are leaving care. We don't know where we're going, what we're doing, how's it going to work. You know, [with this pilot] the government take away the financial worry side of it, [which] does massively help with a lot of anxiety problems that most of us have, and any of the mental health problems.[374]

Basic income has the potential to reduce crime through its impact on poverty, economic security, and the sense of agency it gives to people. UBI schemes and cash transfers have been linked to reduced rates of property-related crime, and in some circumstances less child maltreatment and domestic violence.[375] The mental health improvements that flow from basic income would also reduce crime rates, and basic income would mean that those leaving prison would have a level of support that could help to prevent re-offending.

And what about the environmental and climate crises? The international organisation Basic Income Earth Network suggests that a universal basic income would improve the financial accessibility of climate innovations and technological solutions, such as solar panels, energy-saving appliances and electric vehicles, allow people to reskill for green careers, and provide a safety net to those most vulnerable to environmental impacts.[376]

The think tank New Economics Foundation (NEF) are not keen on UBIs, instead advocating for universal basic services

(UBS) – the idea that, instead of giving people cash, we should provide free access to essential services such as transport, housing, childcare, adult social care, education and digital communications. Think of how the NHS already works in the UK, but extended to cover the basic necessities of life. NEF argues that this approach would be more environmentally sustainable than cash payments because shared public services – like public transport instead of private cars, or community centres instead of individual entertainment purchases – have a smaller environmental footprint per person.

The potential to tackle the climate crisis that NEF extols for universal basic services applies to universal basic incomes as well: the idea that when people have their basic needs secured (whether through cash or services), it builds broad support for policies that limit consumption and constrain excess.[377, 378] UBIs could also underpin a shift from status-based consumption to pro-environmental activities, such as volunteering with environmental organisations, although there is little research evidence demonstrating this as yet, as environmental impacts haven't so far been outcomes of interest in most trials of basic income.[379] Pilot interventions in India did lead to more households switching to clean fuels. There are, increasingly, calls for a global UBI to be funded by taxes on land, mining or artificial intelligence, perhaps through a 'cap and share' scheme on fossil fuel extraction. The think tank Equal Right calculates that a $135 charge on each tonne of fossil fuel extraction would raise up to $5 trillion annually, which would be enough to pay $30 each month to every person on the planet.[380]

A targeted basic income, given to residents of important conservation areas, has also been suggested as a mechanism to protect biodiversity,[381] but the transition to sustainability needs all of us on board. It's the universality of UBI that makes it such an attractive proposition for increasing social solidarity – for making us all feel we really are in it together.

Paying for it

The affordability of a universal basic income obviously depends on the level at which it is set, and how it is funded. In the UK we're not sitting on top of fossil fuel resources that we could exploit to this level, and anyway we should be leaving those in the ground. We could, however, as a society, decide to start small and then build progressively towards a higher level of universal basic income.

The research group Basic Income Health, based at Northumbria University and to which I belong, has developed models for the fully costed implementation of three UBI schemes that could move in stages towards a ten-year goal of providing the Minimum Income Standard that I described in Chapter 1, to everyone.[382] Even in its initial phase, paying just £75 per week to all adults under sixty-five, £50 to every child to replace Child Benefit, and £205 to all those over the age of sixty-five (close to the current state pension), a starter-level UBI would more than *halve child poverty* – bringing it to the lowest level since we began keeping records in 1961 – alongside precipitating falls in pensioner poverty of around 60 per cent and working-age poverty by around 30 per cent. I'm going to have to use some bold text to really emphasise this potential: **child poverty down from almost a third of UK children to 12.5 per cent; working age poverty down to 15 per cent.**

Such a scheme would be fiscally neutral (the government would not have to find any new money), if funded through an abolition of personal allowances for income tax and National

Insurance, equalisation of National Insurance for the employed and self-employed, and a three-percentage-point (3p in the £) increase in the rates of personal income tax; only those in the top 20 per cent of earners would be paying (slightly) more tax than now. If we implemented the Minimum Income Standard for everyone, we'd **cut working age poverty by 75 per cent and our income inequality would be the lowest in the world**. In addition, we'd save all of the costs of implementing our current complicated system of means-testing, managing people's applications for benefits, monitoring their ongoing eligibility and compliance with rules, and, most importantly, all of the costs of the problems we will have prevented. Our research group, using what are called microsimulation methods, has found that even the basic starter UBI scheme would prevent or postpone around 124,000 cases of depression and 118,000 cases of physical health problems in the UK every year. Using standard methods of health economics, this translates into a health benefit, via poverty reduction alone, of £3.87 billion per year for a scheme that was already fiscally neutral.[383] The payoffs for the Minimum Income Standard-level UBI would be even higher and worth almost £20 billion per year.

We need transparent and well-informed public debate about such a radical transformation of our society, and it's high time that universal basic income received that kind of discussion, rather than being dismissed, as it used to be, as unrealistically 'utopian'. Introducing a basic income is undeniably a costly proposition, but what is the cost of doing nothing? The welfare system we have is already an enormous financial burden, and it entrenches the poverty and inequality that are at the root of all the problems described in this book. The costs of dealing with the fallout from our broken society – through the health system, education system, social care and criminal justice – exceed even the generous UBI that would guarantee a Minimum Income Standard. We know that governments can find the money for the things they want to do – paying for wars, bailing out the banks, keeping the economy going through a pandemic.

The case for UBI will become even more compelling with time. As technological progress, including AI, transforms jobs and the labour market, there will be more and more reasons to implement universal basic income. One final thought on UBI: it has well over majority support from the British public. Researchers found that, nationally, 69 per cent of people approved of it, including more than half of those who were planning to vote Conservative in the 2024 general election and 75 per cent of those planning to vote Labour.[384] There are also very high levels of support for the kinds of actions that could be taken to fund it, including taxing excessive corporate profits, removing amoral (in that they do not benefit society) tax reliefs, introducing carbon taxes and, most importantly, taxing wealth.

Talking of wealth . . .

If UBI were to be my first choice for a comprehensive social policy – the warp on which to weave a good society – my second would be taxing wealth.

As I've already noted, in the UK we don't, unlike Norway, Alaska or Iran, have oil wealth to put into a sovereign wealth fund to bolster a good society; the so-called National Wealth Fund established in 2024, mentioned in Chapter 2, is funded through borrowing. And although UBI would be foundational, we still need to put sufficient resources into public services to provide the health care, social care, education and reforms to the criminal justice system that I've outlined in this book. If, as well as the National Health Service of which we are so proud, we want a National Care Service, a National Children's Service, a National Education service (or some combination of these), as well as the resources to transform our criminal justice system with a rehabilitative culture, we will need to invest *before* we start to see the benefits of shifting towards prevention and addressing the causes of the causes.

In the long term, if we have a Minimum Income Standard UBI and well-resourced preventive national public services, we won't need to spend as much on treating crises and chronic problems. In effect, I'm saying that we need *both* the universal basic services (UBS)[385, 386] – as championed by the New Economics Foundation – *and* UBI, so that over time the need for investment in services tapers downwards. We will have to kick-start this transition with a huge initial investment. Wealth taxes can generate this revenue for government, enabling it to invest in UBI, infrastructure, social services, and other public goods that would build this good society, like housing, transport, and digital access for all.

As our population ages and challenges society's capacity to meet increasing needs, wealth taxes are going to be an essential source of revenue for everything. We won't have enough from a tax base when the tax-receipts balance starts shifting towards younger earners and lower-income earners. Population ageing will increase the demand for health and social care services, while at the same time reducing the proportion of the population who are of working age and contributing income tax to the government purse. Economists call this a growth in the dependency ratio that measures the economic pressure on the labour force to support everyone who is not of working age. The UK's dependency ratio is growing more slowly than other rich, developed countries, because we have a higher birth rate and more people immigrating than emigrating, even after Brexit; yet if either of those patterns change, our dependency ratio could shoot up.[387]

Another good argument for taxing wealth is that it could unleash greater investment by the wealthy into society. If we built in the right incentives to a wealth tax, we could incentivise the rich to use their assets for the public good, rather than hoarding them or using them to display their status or buy political power. Of course, some rich people do contribute to society through philanthropy and some very wealthy people are very aware of, and concerned about, the damage their wealth imposes on society (I'm thinking of organisations such as Patriotic Millionaires, founded in the US in 2010 with a strapline of 'Tax the Rich, Pay the People and Spread the Power'; it also has a UK branch). But we can't rely on rich people's private values and ethics because most of them *don't* use their wealth for the common good. While groups like Patriotic Millionaires advocate for proper taxation of private wealth for investment in common wealth, most of the rich continue to put their efforts into sequestering their wealth away from the tax authorities.

Government could encourage the wealthy to invest in the good society and give them a wealth tax break in return for investment in sectors and projects that align with good social goals, such as encouraging investment in renewable energy, affordable housing, or community development. Similarly, wealth tax incentives could be used to promote economic democracy and sustainability, with rewards for investment in companies that prioritise social responsibility. There are real opportunities for win-win-win scenarios here, where the wealthy reduce their taxable wealth, bringing down inequality, while simultaneously contributing to the common good.

Is it fair to tax wealth? It depends on who you ask, of course! Some would distinguish between earned and unearned wealth, but there is a strong fairness argument to be made that those who have benefited the most from society, whether it is through luck, their own efforts, or those of their ancestors, should contribute a fair share in taxes, both of their higher incomes and their accumulated or inherited wealth. Researchers, including economist Professor Mariana Mazzucato from University College London, have shown how far private wealth creation is underpinned by public investment in education, research and infrastructure.[388] We, the people, through *our* taxes, help to make people rich, and so it is indeed right that they should contribute *their* fair share in return. Rich people like to think of themselves as wealth creators – by which they mean they create businesses and jobs and economic growth; this is how they defend their wealth. But the economic story of recent times, of neoliberalism, is of an economy characterised by what economists call *wealth extraction* (in econo-speak, this means asset control and *rent-seeking behaviour*; and that means growing one's wealth by manipulating the social or political environment without creating new wealth) – concentrating wealth among a smaller section of society and away from the rest of us.

While UBI has potential for creating immediate societal benefit through its impact on poverty, the only way to tackle the root cause of all of the problems caused by inequality is by targeting the top end of the socioeconomic ladder through progressive taxation of income and wealth. Recent increases in inequality have been primarily driven by what is happening at the top, by the 10 per cent, the 1 per cent and the 0.1 per cent pulling away from the rest of society. In order to realise all the benefits of more economic equality for improved social cohesion, better population health, a more sustainable economy and enhanced life chances for children and young people, we have to tax wealth.

A final argument to be made in favour of wealth taxes has to do with power. The actor Brian Cox was born working class but is now a member of Patriotic Millionaires. He is best known for playing the billionaire Logan Roy (a fictional character based on Rupert Murdoch) in the TV series *Succession*. Cox calls the gang of real billionaires backing, and benefiting from, Donald Trump's presidency the 'broligarchs', pointing out that they have undemocratically grabbed political power by paying for it – Elon Musk alone put $277 million into Trump's 2024 campaign, and in the first three months of Trump's second term Musk saw his wealth jump by more than $170 billion.[389] The 'broligarchs' are just the worst – and as labelled by Cox, 'obscene'[389] – example of the long-term trend of political capture by the rich.

In the UK, those vested interests might look different from the tech broligarchs – Elon Musk, Jeff Bezos and Mark Zuckerberg – but the unequal power dynamics are no different. Here, extreme wealth is more likely to be rooted in centuries of inherited land ownership and property, passed down through generations of aristocratic and landed families who have shaped policy to protect their interests. Think of the vast estates that still dominate the British countryside, the hereditary peers who sit in the House of Lords, or the property empires built on land that was enclosed from common ownership hundreds of years ago. This old money may be less flashy than Silicon Valley billions, but it wields influence just as effectively – through networks, institutions, and the quiet preservation of systems that keep wealth concentrated in the same hands, generation after generation.

One simple way to reverse this trend is to tax wealth. There are about 3,000 billionaires on the planet; if we only taxed them a 2 per cent super-rich tax, we would raise $250 billion a year, enough to do a lot of good things. But even if we did nothing with that money, even if we locked it all away for a rainy day, we would be making a dent in the inequality that damages us all and denting their hold on power. We are truly in a Catch-22 situation: those in power have vested interests in government not doing what is needed to create the good society. A wealth tax could help us break free of their stranglehold.

All the good ideas and then some

Although I'm not an economist, I spend an awful lot of time with them, in the various institutes, councils, commissions and think tanks that I'm part of. And it is their expertise on ways to tax wealth that I'm drawing on here. Let's listen to a bevy of Nobel Prize-winning economists,* among them Joseph Stiglitz, Esther Duflo and James Meade, who have called for various kinds of wealth taxes. As have Thomas Piketty, Gabriel Zucman and twenty-eight organisations, including Greenpeace, Oxfam, and the Patriotic Millionaires, in an open letter to the UK Chancellor in 2024.[390] Tax is a very technical subject, so I'll keep it snappy: the main take-home message is that there are myriad ways to tax wealth, so the key question shouldn't be *Can we do it?* – but *When and how shall we do it?*

In 2022, I contributed to a short book commissioned and published by the Tribune group of Labour MPs, *The Change We Need*, in which experts of various kinds were asked to suggest bold policy solutions for the next Labour government. The book

---

* *The Economist* suggests that the collective noun for a group of economists could be a gloom, a regression or an assumption . . .

included an essay on tax by Associate Professors Arun Advani, of the University of Warwick, and Andy Summers, of the London School of Economics. Together, Advani and Summers had been the economist commissioners on the independent UK Wealth Tax Commission, and their essay was brim-full of ideas for taxing wealth that, as they put it, 'if done properly . . . are an effective tool against inequality and can be implemented without harming the economy'.[391]

Advani and Summers' research showed that the 'average' person with a total income of £10 million per year paid 21 per cent in tax – less than what someone was then paying on the median income of £30,000 per year. They found that 1 in 10 of those earning more than £1 million were paying a lower tax rate than someone on £15,000 per year. And the effective tax rate on estates worth more than £10 million was just 10 per cent. They proposed taxing capital gains at the same level as income, and immediately, so that people could no longer hang on to those assets without paying tax – nonsensically – until they died. Gaps in inheritance tax needed to be plugged, including the reliefs on agricultural and business property, gifts and untouched pension pots.* Council tax, which is based on long-ago property values (from 1991 in England and 1993 in Wales), and which is regressive, with people in the lowest valuation band paying a higher percentage than those in the highest band, could be restructured so that everyone paid 0.5 per cent of an updated value. Advani and Summers' most radical proposal was for a 1 per cent tax on wealth above £10 million, which would raise £10 billion annually from the wealthiest 0.04 per cent of the population. All in all, they described their tax proposals as a win-win-win,

---

* The Labour government has announced an intention to reform exemptions for family businesses and farms, to be implemented from April 2026.

bringing in £60 billion a year, reducing inequality and improving economic efficiency with more streamlined schemes. They ended their essay thus: 'What's not to like?'[391]

Tax expert Richard Murphy, who was Professor of Practice in International Political Economy at City University, has a different idea for reforming the outdated and regressive council tax system. He is one of the many experts proposing that land value, another wealth asset, should be taxed, ideally by regional government, to replace council tax. Murphy points out five (somewhat technical) advantages of a land tax: you can't hide land or squirrel it away in offshore tax havens, so it is identifiable as an asset; it encourages productive use of land because it is taxed even if unused; the taxing authority can encourage environmental policy goals through land tax incentives; it shifts a tax burden from land occupiers to land owners, so is progressive; and finally, it provides economic gains beyond the tax raised, because land yields rise and the social costs of unused land fall.[392]

Taxing wealth isn't the only progressive reform that is needed for the good society, and which could help finance its development. The Grantham Research Institute for Climate Change and the Environment, based at Imperial College, London, recommends a tax on carbon (rising from £55 to £75 per tonne through to 2030) to bring the UK to net-zero emissions by 2050.[393] Luxury consumption taxes are among other approaches called for by campaigning charity the Equality Trust.[394] Even better, we could combine the two with a luxury-focused carbon tax on things like flights and large cars.[395] Many economists back a financial transaction tax (the so-called Tobin tax), reforms to corporation tax, and measures to deal with tax havens. These latter two could both be accomplished with a move to 'unitary taxation', in which companies are taxed where their economic activity – manufacturing, buying and selling, etc. – takes place, rather than where (so often a tax haven) their business is registered.[396] We, the public, are always shocked when we find out how little tax is paid on profits by many big multi-national companies, such as when Amazon's main UK division paid zero tax in 2022 despite making a £222 million profit (since Rishi Sunak's Conservative government ended a particular allowable tax deduction, Amazon is once again paying some tax in the UK, although not enough, according to the Fair Tax Foundation). Unitary taxation could raise significant amounts of money to invest in good society policies.

I'm not trying to give a comprehensive list here of options for taxing wealth; rather, I'm pointing out the frequency and consistency with which progressive economists and policymakers stress the need to do it, one way or another.[397] They also caution, however, about the challenges involved in selling such reforms to other policymakers and to the public. Council members of the Progressive Economy Forum, when debating taxing wealth to fund social care, suggested various wealth taxes and also pointed out the need to reduce existing unfair tax burdens and grow public spending at the same time, to get public support for the changes.[398]

In 2022, after the publication of *The Change We Need*, I joined academic tax expert Arun Advani, and British economist, former financial trader and Patriotic Millionaire Gary Stevenson, for a panel discussion before MPs at Parliament's Portcullis House. With what I like to think was a comprehensive and passionate case for taxing wealth and reducing inequality, we argued that there was no other way for government to be able to reduce the harms of inequality and fund the public services that would build a better society. We were not, I am afraid, received with widespread enthusiasm. The mainly Labour MPs attending the event did not, they said, fancy knocking on doors at the next election having to sell a manifesto promise of a wealth tax.

This reluctance reflects a fascinating political paradox. In reality, very few people would actually pay wealth taxes – inheritance tax, for instance, currently only affects about 4 per cent of estates because the threshold is so high (£325,000 for individuals, £500,000 if a house is left to children or grandchildren, and up to £1 million for couples). But polling consistently shows that far more people think they might have to pay it. Many ordinary homeowners, particularly in areas where house prices have risen, worry that their family home might push them over thresholds that are actually much higher than they realise. This means politicians fear electoral backlash from voters who would never actually be affected by the policies they're opposing. It's a triumph of perception over reality – and it helps explain why wealth taxes remain politically difficult, despite affecting only the genuinely wealthy.

The joy of tax

One of my proudest moments as a parent was when my teenaged daughter opened her first payslip from her first part-time job. 'Oh good,' she said. 'I've been taxed!'

I echo her pride and pleasure: I actually enjoy paying my taxes each year; it really does feel like a privilege to me to be able to contribute to society, to keep my end of the social contract. I know this is fairly unusual, and it's not (I hope) because I'm a pious goody-two-shoes. It's because my research and all the evidence I've laid out in this book shows that we could have a better, fairer society with higher levels of all kinds of wellbeing, if we were taxed, sufficiently and more fairly, to pay for it. When my parents visited Norway for a holiday some years ago, they commented to their waiter in a café on the high price of a cup of coffee (food and drink served in restaurants is subject to a 25 per cent VAT in Norway). 'But think what we are able to do with those tax revenues,' replied the waiter. 'Libraries, road repairs and more.' It's hard to imagine that same conversation playing out in our neighbourhood coffee shops in the UK.

We Brits tend to view tax as the government robbing us of what is rightfully ours, instead of valuing our contributions to the public good. Obviously, we might all feel very different if the tax system was less pockmarked with unfairness and injustice; if the tax burden fell more squarely on the broadest shoulders. As it is, the Common Sense Policy Group found that the public would not support income tax rises beyond 3 per cent, but they were overwhelmingly in favour of taxing wealth, taxing corporations and taxing carbon: national approval for a progressive programme of reform that included UBI and wealth taxes was around three-quarters across multiple polls – with a majority of Labour *and* Conservative voters in favour.[399] What's not to like, indeed.

A body of persons

> 'History suggests that what is not "politically possible" can change quite radically and quite rapidly over the years; and nothing can become politically possible unless it is first proposed and discussed by some body of persons.'
>
> James Meade[400]

Just who are the 'body of persons' who should be proposing and discussing how to build a good society? This book is my contribution, but how do we make other people's voices heard, and how do we bring more evidence into policy-making?

I'm on the home straight now; I've set out my good society stall and assembled as best I can the evidence from the social sciences and other disciplines that suggests solutions to our biggest social problems; and I've given you my top two radical shifts: universal basic income scaffolded by wealth taxes. I'm going to finish by suggesting some mechanisms and institutions that could be the weft of the good society, some that allow the 'body of persons' proposing and discussing change to be all of us, the general public, and some that would allow for an expert 'body of persons'. In other words, bottom-up and top-down ways to make the radical change we need politically possible.

Let's start with bottom-up. You might find it easier to agree that it would be a good idea to have ways of getting more evidence into policy, than be convinced that we need to find ways to get more so-called ordinary people engaged in the policy process. After all, don't we vote for politicians exactly so they can represent us in policy-making?

Leaving it to politicians would be fine *if* they were really representatives of the whole spectrum of society, and *if* they listened hard to what their constituents want, but they aren't and they often don't. Just look at voter turnout in the last few general elections in the UK: in 2024 only 60 per cent of eligible voters went to the polls, down from 67 per cent in 2019, lower than voter turnout through the entire twentieth century; 84 per cent of the electorate turned out in 1950. These days, older people are much more likely to vote than younger people, although this was not the case historically. Young women seem especially disengaged, as are poor people, and people in many constituencies in the North of England. This pattern of 'democratic malaise' has been linked to income inequality; many of the groups most affected by health, care, education, criminal justice and environmental inequalities are least likely to have trust in politics or believe that those in power will work in concert with citizens' opinions or wishes. This mistrust does not seem misplaced when you consider that about three-quarters of the public support a wealth tax and a universal basic income, and stronger measures to tackle poverty – but still nothing gets done. The public are more ambitious for a good society and more progressive than is generally believed. So how do we get things moving?

Assemblies for grown-ups

You may not have enjoyed having to go to school assemblies in your youth, but imagine having a chance to get together with other people to change the world . . .

Abortion is an issue that can create the deepest of political divides. Author and filmmaker John de Graaf, who has spent much time in recent years trying to engage in dialogue and build bridges across the polarisation of American politics, once told me that abortion was the one issue on which it was impossible to find common ground between those on all sides of the issue. In Ireland, in 1983, under the influence of the Catholic Church and approved by a referendum, an Eighth Amendment was added to the Irish constitution which established a near complete ban on abortion. That was a position which appeared immovable – until 2018, when ninety-nine Irish citizens, chosen at random, and including pro-lifers, pro-choicers and undecideds, met for five weekends across five short months and made history. After listening to medical, legal and ethical experts from various sides of the abortion debate, and testimony from people affected by the issue, much of which was streamed online, these ninety-nine citizens deliberated and reflected, and finally recommended the repeal of the Eighth Amendment. The Irish government listened and held another referendum; when two-thirds of the population voted in favour, they repealed the amendment and opened the door to legal abortion. In less than two years, a deliberative democratic process brought Irish law and politics into line with Irish opinion, which turned out to be much more progressive and secular than many had realised. The Irish taoiseach, Leo Varadkar, described the referendum result as a 'quiet revolution'.

Citizens' assemblies are an idea with the potential to dissipate our democratic malaise and re-energise our politics and policy-making. They are a form of representative democracy and open government that can lead to unexpectedly radical change. The first citizens' assembly of modern times took place in British Columbia, Canada in 2004, set up by the state government to consider electoral reform. The assembly recommended replacing British Columbia's first-past-the-post voting system with a single transferable vote, a form of proportional representation. This was then voted on in a provincial-level election, needing 60 per cent of the vote to be passed into law; the proposal got 58 per cent of the votes, so fell just short.

The model of the citizens' assembly has been replicated more than a thousand times across the world since then, with transformative success at times. In Ireland, another citizens' assembly led to the legalisation of same-sex marriage – again an issue that must have seemed out of reach just a few years previously. In France, a citizens' assembly was held to develop the details to allow medically assisted dying. Japan has held city-based citizens' assemblies on climate issues, including in Sapporo, where citizens' recommendations fed into the city's plan to reduce net emissions to zero by 2050. Canada still leads the way, though, with more than fifty assemblies involving over half a million households. We've had a few in the UK too. In

2020 the government commissioned 'Climate Assembly UK', which recommended ways to achieve net zero by 2050, including a ban on the sale of new petrol, diesel and hybrid cars by 2030–35 (a policy brought forward by the Labour government in early 2025) and support for onshore wind farms (also now receiving governmental support, with a ban lifted in mid 2024).

Citizens' assemblies are composed of members of the public – selected at random, just as we do for jury service – who come together to *study* and give recommendations on a specific issue. But, unlike a jury, the sampling can be set up to make sure that the assembly is representative of society in terms of age, gender, ethnicity, geography, or any other characteristic that we might want to make sure is proportionally represented. An assembly could be set up, for example, with attention to the socioeconomic background of participants. I use the word *study*, because the point of the assembly is that it engages citizens to learn from experts, so that they can give thoughtful consideration to an issue before making recommendations. Ideally, a citizens' assembly, even if commissioned by government, is organised by independent, trusted organisers with the aim of running a non-partisan and non-biased process. That's why citizens' assemblies are considered to be 'deliberative democracy in action'.

Peter MacLeod and Richard Johnson run the Toronto-based public engagement firm MASS LBP, which trains people to lead collaborative, participatory and deliberative projects. They have organised citizens' assemblies across Canada, on issues as diverse as health care, digital rights and transportation, and describe three kinds of benefits of this form of 'activated citizenship'. First, because they offer a space in which the public are presented with quality information, given time for dialogue and debate, and are obliged to work through trade-offs and disagreements, assemblies tend to come up with practical, non-ideologically driven solutions to thorny issues. Second, they give the public a chance to serve – a 'second franchise' – and to develop skills in compromise and open-mindedness. Third, they encourage the same open-mindedness among politicians, encouraging them to put aside their sense that they alone are in control of policy, and to listen to their constituents. Citizens' assemblies, say MacLeod and Johnson, 'up-end our assumptions about an allegedly apathetic, ill-informed public'.[401]

The Iswe Foundation, and the Global Citizens' Assembly Network, backed by the government of Brazil, are setting up what they hope will be a global and permanent citizens' assembly to – in the words of Rich Wilson and David Levaï, from the Iswe Foundation – 'unlock the planet's most valuable asset in tackling the planet's most pressing crises: its billions of citizens, all of whom have knowledge of and care for their local environment and a stake in our collective future'. Wilson and Levaï point out that the same globalisation and technological advances that have accelerated the environmental crisis have also created the capacity to engage millions of people worldwide, enabling citizens to lead the way in a collective platform to shape global negotiations. The goal is for ten million people to be participating annually by 2030.[402]

The European Union is also getting on board with citizens' assemblies – President Ursula von der Leyen announced her support for them in 2022. In 2025, the EU will run a youth assembly for Europeans, aged 18–29, to consider the decline of wild pollinator insects and develop recommendations for the EU institutions. It's heartening to think that young people, who are most likely to be affected by the environmental and climate crisis, will get a chance to feed their concerns directly to the policymakers who could enact change; this assembly is being run online, which also feels like a step towards widening participation in democracy across borders.

The EU has held citizens' panels on food waste, on transnational educational mobility, and on tackling hatred in society. As I write, it is about to launch a randomly selected citizens' panel from countries across Europe to discuss the design of the EU's next long-term budget. This assembly has the potential to influence the priorities and spending of a budget of more than €1 trillion between 2028 and 2035. Which is a great segue into the next idea for getting more of us involved in creating the good society.

How to spend it

The *Financial Times* column 'How to Spend It' suggests how the wealthy can enhance their status through the stuff they buy. But there is a much more democratic process for spending lots of money, and we can harness it in service of a good society.

Dr Kwame McKenzie is Professor of Psychiatry at the University of Toronto and CEO of the Wellesley Institute, a policy think tank. I'm a big admirer of Dr McKenzie – firstly because I was once in a taxi with him when the driver claimed the crime problem in the city was caused by 'the crazies' and Dr McKenzie explained to him, politely but forcefully, that he was wrong (I would have kept cravenly schtum); and secondly because he introduced me to the evidence on participatory budgeting.

In 2014, following the relocation of public health functions out of the NHS and back into local authorities, I sat on a steering group of the British Academy (the UK's national academy for humanities and social sciences) that asked a number of experts to each propose one thing that councils could do to reduce health inequalities. Dr McKenzie put forward participatory budgeting as the best thing he knew of to improve mental well-being, equity, and civic engagement at one stroke. He described mental health as public health's superglue, essential for supporting everything that local policymakers want to achieve, and that by changing the way that they themselves worked they could increase mental capital through community engagement.[403]

These initiatives involve members of the public in making decisions about how to spend public money. They can operate at any scale, in cities for example, or regional or national government, or perhaps, if the EU takes the next step from its citizens' assembly on the long-term budget, at supra-national level. The budget that the public directs can be a percentage of a core budget, or a specified pot of money for a particular place or issue; there are plenty of different models to choose from. In participatory budgeting, citizens set their spending priorities and have the power to direct actual spending; they might have help from official experts to develop the spending proposals in line with rules and regulations, but the spending allocation choices are theirs alone. In most models of participatory budgeting, the spending proposals are voted on to give a ranking of community preferences and the spending authority then funds the top-ranked proposals up to the limit of any designated budget.

Participatory budgeting has been tried and tested all over the world. The process proliferated in Brazil following the end of its dictatorship in 1985 and the adoption of a new constitution in 1988 which gave municipalities much more responsibility for public spending. A notable example comes from the city of Porto Alegre, which in the 1990s began to allow citizens to directly influence how a portion of the city budget was spent on public services and infrastructure. By 1999, citizens were making annual decisions on how to spend $64 million, a fifth of the city's budget. City residents have proposed projects, in public meetings with ballot-box voting, leading to significant improvements in public services, including sanitation, transportation and education, particularly in the poorest areas of the city.[404] But the reason Dr McKenzie is so in favour of participatory budgeting, is not so much what the money is spent on, but how the process makes people feel. In Porto Alegre, participatory budgeting has reduced poverty, for sure, but it has also increased civic participation and strengthened community ties, which can indirectly reduce crime levels.

There has been a fair amount of participatory budgeting in the UK over many years, but mostly on a small scale, in terms of the numbers of citizens participating, the budgets being allocated, and the geographic area affected by the spending choices. The Local Government Association showcases two case studies on its website. In 2008, the Scottish government ran a pilot participatory budget scheme in Govanhill, Glasgow, giving residents £200,000 to spend on local projects. They chose to spend the money on a family support group for addictions, a community justice programme, and the regeneration of a local public swimming baths, with sports and wellness programmes; the process was deemed to be effective in engaging local residents. Tower Hamlets, one of the poorest boroughs in London, held a substantial participatory budgeting process in 2009–10, allocating more than £5 million of council and NHS money to the scheme. In both Govanhill and Tower Hamlets, people who participated developed skills and felt empowered.[405]

There is no doubting that participatory budgeting takes time and money. If public budget holders are going to invest resources in setting up and running a participatory budget process, and citizens are going to put in time and effort to engage in the process, everyone has to believe that it's worth it and that their opinions are being heard. Involve – a charity dedicated to increasing civic participation and deliberative democracy in the UK – suggests that participatory budgeting would work best if it became an established and ongoing part of the budget cycle.[406] Unlike citizens' assemblies, so far the UK schemes have not been based on random and representative selection of participants. But they could be, and if both citizens' assemblies and participatory budgeting were scaled up, we might begin to reverse the trend towards disengagement and disillusionment with our politics, as well as shifting policy and spending to what the public really wants.

The unknown unknowns

Are you well-informed? Do you keep up with current affairs and progress in the sciences and social sciences? And if you think you're well-informed, what are your sources? Do you think the public is helped to understand politics, and social and economic policy, by our media?

In 2010, I took my young son for a haircut. The barber's shop had a stack of newspapers and magazines, and while I was waiting for my boy, I thought I would see what the papers were saying about the Marmot Review of health inequalities, which had just been released. I'd read the very full coverage in the *Guardian* that morning and I wanted to compare reactions to this major report. Except there weren't any. *The Times* had a very short, pretty uninformative, piece. There was nothing at all in the tabloids.

On that day in February 2010, you could have read any of several newspapers cover-to-cover and you would not have known that an independent review had proposed a set of effective, evidence-based strategies for reducing health inequalities in England, nor would you have known the scale and extent of those inequalities.

In 2013 a group of churches, the Baptist, Methodist, United Reformed Church, and the Church of Scotland, published a report titled *The Lies We Tell Ourselves: Ending comfortable myths about poverty*, because they felt that churchgoers and the general public had come to believe that the key factors driving poverty in the UK were the personal failings, including idleness, of the poor. They wanted to expose the myths that they saw being reinforced by politicians and the media that amounted to a systematic misrepresentation of the facts about poverty. The myths that they chose to debunk with hard facts were that: the poor are idle; they are addicted to drink and drugs; they simply don't manage their money properly; they are on the fiddle; they have an easy life; they cause the deficit.[407] The churches wanted to face up to their own blindness and to seek the facts beyond the accepted truth promulgated by newspapers. Reading much of the press coverage was uncomfortable, the churches' report concluded, because parts of the media misrepresent the truth and tell us what we want to hear (or what they think we want to hear).[407]

Or do they tell us what *they*, the media, want us to hear?

In 2023 the Media Reform Coalition reported that just three companies – DMG Media (publishers of the *Daily Mail*, *Metro* and *i*, owned by billionaire Viscount Rothermere); News UK (the *Sun* and *The Times*, owned by the billionaire Murdoch family); and Reach Plc (*Daily Mirror*, *Daily Express*, *Daily Star*, publicly traded but with hedge-fund and other investment shareholders) – account for 90 per cent of national newspaper circulation and more than 40 per cent of the audience reach of the UK's top fifty online news brands. This, they said, gives 'a handful of dominant publishers an unrivalled position for setting the news agenda across print, broadcast and online formats'.[408] Two-thirds of the top online news platforms are owned by Meta (owned by billionaire Mark Zuckerberg), Alphabet (a substantial chunk of their shares are owned by BlackRock, the world's largest investor in fossil fuels, and they own Google), and X Corp (owned by billionaire Elon Musk). Meta (who own Facebook, Instagram and WhatsApp) and Google command 80 per cent of all online advertising spend, 'giving these two tech giants unparalleled power over how online news is found and funded'.[408]

Are we happy with this concentration of power over the news agenda in so few hands, and in the hands of those who may not have our best interests at heart?

In February 2025, billionaire Jeff Bezos, founder of Amazon, declared that the *Washington Post*, which he has owned since 2013, would confine the paper's opinion pages to supporting personal liberties and free markets, with no dissenting views allowed.

Now, if you've got this far in this book you know exactly how to read that story: the *Washington Post* will be turning its face against new economic thinking and our best understanding of the causes of the causes of human wellbeing. As former *Washington Post* journalist Kate Woodsome points out, this is 'gaslighting people to believe that unchecked capitalism delivers personal liberty, when decades of research show it shackles people to financial and emotional insecurity'.[409]

If the stranglehold of the billionaires on what we see, read and hear feels hopeless, cheer up. There *are* alternatives that a good society can nurture and disseminate. Independent publisher and philosopher Dan Hind argues for media reform to underpin social change. Most of us, he says, 'have been living with an inadequate account of the world' for decades, with a media unable to properly describe reality to us because of

THE BUILDING BLOCKS: EVIDENCE AND EQUALITY

pressures on them from the state, from powerful owners and from advertisers. Why not, he suggests, democratise the media through public funding and cooperative models of community ownership, with the public prioritising, through deliberative democratic processes, what they would like to know more about and then commissioning investigative journalism? These reforms would strengthen local journalism and communities, and grow more diverse voices and perspectives and relevant news coverage, with the freedom to hold the powerful to account.[410]

I was struck by these ideas when I first heard about them, and then intrigued to learn that the Croatian government had decided to give them a try. In 2013 the Croatian Ministry of Culture used national lottery money to fund investigative journalism projects, proposed by journalists and chosen by the public. Fifty proposals for journalist projects were received, were voted upon by 1,764 citizens, and fifteen projects funded for a month, and three for three months. The chosen topics included investigations into the finances of the Catholic Church, the destruction of the working class, and the criteria used to select reading lists for schools.[411] Although it was a small and short-lived pilot project, it was proof that the concept could work.

Other systems are available. Professor Julia Cagé, economist at the Paris Institute of Political Studies, proposed another model to transform ownership of the media: the non-profit media organization (NMO) – a democratically controlled charitable foundation in which the public and journalists would crowdfund investments and gain voting rights in news publishing.[412] And playing fantasy society once again, we can look to the usual suspects for examples of a more democratic media. The Swedish press is publicly subsidised: if a newspaper has 2,000 subscribers, it receives government funding, and thus the media is more diverse and broad-based, for instance including newspapers run by trade unions. Norway, Estonia, the Netherlands, Sweden, Finland and Denmark take the top six spots in the 2025 World Press Freedom Index, produced by Reporters Without Borders; the UK is ranked twentieth and the USA fifty-seventh.[413]

Making evidence work in policy

None of this is easy – citizens' assemblies, participatory budgeting, democratically organised and funded media – but it is all worth it in service of a good society. Our impoverished democracy and culture could be revitalised and enriched if we all played more of a part in shaping our world. Our opinions matter and we need to find other mechanisms, if not these, to feed our perspectives into policy-making. But we do need the experts and the evidence as well.

In 2009, Alex Stevens, Professor of Criminal Justice at the University of Kent, spent six months on a placement in a policy-making section of the civil service, in a team responsible for advising government at the highest levels. With ethical approval from his university, Professor Stevens not only interviewed some of the civil servants he worked with; he also conducted what is known as 'covert ethnographic research', observing the work of the team and their interactions with ministerial advisors. He found that 'evidence was ever-present in the development, discussion and presentation of the policies' he observed being formulated, yet all of his interviewees described instances when evidence was not used. Writing about his experiences in an academic paper, Stevens analysed how civil servants attempt to make use of the wealth of evidence they have access to by creating compelling narratives, preferably condensed into a 'killer graph', that often blurred any uncertainty in the evidence or ignored methodological weaknesses in favour of selling a policy to ministers. Stevens' paper came to my attention because he also describes asking his civil service colleagues how *The Spirit Level* research could be translated into policy proposals, only to be met by what he described as 'a tumbleweed-blowing silence'![414]

In 2013, the government established the What Works Network, which now consists of thirteen centres, to supposedly embed evidence into policy-making. Yet after ten years of the programme, the government's own evaluation concluded that 'high-quality evidence on the impact of government policies remains the exception rather than the rule' and that much government spending is not currently evaluated. And the What Works centres and the government-funded policy units only do what government asks of them; their priorities are limited to its priorities. It all feels a bit haphazard, and yet we have a shining example of how to do evidence-based decision-making in the UK, in the National Institute for Health and Care Excellence, widely known as NICE. It's so good that we export the model all over the world, advising international health organisations, ministries and government agencies on how to do evidence-based decision-making. So what does NICE do, and how can we borrow its methods?

The 'art of medicine'

Up until the 1980s, medicine was a bit haphazard. Doctors made decisions about treatments based on their own opinions, experience, dogma and anecdote. Sometimes they made good decisions, sometimes they didn't, but they didn't have frameworks for assessing the available research evidence or the success of their decision-making. It wasn't until the 1970s that Dr Archie Cochrane began to promote the use of randomised controlled trials of treatments, leading to the development of systematic reviews and meta-analysis which sit at the heart of what NICE now does. Up until then, you might have been lucky with respect to your doctor's decisions, but you might well not have been. We don't have to go as far back as leeches and bloodletting to find examples of treatments or medical recommendations that did more harm than good or were simply ineffective – think of thalidomide, the higher rates of Sudden Infant Deaths caused by putting babies to sleep on their tummies, radiation for the common cold (!), prolonged and heavy hormone replacement therapy . . . When I was training as a childbirth doula in the early 1990s vast swathes of normal obstetric practice had no evidence base whatsoever.

Things are different now. Established in 1999, NICE publishes guidelines for medicines, treatment and procedures, on the appropriate care for particular diseases, and on public health practice and social care, all based on evidence of effectiveness (does it work?), safety and cost-effectiveness (is it good value for money?).[415] Obviously, if a treatment isn't effective, it will never be cost-effective. Cost-effectiveness is very important: because we can't fund everything we might want to through the NHS. We have to 'ration' our spending, and we do this by NICE deciding whether or not a treatment provides sufficient value in 'units of health' gained, relative to cost, using a measure called the Quality-Adjusted Life Year. A QALY is equal to one year in perfect health, and treatments are currently considered cost-effective, and so made available, if they fall below the rough threshold of £20,000–30,000 per QALY.

This kind of cost-effectiveness method was developed by health economists, including many important contributions from my colleagues at the Centre for Health Economics (CHE) at the University of York. CHE researchers have helped NICE and health policymakers to think about the benefits that other patients do *not* get if we spend limited resources elsewhere. So, if an expensive new treatment becomes available (and some new drugs cost thousands of pounds per month), who will not get something if we decide to pay for that treatment? Health economists have the tools to look at things like 'the effectiveness of public health campaigns targeting smoking and alcohol . . . waiting times, hospital efficiency, health system productivity, and the costs and benefits of many surgical techniques and interventions'.[416] The methods developed by health economists help us to do the fairest job possible of allocating resources and help policymakers understand the distribution of the benefits and opportunity costs.

I had been thinking for some time that what we need to support evidence-based social policy-making is something similar to NICE, perhaps a National Institute for Social Change (NISC isn't such a good acronym as NICE, but better minds than mine could be brought to bear on that). I was wondering if I was out on a very shaky limb on this, when I went to a conference in 2024 and talked about the difficulty of getting all the evidence I've laid out in this book into policy guidelines, perhaps with a threshold of benefit beyond which government would be obliged to implement a policy. A professor of health economics immediately responded positively, telling me 'we need a social sciences NICE'.

It would take some planning, and it would take some time, but we've done it once and set up a world-leading process for evidence-based medicine, so we can surely replicate that success for other kinds of policy? A social-sciences-based NICE-like body could help us quantify the payoff of investment in social and environmental infrastructure like childcare, schools and universities, culture and the arts, parks, and more. I described the long-term effects of investing in early childhood and in social care in earlier chapters, where paying for services now pays dividends to society later in health and productivity. We need to put these sorts of analyses onto a proper institutional footing and expect governments to follow the (long-term) money; this would help get around the problem that governments think short term, in electoral cycles, and not in the medium and long term.

Getting evidence off the shelves

In 2021, with my colleagues Professor Danny Dorling and Stewart Lansley from the Progressive Economy Forum, I wrote a briefing for Labour's then-shadow Cabinet, asking them, post-pandemic, to set up an independent advisory group of social scientists. We argued that social science advice was vital for what needed to be done to care for and repair the health of the economy and the health of the people following Covid. We wanted political leaders to have better access to the wider evidence that would promote the wellbeing of society. We suggested that if, over the past half century, UK governments had taken the advice of social scientists on just two issues – health inequalities and austerity – the UK would have been more resilient in the face of the Covid-19 pandemic. It was not, we said, enough to 'listen to the science' only during a crisis; robust and rigorous research from across the social sciences should be shaping political decision-making. A Social Science Advisory Group (SSAG – a slightly better acronym?)

THE BUILDING BLOCKS: EVIDENCE AND EQUALITY

could provide consensus advice on key issues and answer questions. The Academy of Social Sciences could support such a group, perhaps with rotating service from its fellows.[417] This would be relatively easy and inexpensive to run, easier and cheaper than a National Institute for Social Change, but perhaps one of its first tasks could be to make recommendations on how to set such an institute rolling. And the institute's priorities could be shaped by the priorities of the people, set through citizens' assemblies, its spending allocations determined through participatory budgeting. We could be putting the contributions of an invigorated public domain and participatory democracy directly in service of policy development and the good society. Together, a Social Science Advisory Group and a National Institute for Social Change could get all the evidence I've been showcasing in this book off the shelves and into policy.

And just one more new institution to think about: what about an independent Office for Social Responsibility, to parallel the independent Office for Budget Responsibility, to provide independent and authoritative analysis of the UK's public policy and political party manifestos, holding government accountable for acting on the evidence?

Facts are facts

It's a strange time to be writing a book so centred on evidence, living as we are in a context and a climate where facts are contested; fake news and disinformation permeate the media and (especially) social media; and, in some circles, being knowledgeable about facts is devalued. As literary critic Michiko Kakutani writes:

The term 'truth decay' has joined the post-truth lexicon that includes such now familiar phrases as 'fake news' and 'alternative facts'. And it's not just fake news either: there's also fake science (manufactured by climate change deniers and anti-vaxxers, who oppose vaccination), fake history (promoted by Holocaust revisionists and white supremacists), fake Americans on Facebook (created by Russian trolls), and fake followers and 'likes' on social media (generated by bots).[418]

So I'm going to suggest one final recommendation, a formal system of science- and social science-checking. Professor Paul Shrivastava of Pennsylvania State University and his colleagues suggest that we need 'science checks' just like the news media does 'fact checks'.[419] They propose that national academies and international councils, perhaps even UNESCO, the United Nations Educational, Scientific and Cultural Organization, could offer that sort of service to governments. We need to keep things real.

EPILOGUE

Living Proof

Too many people, if asked to describe Bradford, the UK's fifth-largest metropolitan area, would probably call to mind its persistent economic challenges, high levels of deprivation, and history of social tensions, perhaps remembering the 2001 riots which drew considerable negative media attention. But in 2025, this northern city exploded with art, music and more, much of it happening in a disused storage depot transformed into a vibrant cultural hub. Bradford was the UK City of Culture for 2025 – and it couldn't have been more proud of its metamorphosis.

But Bradford is also a City of Research, where more than 60,000 residents take part in a trail-blazing research programme, Born in Bradford, that has committed to using research evidence to improve lives and to build a good society. Professor John Wright, Born in Bradford's founder, describes the research as being like a Large Hadron Collider for wellbeing. At its heart is a vast epidemiological study, like a giant scientific version of the television series *Seven Up!*, following the lives of thousands of children and their parents.

Born in Bradford was itself born into a city with very little research capacity in its university or hospitals, low levels of life expectancy, high rates of chronic disease, and the UK's highest rate of infant mortality. But as John Wright describes it, Bradford had the asset of vibrant and diverse communities and a dedicated local NHS. Funded on a shoestring and built from the ground up on public engagement and community conversations, Born in Bradford, affectionately known as BiB, harnessed every parent's desire for a better future for their children and successfully recruited 80 per cent of the families who were invited to take part. These are families who are seldom included in research studies, almost half of them of South Asian heritage and over two-thirds from the poorest fifth of neighbourhoods in England and Wales.

Born in Bradford now sits at the centre of an international network of researchers and has fostered a large and diverse research team in the city, and an ever-growing programme of spin-off projects. BiB researchers have contributed to understanding the ill-health effects of air pollution and the benefits of access to green space for mental and physical health. They have made discoveries about the early pathways that lead to diabetes and heart disease. They have led educational research on early detection of autism within schools. Genetic research has led to new drugs and better understanding of the molecular basis of disease. BiB also links its research data to all the data that are routinely collected in health, education, social care and other systems: the Connected Bradford database now includes 600,000 citizens, whose data is harnessed for new discovery science and the evaluation of improvement initiatives.

Born in Bradford's goal was always to be a research programme that could change a city, a pipeline of evidence that would actually be used to improve people's lives. BiB research led the local authority to change its policy on 'age at school admission' for premature babies, and to start to screen children early for autism diagnosis and intervention. Driven by a strong social-determinants perspective, BiB now also works regionally and nationally, as well as locally, influencing politics, policy and practice. During the Covid pandemic, the research team formed an award-winning scientific advisory group for the city, helping, among other things, to get life-saving vaccinations to communities being bombarded with 'anti-vax' propaganda. Now a scientific advisory group is bringing evidence to the wider West Yorkshire Combined Authority and the regional Health and Care Partnership on issues like school absence and flexible working.

BiB has brought in over £100 million of investment to the city, from Big Lottery, Sport England, the Arts Council, government and the research councils. BiB has hosted artists and poets in residence, as well as festivals of science and culture. Thanks to BiB, the city has an ambitious Clean Air Zone, with over £30 million in funding to support the transition to less polluting vehicles; improved urban parks and green spaces; science-based early life interventions for diet, physical activity, speech and language, and parenting; a Digital Creatives project for young people; a Centre for Applied Education Research; and obesity prevention programmes in Islamic faith settings. There is so much more, it could fill a book.

So, has Born in Bradford lived up to its vision? Can a research project change a city? It is certainly changing lives, and it gives hope and aspiration to both citizens and leaders. I've played 'fantasy society' throughout this book, drawing pictures of a good society by bringing together real-world elements that are all happening somewhere, just not in the same place. Born in Bradford shows how in one real-world place, evidence and ambition can come together and set a city firmly on a path to actively creating a good society.

This is a story that could come to belong to all of us.

Acknowledgements

This book has been in my mind for quite some time, so I have a lot of people to thank.

Many thanks to my lovely agent, Rebecca Carter, for taking me on and believing in this project – I'm really looking forward to working with you on more ideas. This book has been given scope, scale and shape by the care and attention of my wonderful editor, Will Hammond, and by the equally wonderful Juliet Brooke while Will has been on paternity leave. Thank you both for giving me confidence in what I had to say and how I say it. Thank you also to managing editor Leah Boulton, to Kate Johnson for meticulous copy-editing and to Laura Reeves for help with figures.

At the University of York, a big thank you to all my colleagues in the Public Health and Society Research Group, the Cost of Living Research Group, the York Policy Engine, the BiB Centre for Social Change and the Leverhulme Centre for Anthropocene Biodiversity, with special thanks to Amy Barnes, Sarah Blower, Maria Bryant and Anthonia James. Thank you to my vice-chancellor, Charlie Jeffery, for understanding what a university is for (it's for the public good!).

Thank you to everyone at Born in Bradford – as the logo says, 'We Are Family' – especially John Wright, Rosie McEachan and Josie Dickerson. And thank you to my colleagues in INRICH, the International Network for Research on Inequalities in Child Health. Thank you also to the Progressive Economy Forum, enlightened economists all, especially Guy Standing and Susan Himmelweit for your discussion of what a care economy could look like. Thank you to the Common Sense Policy Group, especially Matthew Johnson, Daniel Nettle and Elliott Johnson, for making an unassailable case for UBI and including me in so many projects. And thank you to all at the Equality Trust and the Wellbeing Economy Alliance for your tireless work and dedication to forging a good society. Thank you to the Bhutan Bus Family (Bob Costanza, Sandrine Dixson-Declève, Lorenzo Fioramonti, Enrico Giovannini, Ida Kubizewski, Hunter Lovins, Jacquie McGlade, Lars Fogh Mortensen, Kristín Vala Ragnarsdóttir, Debra Roberts, Katherine Trebeck, Roberto De Vogli, Stewart Wallis) for working on wellbeing and contributing to mine.

Thanks to my colleagues at Health Equity North: Hannah Davies, David Taylor-Robinson, Clare Bambra and Luke Munford, and all of the authors and staff who have contributed to our many reports on health inequalities.

A lot of people have shared research findings and ideas over a number of years; thank you: Robin Alexander, Claire Cameron, Danny Dorling, Bill Kerry, Neal Lawson, Martin O'Neill, Steven Pittam, Laura Quick and Roberto De Vogli.

Friends matter for wellbeing; thank you: Karen Bloor, Rachel Curwen and Deborah Smith, Lesley Jones and Robin Bunton, Maddy Power and Sky Duthie, Georg'ann Cattelona and David Pace. Thank you also to family for walks, swims, skiing and very many happy times: Sarah and Paul Colebourne, Helen and Richard Holman, George and Geraldine Wilkinson, Annie Wilkinson and Tom Mustill. Special thanks to Sarah Colebourne and Imogen Colebourne for input into the chapter on social care. I hope that my children, grandchildren, nieces and godchildren will all be able to enjoy a good (better) society: Harry, Bronwen, Sophie, Imogen, Juliet, Josie, Owen, Jenny, Stella and the two Astrids.

Finally, in memory of my dad, Don Chapman (1932–2024), mountaineer and great reader, who was often in my thoughts as I was writing, and with gratitude to my mum, Marion Chapman, who has talked to me about books and writing all of my life. Last but most, thanks to my beloved husband, co-author and best friend, Richard Wilkinson, who has supported every moment of this book's journey while also working tirelessly for the Good Society. A shared purpose is a very good thing.

Note on Methods

Much of the time the evidence that policymakers have before them is *observational* rather than *experimental*. This is an issue for almost all the evidence in this book about what works; it applies just as much to thinking about what to do in the criminal justice, education and social care systems as it does in the health sector, where many of the methods originated.

We have what we call a 'hierarchy of evidence' in medicine and public health, giving more weight to some kinds of evidence than others when it comes to decision-making. The exact structure of the hierarchy of evidence has been modified over time, but traditionally, at the top, sit randomised double-blinded controlled trials or experiments, often synthesised in systematic reviews of evidence and so-called meta-analyses, where data are pooled and analysed across several studies.

The hierarchy of evidence pyramid.

NOTE ON METHODS

This is the classic scientific way of deciding whether an intervention, whether it is a medical treatment or a crop treatment in agriculture, and so forth, is better than either doing nothing, or doing what you would usually do. When considering introducing a new medical treatment, such as a drug, a new clinical practice or technology, outcomes can be compared between people who have received it and those who were given nothing (which usually entails giving people a placebo, something that looks like the new drug but is thought to have no effect) or those who got the standard or previous treatment (this is a tougher test of the new treatment). As we want to make sure that the groups of people being compared are not different to each other in some way, which might introduce factors that have an impact on the new treatment's efficacy, including in ways that we cannot observe or measure, we choose who gets the new drug and who gets the placebo or usual treatment at random. And to make sure that our assessment of the outcomes and patients' responses is not biased by either the researchers or the patients knowing who got what, both groups are blinded to the random allocation until after the data have been analysed.

This kind of study is the best and is designed to remove doubts as to whether or not a new treatment works at all and/or works better than usual treatment options. Large-scale randomised trials with a big sample of people are better than small ones, because it is statistically less likely that you might miss seeing a true effect purely down to the numbers of people in your trial. If you have results from several small trials there are ways to combine them into what's called a meta-analysis or a systematic review, which effectively makes a big trial; these sorts of evidence synthesis also sit at the top of the hierarchy of evidence.

There are plenty of well-known problems with the randomised controlled trial, not least that is a very artificial set-up and quite often produces results that are hard to replicate in the messy real world. But a bigger problem in medicine, and in public health (and in most social sciences) in particular, is that quite often we simply cannot do this kind of experiment for ethical reasons. For example, we cannot allocate people to take or do things that might be harmful for them, such as encouraging people to smoke cigarettes when we now know it causes lung cancer. And we (usually) cannot, for practical and/or ethical reasons, randomise people to live in a more equal society or a less-deprived neighbourhood, or be paid a higher salary, or live in isolation from social support, in order to understand better the impact of those conditions.

It's not impossible to get experimental evidence of a sort on social policy. There is a famous American experiment from the 1990s called 'Moving to Opportunity'. More than 4,500 poor families with children, living in what Americans call public housing projects and what we would call council estates, volunteered to take part, and were then randomly assigned to three groups. One group got housing vouchers and help to find appropriate housing in an area without high levels of poverty; after one year they could use those housing vouchers to move anywhere they liked. The second group got housing vouchers for any kind of neighbourhood but with no assistance. The third group got nothing beyond the usual entitlement to social security and welfare benefits. Some families moved out of poor neighbourhoods and others didn't. This was a huge and complex study, and it has taken a long time to evaluate all of its impacts.

Families in the first group did end up living in better housing, and in better neighbourhoods, at least in terms of levels of neighbourhood crime. The disruptions and stresses of moving, however, combined with a reduction in social support from family or friends who no longer lived nearby, led to some initial drops in employment. These levelled out, but in the long term there were no positive effects of the experiment on employment or incomes. There were reductions in obesity and mental illness for parents, but in-depth interviews with families who had moved away from poor neighbourhoods found that they hadn't established new 'communities'. Among the children, those who moved before they were teenagers did better than children who didn't move at all; but children who moved when they were already teenagers in fact did worse.

Of course, what was not being 'trialled' here was any intervention to address the root causes of poverty, such as structural inequality or racism, and there was no trial of neighbourhood development or what is sometimes called community wealth-building. Instead, families were being incentivised to exchange one location characterised by poverty, but where they might have deep ties, for another location which was not poor, but where they might have no social support or sense of belonging. Moving to Opportunity has been criticised for naivety in its assumptions and the harm it caused to some, but it is still often cited in textbooks as a rare example of a social policy experiment.[420]

It's a lot easier to think about experimenting on things that sit closer to the outcome in the chain of causation, rather than root causes, and so we tend to have more *experimental* evidence for things like getting people to stop smoking, or for using phonics to teach children to read, or for interventions to reduce violence in prisons, than we do for preventing people from starting to smoke, or ensuring that children from deprived areas are school-ready, or preventing people from becoming criminals.

What we have got is a large body of evidence from just a bit further down the hierarchy of evidence, from *observational* rather than experimental studies. We have a lot of evidence from studies that follow groups of people over time, called cohort studies. In the UK, we have many of these, including studies of large numbers of people who are representative of the country as a whole. Some start at birth – we have national studies of people who were born in 1946, 1958, 1970 and around the turn of the millennium. Some are studies of households and include both adults and children. Some are studies of particular groups of people, like civil servants, or those born in particular places, like the Avon region of South West England, and the city of Bradford in the North. In cohort studies we can measure social conditions at the start and throughout a study and see how they relate to any outcomes that people experience over time, such as getting a particular disease or achieving a particular level of education. In cohort studies like these we can get the causal ordering of things right, and control with statistical methods the differences between different groups of people, in place of randomising them like in a trial. It's not perfect, but it can come close.

We have other kinds of evidence as well. There are studies that compare outcomes in different places, comparing, for example, different countries; this is the kind of data that I've spent a lot of my research career analysing. There are large surveys, sometimes based on randomly selected groups that are representative of populations. There are studies of important cases, and research that asks, in depth, about people's experiences, attitudes and so on. Usually, the evidence that is relevant to a particular issue will come from a large body of research, including studies of different kinds. And careful assessment of that body of research allows experts to infer, rather than prove, causality.

What should we do, then, when we have mostly observational evidence to work with? Emeritus Professor of Global Health at the University of Newcastle Ted Schrecker has thought a lot about standards of proof for making policy. He suggests that we need to think about the difference (the risks and the benefits) between doing something to address a problem when we are wrong about the evidence, and not doing anything because we haven't got strong evidence. And, he argues, this is an ethical issue, one that must be decided upon values, and sometimes in the face of vested interests that are happy to manufacture uncertainty.[421] Think of how tobacco manufacturers spent decades contesting the health damage caused by smoking by casting doubt on the non-experimental observational evidence. The 'precautionary principle' means that we should take action to prevent harm even when scientific evidence is uncertain; lack of scientific certainty shouldn't be used as a reason to delay doing something, as long as that something is unlikely to cause harm. Schrecker quotes Professor Sir Michael Marmot: 'While we should not formulate policies in the absence of evidence to support them, we must not be paralysed into inaction while we wait for the evidence to be absolutely unimpeachable.'[422]

We have a vast library of mostly observational research evidence. This is good news. We can, and should, be using it.

Notes

1. W. Beveridge, *Social Insurance and Allied Services, The Beveridge Report 1942* (Stationery Office, London, 1942).
2. M. Thatcher, 'No Such Thing as Society', interview for *Woman's Own*, Margaret Thatcher Foundation: Speeches, Interviews and Other Statements, Thatcher MSS (Churchill Archive Centre): THCR5/2/262 [COI transcript], London, 1987.
3. Z. Williams, *Get It Together: Why we deserve better politics* (Hutchinson, London, 2015).
4. E. Musk, *The Joe Rogan Experience* (podcast), #2281, 2025.
5. R. G. Wilkinson, 'Income distribution and life expectancy', *BMJ*, 1992;304(6820):165–8.
6. Editor's Choice, 'The big idea', *BMJ*, 1996;312(7037):0.
7. R. Wilkinson, K. Pickett, *The Spirit Level: Why more equal societies almost always do better* (Allen Lane, London, 2009).
8. R. Wilkinson, K. Pickett, *The Inner Level: How more equal societies reduce stress, restore sanity and improve everybody's well-being* (Allen Lane, London, 2018).
9. R. Layte, C. T. Whelan, 'Who feels inferior? A test of the status anxiety hypothesis of social inequalities in health', *European Sociological Review*, 2014;30(4):525–35.
10. K. Pybus, M. Power, K. E. Pickett, et al., 'Income inequality, status consumption and status anxiety: An exploratory review of implications for sustainability and directions for future research', *Social Sciences & Humanities Open*, 2022;6(1):100353. doi: doi.org/10.1016/j.ssaho.2022.100353.
11. R. Wilkinson, K. Pickett, 'From inequality to sustainability', Earth4All: Deep-Dive Paper 01, Winterthur, Switzerland: Club of Rome, 2022.

12. R. G. Wilkinson, K. E. Pickett, 'Why the world cannot afford the rich', *Nature*, 2024;627(8003):268–70.
13. K. E. Pickett, R. G. Wilkinson, 'Income inequality and health: A causal review', *Social Science & Medicine*, 2015;128:316–26.
14. A. Simms, 'Let's play fantasy economics. Things could really get better', *Guardian*, 17 February 2013.
15. L. Fioramonti, E. Giovannini, R. Costanza, et al., 'Say goodbye to capitalism: Welcome to the Republic of Wellbeing', *Guardian*, 2 September 2015.
16. The Report of the Greater Manchester Independent Inequalities Commission, *The Next Level: Good lives for all in Greater Manchester* (Greater Manchester Combined Authority, Manchester, 2021).
17. J. Rawls, *A Theory of Justice* (Harvard University Press, Cambridge, MA, 1971).
18. D. Chandler, *Free and Equal: What would a fair society look like?* (Allen Lane, London, 2023).
19. Miro Aurela, *Veil of Ignorance* (role-playing game): lrdazrl.itch.io/veil-of-ignorance [accessed 2 September 2025].
20. T. Pearce, 'The Thick Of It's creator Armando Iannucci talks creepy show predictions of bizarre policies that have become law', *Metro*, 22 January 2020.
21. Office for National Statistics (ONS), 'National life tables – life expectancy in the UK: 2020 to 2022', released 11 January 2024, ONS website, statistical bulletin.
22. UNICEF, *Child Poverty in the Midst of Wealth* (UNICEF, Innocenti Centre, Florence, Italy, 2023): www.unicef.org/innocenti/media/3296/file/UNICEF-Innocenti-Report-Card-18-Child-Poverty-Amidst-Wealth-2023.pdf [accessed 2 September 2025].
23. University of York Cost of Living Research Group, *Getting the Child Poverty Strategy Right: Key lessons from research evidence for an effective, ambitious approach* (York Policy Engine, York, 2024).
24. 'Pupil absence in schools in England', Department for Education, London, 2025: explore-education-statistics.service.gov.uk/find-statistics/pupil-absence-in-schools-in-england/2024-25-autumn-term [accessed 2 September 2025].

25. The King's Fund, 'Key facts and figures about adult social care', 19 June 2025: www.kingsfund.org.uk/insight-and-analysis/data-and-charts/key-facts-figures-adult-social-care [accessed 2 September 2025].
26. S. Hoddinott, *General Practice Across England* (Institute for Government, London, 2025): www.instituteforgovernment.org.uk/sites/default/files/2025-04/performance-tracker-local-gp-england_2.pdf [accessed 2 September 2025].
27. A. Darzi, *Independent Investigation of the National Health Service in England* (Department of Health and Social Care, London, 2024).
28. M. Marmot, 'Health Inequalities, Lives Cut Short', press release, Institute for Health Equity, London, 2024: www.instituteofhealthequity.org/in-the-news/press-releases-and-briefings-/health-inequalities-lives-cut-short [accessed 2 September 2025].
29. R. Boyle, D. Eyre, 'Will Scotland be the first to guarantee a minimum income?', *Open Democracy*, 6 November 2024.
30. S. Szreter, 'Rethinking McKeown: The relationship between public health and social change', *American Journal of Public Health*, 2002;92(5):722–5. doi: 10.2105/ajph.92.5.722 [published online first: 4 May 2002].
31. N. Cartwright, 'Causation: One word, many things', *Philosophy of Science*, 2004;71(5):805–19. doi: 10.1086/426771 [published online first: 1 January 2022].
32. J. P. Mackenbach, M. H. Bouvier-Colle, E. Jougla, '"Avoidable" mortality and health services: A review of aggregate data studies', *Journal of Epidemiology and Community Health*, 1990;44(2):106–11. doi: 10.1136/jech.44.2.106 [published online first: 1 June 1990].
33. H. Krelle, M. Stafford, F. Cavallaro, et al., 'How do people estimate the contribution health care makes to our health?', Health Foundation, 16 January 2024: www.health.org.uk/news-and-comment/blogs/estimate-contribution-healthcare-to-health [accessed 2 September 2025].
34. K. E. Lasser, D. U. Himmelstein, S. Woolhandler, 'Access to care, health status, and health disparities in the United States and Canada: Results of a cross-national population-based survey',

American Journal of Public Health, 2006;96(7):1300–07. doi: 10.2105/ajph.2004.059402.

35. J. Tudor Hart, 'The inverse care law', *The Lancet*, 1971;297(7696):405–12. doi: 10.1016/S0140-6736(71)92410-X.

36. X. Luta, K. Diernberger, J. Bowden, et al., 'Healthcare trajectories and costs in the last year of life: A retrospective primary care and hospital analysis', *BMJ Supportive & Palliative Care*, 2024;14(e1):e807-e15. doi: 10.1136/bmjspcare-2020-002630.

37. G. Dahlgren, M. Whitehead, *Policies and Strategies to Promote Social Equity in Health* (Institute for Futures Studies, Stockholm, Sweden, 1991).

38. G. Dahlgren, M. Whitehead, 'The Dahlgren-Whitehead model of health determinants: 30 years on and still chasing rainbows', *Public Health*, 2021;199:20–24. doi: https://doi.org/10.1016/j.puhe.2021.08.009.

39. K. E. Smith, M. Kandlik Eltanani, 'What kinds of policies to reduce health inequalities in the UK do researchers support?', *Journal of Public Health*, 2015;37(1):6–17. doi: 10.1093/pubmed/fdu057 [published online first: 1 September 2014].

40. J. Popay, M. Whitehead, D. J. Hunter, 'Injustice is killing people on a large scale – but what is to be done about it?', *Journal of Public Health*, 2010;32(2):148–9. doi: 10.1093/pubmed/fdq029 [published online first: 29 April 2010].

41. K. Pybus, M. Power, K. E. Pickett, '"We are constantly overdrawn, despite not spending money on anything other than bills and food": A mixed-methods, participatory study of food and food insecurity in the context of income inequality', *Journal of Poverty and Social Justice*, 2021;29(1):21–45. doi: 10.1332/175982720X15998354133521.

42. A. McKnight, 'Estimates of the asset-effect: The search for a causal effect of assets on adult health and employment outcomes', Paper Number CASE 149, Centre for Analysis of Social Exclusion, London School of Economics, London, 2011: sticerd.lse.ac.uk/case/_new/publications/abstract/?index=3851 [accessed 2 September 2025].

43. A. Panjwani, 'Child Trust Funds', Research Briefing, House of Commons Library, 15 October 2022: commonslibrary.parliament.

44. S. McKay, L. Tian, A. Lymer, 'Whatever happened to the Child Trust Fund? The abandonment of universal savings for UK children', *Social Policy & Administration*, 2024;58(1):18–38. doi: doi.org/10.1111/spol.12941.
45. K. E. Pickett, R. G. Wilkinson, 'The health costs of political failure', *BMJ*, 2024;384:q379. doi: 10.1136/bmj.q379.
46. A. Page, S. Morrell, R. Taylor, 'Suicide and political regime in New South Wales and Australia during the 20th century', *Journal of Epidemiology & Community Health*, 2002;56(10):766–72.
47. M. Shaw, D. Dorling, G. D. Smith, 'Mortality and political climate: How suicide rates have risen during periods of Conservative government, 1901–2000', *Journal of Epidemiology & Community Health*, 2002;56(10):723–5. doi: 10.1136/jech.56.10.723 [published online first: 20 Septemner 2002].
48. J. Gilligan, *Why Some Politicians Are More Dangerous Than Others* (Polity Press, Cambridge, 2011).
49. J. Winter, *The Great War and the British People* (Palgrave Macmillan, New York, 2003).
50. https://herbalapothecary.co.uk/vitamins/vitamins/executive-b-stress-formula-now-called-unwind.
51. R. Wilkinson. 'Dear David Ennals', *New Society*, London, 1976: sochealth.co.uk/national-health-service/public-health-and-wellbeing/poverty-and-inequality/the-black-report-1980/the-origin-of-the-black-report/dear-david-ennals/ [accessed 2 September 2025].
52. P. Townsend, M. Whitehead, N. Davidson, 'Introduction' in P. Townsend, N. Davidson, M. Whitehead (eds), *Inequalities in Health: The Black Report and The Health Divide* (new third edition, Penguin, London, 1992).
53. P. Townsend, N. Davidson, M. Whitehead (eds), *Inequalities in Health: The Black Report and The Health Divide* (new third edition, Penguin, London, 1992).
54. M. Whitehead, *The Health Divide* (Health Education Council, London, 1987).

55. D. Acheson, *Independent Inquiry into Inequalities in Health Report* (Stationery Office, London, 1998).
56. M. Marmot, J. Allen, P. Goldblatt, T. Boyce, D. McNeish, M. Grady, I. Geddes, *Fair Society, Healthy Lives: The Marmot Review of Health Inequalities* (Institute of Health Equity, London, 2010).
57. M. Marmot, J. Allen, T. Boyce, P. Goldblatt, J. Morrison, *Health Equity in England: The Marmot Review 10 Years On* (Institute of Health Equity, London, 2020): www.health.org.uk/reports-and-analysis/reports/health-equity-in-england-the-marmot-review-10-years-on-0 [accessed 2 September 2025].
58. B. Barr, J. Higgerson, M. Whitehead, 'Investigating the impact of the English health inequalities strategy: Time trend analysis', *BMJ*, 2017;358:j3310. doi: 10.1136/bmj.j3310.
59. R. Tomos, B. Heather, D. N. Paul, et al., 'The impact of New Labour's English health inequalities strategy on geographical inequalities in infant mortality: A time-trend analysis', *Journal of Epidemiology & Community Health*, 2019;73(6):564. doi: 10.1136/jech-2018-211679.
60. H. Graham, S. de Bell, N. Hanley, et al., 'Willingness to pay for policies to reduce future deaths from climate change: Evidence from a British survey', *Public Health*, 2019;174:110–17. doi: doi.org/10.1016/j.puhe.2019.06.001.
61. K. Pickett, D. Taylor-Robinson, et al., *The Child of the North: Building a fairer future after COVID-19* (The Northern Health Science Alliance and N8 Research Partnership, 2021): www.thenhsa.co.uk/app/uploads/2022/01/Child-of-the-North-Report-FINAL-1.pdf.
62. S. Cattan, G. Conti, C. Farquharson, et al., *The Health Effects of Sure Start* (Institute for Fiscal Studies, London, 2019).
63. J. Hayre, H. Pearce, R. Khera, et al., 'Health impacts of the Sure Start programme on disadvantaged children in the UK: A systematic review', *BMJ Open*, 2025;15(2):e089983; doi: 10.1136/bmjopen-2024-089983.
64. S. Cattan, G. Conti, C. Farquharson, R. Ginja, M. Pecher, 'The health effects of universal early childhood interventions: Evidence from Sure Start', Working Paper 22/43, Institute for Fiscal Studies, London, 2022.

65. P. Carneiro, S. Cattan, N. Ridpath, 'The short-and medium-term impacts of Sure Start on educational outcomes' (Institute for Fiscal Studies, London, 2024): ifs.org.uk/publications/short-and-medium-term-impacts-sure-start-educational-outcomes [accessed 2 September 2025].
66. J. Heckman, 'Invest in early childhood development: Reduce deficits, strengthen the economy', Chicago, 2013: heckmanequation.org/wp-content/uploads/2013/07/F_HeckmanDeficitPieceCUSTOM-Generic_052714-3-1.pdf [accessed 2 September 2025].
67. R. Joyce, L. Sibieta, 'Labour's record on poverty and inequality', Institute for Fiscal Studies, London, 2013.
68. D. Taylor-Robinson, M. Whitehead, B. Barr, 'Great leap backwards', *BMJ*, 2014;349:g7350. doi: 10.1136/bmj.g7350.
69. Joseph Rowntree Foundation, 'UK Poverty 2025', York, 2025: www.jrf.org.uk/uk-poverty-2025-the-essential-guide-to-understanding-poverty-in-the-uk [accessed 2 September 2025].
70. OECD, 'Life expectancy at birth (indicator)'. doi: 10.1787/27e0fc9d-en2023 [accessed 30 March 2023].
71. OECD, 'Infant mortality rates (indicator)'. doi: 10.1787/83dea506-en2023 [accessed 30 March 2023].
72. OECD, 'Obesity update 2017': web-archive.oecd.org/2022-02-09/305367-obesity-update.htm [accessed 2 September 2025].
73. OECD, 'National estimates of prevalence of depression or symptoms of depression, 2019–22', 2024: www.oecd.org/en/topics/sub-issues/mental-health.html [accessed 2 September 2025].
74. Office for National Statistics (ONS), 'Coronavirus (COVID-19) latest insights: Deaths 2023': www.ons.gov.uk/peoplepopulationandcommunity/healthandsocialcare/conditionsanddiseases/articles/coronaviruscovid19latestinsights/deaths#deaths-by-vaccination-status [accessed 2 September 2025].
75. D. Taylor-Robinson, B. Barr, 'Death rate now rising in UK's poorest infants', *BMJ*, 2017;357:j2258.
76. D. C. Taylor-Robinson, E. T. Lai, M. Whitehead, et al., 'Child health unravelling in UK', *BMJ*, 2019;364:l963. doi: 10.1136/bmj.l963 [published online first: 7 July 2019].

77. L. Akanni, K. Udu, O. B. Esan, et al., *Infant Mortality in England* (NHSA, Newcastle, 2024).
78. ONS, *Child and Infant Mortality in England and Wales: 2020*, Statistical Bulletin, 2022: www.ons.gov.uk/peoplepopulationand community/birthsdeathsandmarriages/deaths/bulletins/ childhoodinfantandperinatalmortalityinenglandandwales/2020 [accessed 2 September 2025].
79. C. Baker, E. Kirk-Wade, 'Mental health statistics: Prevalence, services and funding in England', Research Briefing, House of Commons Library, 1 March 2024: researchbriefings.files. parliament.uk/documents/SN06988/SN06988.pdf [accessed 2 September 2025].
80. World Health Organization, 'Mental health and COVID-19: Early evidence of the pandemic's impact', Scientific Brief, 2 March 2022: www.who.int/publications/i/item/WHO-2019-nCoV-Sci_Brief-Mental_health-2022.1 [accessed 2 September 2025].
81. G. Iacobucci, 'Covid-19: Pandemic has disproportionately harmed children's mental health, report finds', *BMJ*, 2022;376:o430. doi: 10.1136/bmj.o430.
82. J. L. Ward, A. Vázquez-Vázquez, K. Phillips, et al., 'Admission to acute medical wards for mental health concerns among children and young people in England from 2012 to 2022: A cohort study', *The Lancet Child & Adolescent Health*, 2025;9(2):112–20. doi: 10.1016/ S2352-4642(24)00333-X.
83. A. Jones, K. Abdinasir, *Future Minds: Why investing in children's mental health will unlock economic growth* (Centre for Mental Health, 2025): www.centreformentalhealth.org.uk/publications/future-minds/ [accessed 2 September 2025].
84. OECD, *The Heavy Burden of Obesity*, 2019. doi:doi.org/10.1787/ 67450d67-en.
85. S. Stiebahl, 'Obesity Statistics', Research Briefing, House of Commons Library, 10 February 2025: researchbriefings.files.parliament.uk/ documents/SN03336/SN03336.pdf [accessed 2 September 2025].
86. National Institute for Health and Clinical Excellence, 'Health inequalities briefing: Obesity and weight management (draft for consultation)', NICE, 2023: www.nice.org.uk/guidance/cg189/

documents/health-inequalities-briefing-2 [accessed 2 September 2025].

87. E. J. Howard, *Casting Off* (Macmillan, London, 1995).
88. The Health Foundation, 'Relationship between income and health, 2025': www.health.org.uk/evidence-hub/money-and-resources/income/relationship-between-income-and-health [accessed 2 September 2025].
89. N. J. MacKinnon, V. Emery, J. Waller, et al., 'Mapping health disparities in 11 high-income nations', *JAMA Network Open*, 2023;6(7):e2322310-e10. doi: 10.1001/jamanetworkopen.2023.22310.
90. F. Popham, C. Dibben, C. Bambra, 'Are health inequalities really not the smallest in the Nordic welfare states? A comparison of mortality inequality in 37 countries', *Journal of Epidemiology & Community Health*, 2013;67(5):412–18. doi: 10.1136/jech-2012-201525.
91. D. Nettle, C. Chevallier, B. de Courson, et al., 'Short-term changes in financial situation have immediate mental health consequences: Implications for social policy', *Social Policy & Administration*, 2025;59(2):293–308. doi: doi.org/10.1111/spol.13065.
92. C. Thomas, *The Disease of Disparity: A blueprint to make progress on health inequalities in England* (IPPR, 2021): www.ippr.org/research/publications/disease-of-disparity [accessed 2 September 2025].
93. C. Bambra, K. E. Smith, C. Nwaru, N. Bennett, V. Albani, A. Kingston, A. Todd, F. Matthews, *Targeting Health Inequalities: Realising the potential of targets in reducing health inequalities* (Health Equity North, 2023): www.healthequitynorth.co.uk/app/uploads/TARGETING-HEALTH-INEQUALITIES-REPORT.pdf [accessed 2 September 2025].
94. J. Holt-Lunstad, T. B. Smith, J. B. Layton, 'Social relationships and mortality risk: A meta-analytic review', *PLOS Medicine*, 2010;7(7):e1000316. doi: 10.1371/journal.pmed.1000316 [published online first: 30 July 2010].
95. L. Berkman, T. Glass, 'Social integration, social networks, social support, and health', in L. Berkman, I. Kawachi (eds), *Social Epidemiology* (Oxford University Press, New York, 2000).
96. C. Park, A. Majeed, H. Gill, et al., 'The effect of loneliness on distinct health outcomes: A comprehensive review and

meta-analysis', *Psychiatry Research*, 2020;294:113514. doi: doi.org/10.1016/j.psychres.2020.113514.

97. T. Pettersen, 'The ethics of care: Normative structures and empirical implications', *Health Care Analysis*, 2011;19(1):51–64. doi: 10.1007/s10728-010-0163-7.

98. I. Peng, 'The care economy: A new research framework', 2019: sciencespo.hal.science/hal-03456901v1 [accessed 2 September 2025].

99. M. A. Green, D. Dorling, J. Minton, et al., 'Could the rise in mortality rates since 2015 be explained by changes in the number of delayed discharges of NHS patients?', *Journal of Epidemiology & Community Health*, 2017;71(11):1068–71. doi: 10.1136/jech-2017-209403.

100. D. Campbell, 'England and Wales death rate rise linked to longer stays in hospital', *Guardian*, 2 October 2017.

101. J. Belsky, 'The "effects" of infant day care reconsidered', *Early Childhood Research Quarterly*, 1988;3(3):235–72. doi: doi.org/10.1016/0885-2006(88)90003-8.

102. M. Baker, J. Gruber, K. Milligan, 'Universal child care, maternal labor supply, and family well-being', *Journal of Political Economy*, 2008;116(4):709–45. doi: 10.1086/591908.

103. M. Baker, J. Gruber, K. Milligan, 'The long-run impacts of a universal child care program', *American Economic Journal: Economic Policy*, 2019;11(3):1–26. doi: 10.1257/pol.20170603.

104. C. Rey-Guerra, H. D. Zachrisson, E. Dearing, et al., 'Do more hours in center-based care cause more externalizing problems? A cross-national replication study', *Child Development*, 2023;94(2):458-77. doi: doi.org/10.1111/cdev.13871.

105. NICHD Research Network (eds), *Child Care and Child Development: Results from the NICHD study of early child care and youth development* (Guilford Press, New York, 2005).

106. Z. B. Wolf, 'Trump's rambling answer to a child care question, deconstructed', *CNN*, 6 September 2024.

107. ONS, 'Families and the labour market, UK: 2021 (correction)', ONS, London, 2023.

108. M. Costa Dias, R. Elming, R. Joyce, *The Gender Wage Gap* (Institute for Fiscal Studies, London, 2016).

109. V. Pryce, *Women vs Capitalism* (Hurst & Co., London, 2019).
110. L. Hodges, S. Shorto, E. Goddard, *Childcare Survey 2024* (Coram Family and Childcare, London, 2024).
111. P. Lindley, *Raising the Nation: How to build a better future for our children* (Policy Press, Bristol, 2024).
112. Payscale, 'Average child care / day care worker hourly pay in United Kingdom', 2024: www.payscale.com/research/UK/Job=Child_Care_%2F_Day_Care_Worker/Hourly_Rate [accessed 2 September 2025].
113. N. Hendren, B. Sprung-Keyser, 'A unified welfare analysis of government policies', *The Quarterly Journal of Economics*, 2020;135(3):1209–318. doi: 10.1093/qje/qjaa006.
114. J. Sandher, T. Stephens, 'Investing in universal early years education pays for itself', New Economics Foundation, 18 July 2023.
115. R. Asher, *Shattered: Modern motherhood and the illusion of equality* (Harvill Secker, London, 2011).
116. K. Marçal, *Who Cooked Adam Smith's Dinner?* (Simon & Schuster, London, 2016).
117. H. Chung, 'Shared care, fathers' involvement in care and family wellbeing outcomes: A literature review', Women and Equalities Unit, Government Equalities Office, UK Government, 2021.
118. A. Gromada, D. Richardson, *Where Do Rich Countries Stand on Childcare?* (UNICEF Office of Research, Innocenti, Florence, 2021).
119. C. Cameron, P. E. Moss, *Transforming Early Childhood Education: Towards a democratic education* (UCL Press, London, 2020).
120. 'Official statistics for looked after children in the UK. Children looked after in England including adoptions; Children's Social Work Statistics Scotland; Children looked after by local authorities (Wales); Children's social care statistics for Northern Ireland', England: Department for Education; Scotland: Scottish Government; Wales: Welsh Government; Northern Ireland: Department of Health, 2024.
121. D. L. Bennett, D. K. Schlüter, G. Melis, et al., 'Child poverty and children entering care in England, 2015–2013: A longitudinal ecological study at the local area level', *The Lancet Public Health*, 2022;7(6):e496-e503. doi: 10.1016/S2468-2667(22)00065-2.

122. E. T. Murray, R. Lacey, B. Maughan, et al., 'Non-parental care in childhood and health up to 30 years later: ONS Longitudinal Study 1971–2011', *European Journal of Public Health*, 2020;30(6): 1121–27. doi: 10.1093/eurpub/ckaa113.
123. E. T. Murray, R. Lacey, B. Maughan, et al., 'Association of childhood out-of-home care status with all-cause mortality up to 42-years later: ONS Longitudinal Study', *BMC Public Health*, 2020;20(1):735. doi: 10.1186/s12889-020-08867-3.
124. A. Sacker, R. E. Lacey, B. Maughan, et al., 'Out-of-home care in childhood and socio-economic functioning in adulthood: ONS Longitudinal study 1971–2011', *Children and Youth Services Review*, 2022;132:106300. doi: doi.org/10.1016/j.childyouth.2021.106300.
125. J. Sebba, D. Berridge, N. Luke, et al., 'The Educational Progress of Looked After Children in England: Linking care and educational data', Nuffield Foundation, 2015: www.nuffieldfoundation.org/project/the-educational-progress-of-looked-after-children [accessed 2 September 2025].
126. 'The education of children living in children's homes', Ofsted, London, 17 February 2021: www.gov.uk/government/publications/the-education-of-children-living-in-childrens-homes/the-education-of-children-living-in-childrens-homes [accessed 2 September 2025].
127. R. Wearmouth, 'Children in care repeatedly rejected by academies as admissions "scandal" grows', *HuffPost*, 20 February 2020.
128. K. Hunter, B. Francis, C. Fitzpatrick, *Care Experience, Ethnicity and Youth Justice Involvement: Key trends and policy implications*, Research Report, ADR (Administrative Data Research) UK, September 2023.
129. *All-Party Parliamentary Group for Ending Homelessness: Homelessness prevention for care leavers, prison leavers and survivors of domestic violence* (All-Party Parliamentary Group for Ending Homelessness, July 2017): www.crisis.org.uk/media/237534/appg_for_ending_homelessness_report_2017_pdf.pdf [accessed 2 September 2025].
130. P. Mackie, I. Thomas, *Nations Apart? Experiences of single homeless people across Great Britain* (Crisis, London, 2014).

131. D. Bennett, P. Lee, S. Doebler, et al., *Children in Care in the North of England: A report prepared for the Child of the North All-Party Parliamentary Group* (Health Equity North, Newcastle, 2024).
132. Child Poverty Action Group, *The Cost of a Child in 2024* (Child Poverty Action Group, London, 2024).
133. Independent Review of Children's Social Care, *The Independent Review of Children's Social Care – Final Report* (Department for Education, London, 2022).
134. E. Fincham, *Rising Costs of Caring Risks the Stability of Children and Young People in Care* (Coram, 27 October 2022): corambaaf.org.uk/updates/rising-costs-caring-risks-stability-children-and-young-people-care [accessed 2 September 2025].
135. *FosterTalk Cost of Living Report 2022* (FosterTalk, 2022): fostertalk.org/wp-content/uploads/2022/11/FosterTalk-Cost-of-Living-Report-2022.pdf [accessed 2 September 2025].
136. A. Rome, *Profit Making and Risk in Independent Children's Social Care Placement Providers: 4th Update Report* (Revolution Consuting, September 2023): www.revolution-consulting.org/wp-content/uploads/2023/09/Alt-Profit-Making-and-Risk-in-Independent-Childrens-Social-Care-Placement-Providers-final-2023.pdf [accessed 2 September 2025].
137. Competition and Markets Authority, *Children's Social Care Market Study: Final report* (HM Government, London, 2022).
138. H. Baldwin, N. Biehal, V. Allgar, et al., 'Antenatal risk factors for child maltreatment: Linkage of data from a birth cohort study to child welfare records', *Child Abuse & Neglect*, 2020;107:104605. doi: doi.org/10.1016/j.chiabu.2020.104605.
139. D. W. Rothwell, A. Jud, 'On the relationship between economic inequality and child maltreatment: Takeaways from the special issue and future directions', *Child Abuse & Neglect*, 2022;130:105632. doi: doi.org/10.1016/j.chiabu.2022.105632.
140. L. Zhang, C. Simmel, L. Nepomnyaschy, 'Income inequality and child maltreatment rates in US counties, 2009–2018', *Child Abuse & Neglect*, 2022;130:105328. doi: doi.org/10.1016/j.chiabu.2021.105328.
141. C. J. R. Webb, P. Bywaters, M. Elliott, et al., 'Income inequality and child welfare interventions in England and Wales', *Journal of*

Epidemiology & Community Health, 2021;75(3):251–57. doi: 10.1136/jech-2020-214501.

142. J. Davis, *Adultification Bias Within Child Protection and Safeguarding* (HM Inspectorate of Probation, London, 2022).

143. D. Westlake, S. Holland, M. Sanders, et al., 'The basic income for care leavers in Wales pilot evaluation: Protocol of a quasi-experimental evaluation', *PLOS One*, 2024;19(10):e0303837: https://doi.org/10.1371/journal.pone.37.

144. S. Holland, D. Westlake, L. Roberts, et al., 'Basic income for care leavers in Wales pilot evaluation: Annual report, 2023 to 2024', GSR report number 12/2024, Welsh Government, Cardiff, 2024.

145. J. Cribb, J. Karjalainen, T. Waters, *Living Standards of Working-Age Disability Benefits Recipients in the UK* (Institute for Fiscal Studies, London, 2022).

146. Disability Rights UK, 'Nearly half of families with a disabled child living in poverty', 2024: www.disabilityrightsuk.org/news/nearly-half-families-disabled-child-living-poverty [accessed 2 September 2025].

147. Social Metrics Commission, chaired by P. Stroud, *Measuring Poverty 2023* (Social Metrics Commission, London, 2024).

148. N. Bennett, L. Munford, H. Davies, et al., *Economic Impact of the Proposed Changes to Personal Independence Payments (PIP) by Parliamentary Constituency* (Health Equity North, Newcastle, 2025).

149. Census 2021, 'Outcomes for disabled people in the UK: 2021', ONS, 2022: www.ons.gov.uk/peoplepopulationandcommunity/healthandsocialcare/disability/articles/outcomesfordisabledpeopleintheuk/2021 [accessed 2 September 2025].

150. Public Services Committee, *Think Work First: The transition from education to work for young disabled people* (House of Lords, London, 2024).

151. S. Chatzitheochari, S. Velthuis, R. Connelly, 'Childhood disability, social class and social mobility: A neglected relationship', *The British Journal of Sociology*, 2022;73(5):959–66. doi: https://doi.org/10.1111/1468-4446.12974.

152. ONS, 'Disability and housing, UK: 2019': www.ons.gov.uk/peoplepopulationandcommunity/healthandsocialcare/disability/bulletins/disabilityandhousinguk/2019 [accessed 2 September 2025].
153. Equality and Human Rights Commission, *Housing and Disabled People: Britain's hidden crisis*, 2018: www.equalityhumanrights.com/sites/default/files/housing-and-disabled-people-britains-hidden-crisis-main-report_0.pdf [accessed 2 September 2025].
154. Joseph Rowntree Foundation, *From Disability to Destitution*, 2022: www.jrf.org.uk/deep-poverty-and-destitution/from-disability-to-destitution [accessed 2 September 2025].
155. R. Delaney, Endorsement for E. Kenway, *Who Cares: The hidden crisis of caregiving, and how we solve it* (Wildfire, London, 2023).
156. ONS, 'Leading causes of death, UK: 2001 to 2018', 2020: www.ons.gov.uk/peoplepopulationandcommunity/healthandsocialcare/causesofdeath/articles/leadingcausesofdeathuk/2001to2018 [accessed 2 September 2025].
157. 'Adult social care in England, monthly statistics: March 2024', Department of Health and Social Care: www.gov.uk/government/statistics/adult-social-care-in-england-monthly-statistics-march-2024/adult-social-care-in-england-monthly-statistics-march-2024 [accessed 2 September 2025].
158. The King's Fund, 'Social care 360', 21 May 2025: www.kingsfund.org.uk/insight-and-analysis/long-reads/social-care-360-access [accessed 2 September 2025].
159. PolicyBee, 'UK domiciliary care statistics 2024': www.policybee.co.uk/blog/domiciliary-care-statistics [accessed 2 September 2025].
160. Carers UK, 'Key facts and figures about caring': www.carersuk.org/policy-and-research/key-facts-and-figures/ [accessed December 2024].
161. Age UK, *State of Health and Care of Older People in England 2024*: www.ageuk.org.uk/discover/2024/september/state-of-health-and-care-of-older-people-in-england-2024/ [accessed 2 September 2025].
162. Centre for Ageing Better, 'Our ageing population: The state of ageing 2023–24': ageing-better.org.uk/our-ageing-population-state-ageing-2023-4 [accessed 2 September 2025].

163. WHO, 'Ageing and health', 1 October 2024: www.who.int/newsroom/fact-sheets/detail/ageing-and-health [accessed 2 September 2025].
164. C. Bambra, H. Davies, L. Munford, et al., *Woman of the North: Inequality, health and work* (Health Equity North, Newcastle, 2024).
165. R. Booth, '"How would you like to be in this dump?": Families' horror at privately run UK care homes', *Guardian*, 23 March 2023.
166. S. Himmelweit, 'Reforming social care through a care-led recovery', in P. Allen, S. J. Konzelmann, J. Toporowski (eds), *The Return of the State: Restructuring Britain for the common good* (Agenda Publishing, Newcastle, 2021).
167. G. Standing, 'Care and the pandemic: A comment in reply to Sue Himmelweit', Progressive Economy Forum, 2021: progressiveeconomyforum.com/blog/care-and-the-pandemic-a-comment-in-reply-to-sue-himmelweit/ [accessed 2 September 2025].
168. F. Tobi, J. Harris, 'Social care sector faces collapse as NICs and wage rises loom, providers warn', *Guardian*, 20 March 2025.
169. N. Curry, C. Lobont, N. Hemmings, 'Will the Autumn Budget push the social care sector beyond breaking point?', Nuffield Trust, 2024: www.nuffieldtrust.org.uk/news-item/will-the-autumn-budget-push-the-social-care-sector-beyond-breaking-point [accessed 2 September 2025].
170. I. L. C. Connon, *Literature Review of International Models of Social Care: Lessons for social care delivery, sustainability and funding in Scotland* (Scottish Parliament, Edinburgh, 2022).
171. D. Wanless, J. Forder, J.-L. Fernández, et al., *Wanless Social Care Review: Securing good care for older people, taking a long-term view* (King's Fund, London, 2006).
172. Boris Johnson's first speech as Prime Minister, 24 July 2019: www.gov.uk/government/speeches/boris-johnsons-first-speech-as-prime-minister-24-july-2019 [accessed 2 September 2025].
173. S. Kinnock, W. Streeting, 'New reforms and independent commission to transform social care', Department of Health and Social Care, 3 January 2025: www.gov.uk/government/news/new-reforms-and-independent-commission-to-transform-social-care [accessed 2 September 2025].

174. S. Bedford, D. Button, *Universal Quality Social Care: Transforming adult social care in England* (New Economics Foundation and Women's Budget Group, 2022): www.wbg.org.uk/publication/universal-quality-social-care/ [accessed 2 September 2025].
175. E. Kenway, *Who Cares? The hidden crisis of caregiving and how we solve it* (Wildfire, London, 2023).
176. H. Cottam, *Radical Help: How we can remake the relationships between us and revolutionise the welfare state* (Virago, London, 2019).
177. A. Glass, 'Aging in a community of mutual support: The emergence of an elder intentional cohousing community in the United States', *Journal of Housing for the Elderly*, 2009;23:283–303. doi: 10.1080/02763890903326970.
178. H. Cottam, *A Radical New Vision for Social Care: How to reimagine and redesign support systems for this century* (REAL Centre, the Health Foundation, London, 2021).
179. Local Government Association, 'Economic Case for Local Investment in Carer Support', 2015: www.local.gov.uk/sites/default/files/documents/economic-case-investment--7a4.pdf [accessed 2 September 2025].
180. M. C. Nussbaum, *Creating Capabilities: The human development approach* (Harvard University Press, Cambridge, MA, 2011).
181. U. Bronfenbrenner, P. A. Morris, 'The Bioecological Model of Human Development', in R. M. Lerner (ed.), *Handbook of Child Psychology* (John Wiley & Sons, Hoboken, 1998).
182. World Economic Forum, *The Global Social Mobility Report 2020: Equality, opportunity and a new economic imperative – platform for shaping the future of the new economy and society* (World Economic Forum, Geneva, 2020).
183. www.oecd.org/en/about/programmes/pisa/pisa-test.html.
184. OECD, *PISA 2022 Results (Vol. I): The state of learning and equity in education* (PISA, OECD Publishing, Paris, 2023).
185. P. Givord, 'How age at school entry affects future educational and socioemotional outcomes: Evidence from Pisa', 2024, available

at SSRN: ssrncom/abstract=4954708 and dxdoiorg/102139/ssrn4954708.
186. Q. Du, H. Gao, M. D. Levi, 'The relative-age effect and career success: Evidence from corporate CEOs', *Economics Letters*, 2012;117(3):660–62.
187. D. Muller, L. Page, 'Born Leaders: Political selection and the relative age effect in the US Congress', *Journal of the Royal Statistical Society Series A: Statistics in Society*, 2016;179(3):809–29.
188. I. A. G. Wilkinson, R. J. Hamilton, 'Learning to read in composite (multigrade) classes in New Zealand: Teachers make the difference', *Teaching and Teacher Education*, 2003;19(2):221–35. doi: doi.org/10.1016/S0742-051X(02)00105-1.
189. Z. Cronin, 'To mix or not to mix: A critical review of literature on mixed-age groups in primary schools', *Cambridge Open-Review Educational Research e-Journal*, 2019;6:165–79.
190. C. Berry, 'Mixed age classes in urban primary schools: Perceptions of headteachers', *Institute of Education*, University of London, 2018:1–13.
191. T. J. VanderWeele, 'Meaning in Life and Human Flourishing', *Psychology Today*, 26 February 2025: www.psychologytoday.com/intl/blog/human-flourishing/202502/meaning-in-life-and-human-flourishing [accessed 2 September 2025].
192. D. Chollet, A. Turner, J. Marquez, et al., *The Good Childhood Report 2024* (Children's Society, London, 2024).
193. The Children's Society, *The Good Childhood Report 2024: Youth summary* (Children's Society, London, 2024).
194. Common Sense Policy Group, 'A Fairer Education System', in Common Sense Policy Group (ed.), *Act Now: A vision for a better future and a new social contract* (Manchester University Press, Manchester, 2024).
195. Comptroller and Auditor General, *Ofsted's Inspection of Schools* (National Audit Office, London, 2018).
196. 'Child of the North 2024/2025 Campaign report series: A country that works for all children and young people': www.n8research.org.uk/research-focus/child-of-the-north/2024-campaign/ [accessed 2 September 2025].

197. R. Alexander, *Children, Their World, Their Education: Final report and recommendations of the Cambridge Primary Review* (Routledge, Abingdon, 2010).
198. R. Alexander, *Education in Spite of Policy* (Routledge, Abingdon, 2022).
199. D. Greatbatch, S. Tate, *School Improvement Systems in High Performing Countries* (Department for Education, London, 2019).
200. A. Fazackerley, 'Teachers at top academy in Hackney "screamed at" and humiliated pupils, say angry parents', *Guardian*, 23 November 2024.
201. A. Fazackerley, '"Pupils are in fear every day": Parents raise concerns about new schools run by top UK academy', *Guardian*, 2 February 2025.
202. L. Quick, 'The threat of three-fold failure: "Low attainers" in English primary schools', *British Journal of Sociology of Education*, 2024;45(4):639–54. doi: 10.1080/01425692.2024.2351863.
203. J. Owens, T. de St Croix, 'Engines of social mobility? Navigating meritocratic education discourse in an unequal society', *British Journal of Educational Studies*, 2020;68(4):403–24.
204. L. Quick, *Bottom of the Class* (Routledge, Abingdon, 2025).
205. K. Brown, A. Crawford, C. Lloyd, D. Birks, N. Capstick, M. Wood, et al., *A Country That Works for All Children and Young People: An evidence-based plan for addressing childhood vulnerability, crime and justice* (Child of the North & the Centre for Young Lives, 2024): eprints.whiterose.ac.uk/id/eprint/221068/ [accessed 2 September 2025].
206. T. M. F. Newlove-Delgado, T. Williams, D. Mandalia, J. Davis, S. McManus, M. Savic, W. Treloar, T. Ford, *Mental Health of Children and Young People in England, 2022* (NHS Digital, Leeds, 2022).
207. K. J. Lester, D. Michelson, 'Perfect storm: Emotionally based school avoidance in the post-COVID-19 pandemic context', *BMJ Mental Health*, 2024;27(1):e300944. doi: 10.1136/bmjment-2023-300944.
208. E. Sonuga-Barke, P. Fearon, 'Editorial: Do lockdowns scar? Three putative mechanisms through which COVID-19 mitigation policies could cause long-term harm to young people's mental

health', *Journal of Child Psychology and Psychiatry*, 2021;62(12): 1375–78. doi: doi.org/10.1111/jcpp.13537.

209. T. M. F. Newlove-Delgado, T. Williams, D. Mandalia, M. Dennes, S. McManus, M. Savic, W. Treloar, K. Croft, T. Ford, *Mental Health of Children and Young People in England, 2023* (NHS Digital, Leeds, 2023).

210. C. Bond, L. Munford, D. Birks, O. Shobande, S. Denny, S. Hatton-Corcoran, P. Qualter, M. L. Wood, et al., *A Country That Works for All Children and Young People: An evidence-based plan for improving school attendance*, Child of the North, 2024: www.n8research.org.uk/media/CotN_Attendance_Report_10.pdf [accessed 2 September 2025].

211. 'Suspensions and permanent exclusions in England', Department for Education, 2024: explore-education-statistics.service.gov.uk/find-statistics/suspensions-and-permanent-exclusions-in-england/2022-23 [accessed 2 September 2025].

212. Department for Education, *Timpson Review of School Exclusion* (HM Stationery Office, London, 2019).

213. T. Greany, R. Higham, *Hierarchy, Markets and Networks: Analysing the 'self-improving school-led system' agenda in England and the implications for schools* (Institute of Education Press, UCL, London, 2018).

214. S. Farouk, S. Edwards, 'Narrative counselling for adolescents at risk of exclusion from school', *British Journal of Guidance & Counselling*, 2021;49(4):553–64. doi: 10.1080/03069885.2020.1729342.

215. M. Gove, 'Oral evidence taken before the Education Committee: The responsibilities of the Secretary of State for Education', Questions 98–100, Hansard, London, 31 January 2012.

216. International Association for the Evaluation of Educational Achievement, 2024 (all PIRLS and TIMSS reports can be downloaded at: www.iea.nl/) [accessed March 2024].

217. G. Rikowski, 'Why employers can't ever get what they want. In fact, they can't even get what they need', *Fast Company*, 2000;32:82.

218. ACS International Schools and the IB Schools and Colleges Association (IBSCA), *The Future Skills Report: Education for a World of Opportunity*, London, 2023: www.ibsca.org.uk/publications [accessed 2 September 2025].

219. A. Bennett, 'World at One at 50 – celebrating Britain's best', *World at One*, BBC Radio 4, 2 March 2015.
220. T. Piketty, *A Brief History of Equality* (Harvard University Press, Cambridge, MA, 2022).
221. H. Evennett, 'King's Speech 2024: Education', House of Lords Library Briefing, 12 July 2024: researchbriefings.files.parliament.uk/documents/LLN-2024-0033/LLN-2024-0033.pdf [accessed 2 September 2025].
222. A. Reeves, S. Friedman, *Born to Rule: The making and remaking of the British elite* (Harvard University Press, Cambridge, MA, 2024).
223. S. Schagen, I. Schagen, *The Impact of the Structure of Secondary Education in Slough* (National Foundation for Education Research, London, 2001).
224. S. Burgess, E. Greaves, A. Vignoles, et al., 'What Parents Want: School preferences and school choice', *The Economic Journal*, 2014;125(587):1262–89. doi: 10.1111/ecoj.12153.
225. S. Burgess, E. Greaves, A. Vignoles, *School Places: A Fair Choice? School choice, inequality and options for reform of school admissions in England* (Sutton Trust, London, 2020).
226. C. Farquharson, S. McNally, I. Tahir, 'Education inequalities', *Oxford Open Economics*, 2024;3(Supplement_1):i760–i820. doi: 10.1093/ooec/odad029.
227. S. Tuckett, D. Robinson, E. Hunt, et al., *Annual Report* (Education Policy Institute, London, 2024).
228. National Audit Office, *Support for Pupils with Special Educational Needs and Disabilities in England*, 2019: www.nao.org.uk/reports/support-for-pupils-with-special-educational-needs-and-disabilities/ [accessed 2 September 2025].
229. Education Policy Institute and Nuffield Foundation, *Identifying Pupils with Special Educational Needs and Disabilities*, 2021: epi.org.uk/wp-content/uploads/2021/03/SEND-Indentification_2021-EPI.pdf [accessed 2 September 2025].
230. Ofsted and the Care Quality Commission, *Joint Area SEND Inspection in Kirklees*, 2022: files.ofsted.gov.uk/v1/file/50185451 [accessed 2 September 2025].

231. P. Butler, M. Pearce, R. Boyd, 'Ministers plan major changes to Send education in England', *Guardian*, 3 March 2025.
232. M. Benn, *Life Lessons: The case for a National Education Service* (Verso, London, 2018).
233. M. Mon-Williams, M. Wood, D. Taylor-Robinson, *Addressing Education and Health Inequity: Perspectives from the North of England*, A report prepared for the Child of the North APPG (NHSA, Newcastle, 2023).
234. J. García, J. Heckman, D. Leaf, et al., 'Quantifying the life-cycle benefits of a prototypical early childhood program', NBER working paper series (Cambridge, MA, National Bureau of Economic Research, 2017).
235. C. Jeffery, 'It is only because of the international student fee income that we can afford to teach home students', *Yorkshire Post*, 13 April 2024.
236. R. Taylor, 'Higher education: Contribution to the economy and levelling up', *In Focus*, House of Lords Library, 2024: https://lordslibrary.parliament.uk/higher-education-contribution-to-the-economy-and-levelling-up/ [accessed 2 September 2025].
237. R. Adams, 'University courses in creative arts face new funding cuts', *Guardian*, 5 April 2024.
238. E. Holt-White, D. O'Brien, O. Brook, et al., *A Class Act: Social mobility and the creative industries* (Sutton Trust, London, 2024).
239. L. Bakare, 'David Shrigley urges schools to prioritise arts – with aid of giant mantis', *Guardian*, 28 October 2024.
240. D. Reay, 'Schooling for Democracy: A common school and a common university? A response to "Schooling for Democracy"', *Democracy and Education*, 2011;19(1):1–4.
241. D. Reay, 'What would a socially just education system look like? Saving the minnows from the pike', *Journal of Education Policy*, 2012;27(5):587–99. doi: 10.1080/02680939.2012.710015.
242. D. Reay, *Miseducation: Inequality, education and the working classes* (second edition, Policy Press, Bristol, 2025).
243. Centre for Young Lives, *Too Skint for School: Breaking the link between poverty and attendance*, 2024: www.centreforyounglives.org.uk/news-centre/

centre-for-young-lives-report-warns-poverty-and-hardship-are-preventing-some-children-from-attending-school-amid-big-increases-in-persistent-and-severe-absence-among-children-receiving-free-school-meals [accessed 2 September 2025].
244. A. J. E. Barnes, C. J. Snell, A. Bailey, et al., *Child Poverty and the Cost of Living Crisis: A report prepared for the APPG Child of the North* (NHSA, Newcastle, 2023).
245. M. Obama, Comments on visiting Mulberry School for Girls, 2015: www.mulberryschoolforgirls.org/ [accessed 2 September 2025].
246. M. Chase, 'York Castle and Its Political Prisoners: The Luddites in a broader context', Huddersfield Local History Society, 2009: www.huddersfieldhistory.org.uk/wp-content/uploads/2009/02/Political-prisoners-in-York-Castle-Malcolm-Chase.pdf [accessed 2 September 2025].
247. R. Foster, 'A former prisoner reveals what everyday life was like in prison', *Metro*, 29 May 2017.
248. Ministry of Justice, 'Prison education and accredited programme statistics 2022–2023', Official Statistics, 2024: www.gov.uk/government/statistics/prison-education-and-accredited-programme-statistics-2022-to-2023/prison-education-and-accredited-programme-statistics-2022-2023 [accessed 2 September 2025].
249. R. Epstein, 'Mothers in prison: The sentencing of mothers and the rights of the child', Howard League What is Justice? Working Papers 3/2014, Howard League for Penal Reform, London, 2014.
250. His Majesty's Inspectorate of Prisons, *Children in Custody 2022–23*, 2023: www.justiceinspectorates.gov.uk/hmiprisons/inspections/children-in-custody-2022-23/ [accessed 2 September 2025].
251. J. Muncie, 'The "punitive turn" in juvenile justice: Cultures of control and rights compliance in Western Europe and the USA', *Youth Justice*, 2008;8(2):107–21 doi: 10.1177/1473225408091372.
252. D. Taylor, 'Germany refuses to extradite man to UK over concerns about British jail conditions', *Guardian*, 5 September 2023.
253. M. Boone, F. Pakes, S. van Wingerden, 'Explaining the collapse of the prison population in the Netherlands: Testing the theories', *European Journal of Criminology*, 2022;19(4):488–505. doi: 10.1177/1477370819896220.

254. H. Pidd, 'Two-thirds of prisons officially overcrowded in England and Wales', *Guardian*, 15 October 2023.
255. M. Savage, 'Three-quarters of prisons in England and Wales in appalling conditions as overcrowding fears grow', *Observer*, 5 August 2023.
256. K. Ingala Smith, C. O'Callaghan, K. Elliott, et al., *2000 Women*, femicidecensus.org, 2025.
257. ONS, 'Domestic abuse in England and Wales overview: November 2024', Statistical Bulletin, 2024: www.ons.gov.uk/peoplepopulationandcommunity/crimeandjustice/bulletins/domesticabuseinenglandandwalesoverview/november2024 [accessed 2 September 2025].
258. Eyewitness Travel, *Mexico* (Dorling Kindersley, London, 2012).
259. M. Daly, *Killing the Competition: Economic inequality and homicide* (Routledge, New Brunswick, NJ, 2017).
260. The Data Team, 'The stark relationship between income inequality and crime', *The Economist*, 7 June 2018: www.economist.com/graphic-detail/2018/06/07/the-stark-relationship-between-income-inequality-and-crime [accessed 2 September 2025].
261. A. Blumstein, A. J. Beck, 'Population growth in US prisons, 1980–1996', *Crime and Justice*, 1999;26:17–61.
262. F. Pakes, 'The Shallow End: Understanding the prisoner experience in Iceland's open prisons', *Incarceration*, 2023;4:26326663231160343. doi: 10.1177/26326663231160343.
263. Scandinavian Prison Project, 'The Research': scandinavianprisonproject.com/research [accessed 2 September 2025].
264. G. Sturge, 'UK Prison Population Statistics', Research Briefing, House of Commons Library, 8 July 2023: commonslibrary.parliament.uk/research-briefings/sn04334/ [accessed 2 September 2025].
265. Editorial, 'Why British police should focus on victims', *The Economist*, 15 February 2024.
266. Editorial, 'The curious case of the fall in crime', *The Economist*, 20 July 2013.

267. Prison Reform Trust, *Prison: The facts*, Bromley Briefings (Prison Reform Trust, London, 2023).
268. Ministry of Justice, 'Ethnicity and the Criminal Justice System, 2020', National Statistics, 2021: www.gov.uk/government/statistics/ethnicity-and-the-criminal-justice-system-statistics-2020/ethnicity-and-the-criminal-justice-system-2020 [accessed 2 September 2025].
269. R. Jones, E. Hart, D. Scott, *Chorley 'Super Prison': The case against*, Wales Governance Centre, University of Cardiff, Cardiff, 2022.
270. M. Navarro, R. Clare, *Education for Prisoners with Learning Difficulties and/or Disabilities*, Ofsted: Schools and Further Education & Skills (FES), 11 November 2022: educationinspection.blog.gov.uk/2022/11/11/education-for-prisoners-with-learning-difficulties-and-or-disabilities/ [accessed 2 September 2025].
271. HMIP & Ofsted, *Prison Education: A review of reading education in prisons*, 22 March 2022: www.gov.uk/government/publications/prison-education-a-review-of-reading-education-in-prisons/prison-education-a-review-of-reading-education-in-prisons [accessed 2 September 2025].
272. G. Durcan, *The Future of Prison Mental Health Care in England: A national consultation and review*, Centre for Mental Health, 2021: www.centreformentalhealth.org.uk/publications/future-prison-mental-health-care-england/ [accessed 2 September 2025].
273. J. Hillier, A. Mews, 'Do offender characteristics affect the impact of short custodial sentences and court orders on reoffending?', Ministry of Justice, London, 2018.
274. V. Law, *Prisons Make Us Safer: And 20 other myths about mass incarceration* (Beacon Press, Boston, 2021).
275. N. Freudenberg, *Lethal But Legal: Corporations, consumption, and protecting public health* (Oxford University Press, Oxford, 2014).
276. W. K. Black, 'Echo Epidemics: Control frauds generate white-collar street crime waves', UMKC School of Law Institutional Repository, University of Missouri-Kansas City School of Law, 2010: irlaw.umkc.edu/faculty_works/519 [accessed 2 September 2025].

277. K. J. Robinson, 'Savings and Loan Crisis, 1980–1989', Federal Reserve Bank of St. Louis, 2013: www.federalreservehistory.org/essays/savings-and-loan-crisis [accessed 2 September 2025].
278. C. S. Hay, S. Farrall, N. Burke, 'Revisiting Margaret Thatcher's law and order agenda: The slow-burning fuse of punitiveness', *British Politics*, 2016;11(2):205–31.
279. V. Stern, 'Crime policy and the role of punishment', *RSA Journal*, 1993;141(5443):693–705.
280. R. Burnett, S. Maruna, 'So "prison works", does it? The criminal careers of 130 men released from prison under Home Secretary, Michael Howard', *Howard Journal of Criminal Justice*, 2004;43(4):390–404. doi: https://doi.org/10.1111/j.1468-2311.2004.00337.x.
281. G. Lubega, *Lowering the Standard: A review of Behavioural Control Orders in England and Wales* (Justice, London, 2023).
282. K. Clarke, 'The government's vision for criminal justice reform', Centre for Crime and Justice Studies speeches, 2010: www.crimeandjustice.org.uk/governments-vision-criminal-justice-reform.
283. R. Mason, 'Keir Starmer hits out at prison system "mess" caused by Tories', *Guardian*, 6 July 2024.
284. N. Mutebi, R. Brown, 'The use of short prison sentences in England and Wales', POST Brief, Parliamentary Office of Science and Technology (POST), London, 2023.
285. J. Major, 'Speech to the Prison Reform Trust at the Old Bailey, 9 May 2023': prisonreformtrust.org.uk/sir-john-major-we-over-use-prison-and-under-value-alternative-sentences/ [accessed 2 September 2025].
286. V. J. Felitti, 'The relation between adverse childhood experiences and adult health: Turning gold into lead', *Permanente Journal*, 2002;6(1):44–47. doi: 10.7812/tpp/02.994 [published online first: 1 January 2002].
287. A. S. Yoon, H. J. D. Lee, I. Moon, 'Social Determinants of Mental Health', in H. S. Friedman, C. H. Markey (eds), *Encyclopedia of Mental Health* (third edition, Academic Press, Oxford, 2023), pp. 274–85.
288. D. B. Jackson, M. S. Jones, D. C. Semenza, et al., 'Adverse childhood experiences and adolescent delinquency: A theoretically

informed investigation of mediators during middle childhood', *International Journal of Environmental Research and Public Health*, 2023;20(4) doi: 10.3390/ijerph20043202 [published online first: 26 February 2023].

289. B. H. Fox, N. Perez, E. Cass, et al., 'Trauma changes everything: Examining the relationship between adverse childhood experiences and serious, violent and chronic juvenile offenders', *Child Abuse & Neglect*, 2015;46:163–73. doi: doi.org/10.1016/j.chiabu.2015.01.011.

290. Children's Commissioner, 'Childhood vulnerability in England 2019', Children's Commissioner's Office, 2019: www.childrenscommissioner.gov.uk/resource/childhood-vulnerability-in-england-2019/ [accessed 2 September 2025].

291. R. E. Lacey, L. D. Howe, M. Kelly-Irving, et al., 'The clustering of adverse childhood experiences in the Avon Longitudinal Study of parents and children: Are gender and poverty important?', *Journal of Interpersonal Violence*, 2022;37(5–6):2218–41. doi: 10.1177/0886260520935096.

292. A. Karamanos, K. Stewart, S. Harding, et al., 'Adverse childhood experiences and adolescent drug use in the UK: The moderating role of socioeconomic position and ethnicity', *SSM – Population Health*, 2022;19:101142. doi: doi.org/10.1016/j.ssmph.2022.101142.

293. R. M. Johnson, A. V. Hill, V. C. Jones, et al., 'Racial/ethnic inequities in adverse childhood experiences and selected health-related behaviors and problems among Maryland adolescents', *Health Promotion Practice*, 2022;23(6):935–40. doi: 10.1177/15248399211008238.

294. K. Ford, E. R. Barton, A. Newbury, et al., *Understanding the Prevalence of Adverse Childhood Experiences (ACEs) in a Male Offender Population in Wales: The Prisoner ACE Survey* (World Health Organization Collaborating Centre on Investment for Health and Well-being Directorate, Cardiff, 2019).

295. K. Ford, M. A. Bellis, K. Hughes, et al., 'Exploring the intergenerational continuity of ACEs amongst a sample of Welsh male prisoners: A retrospective cross-sectional study', *Child Protection and Practice*, 2024;3:100053. doi: doi.org/10.1016/j.chipro.2024.100053.

296. E. G. Krug, L. L. Dahlberg, J. A. Mercy, et al., *World Report on Violence and Health* (World Health Organization, Geneva, 2002).
297. G. Hassan, *Violence Is Preventable, Not Inevitable: The story and impact of the Scottish Violence Reduction Unit* (Scottish Violence Reduction Unit, Glasgow, 2018).
298. D. J. Williams, D. Currie, W. Linden, et al., 'Addressing gang-related violence in Glasgow: A preliminary pragmatic quasi-experimental evaluation of the Community Initiative to Reduce Violence (CIRV)', *Aggression and Violent Behavior*, 2014;19(6):686–91. doi: doi.org/10.1016/j.avb.2014.09.011.
299. Prison Reform Trust, *The Woolf Report: A summary of the main findings and recommendations of the inquiry into prison disturbances*, 1991: https://prisonreformtrust.org.uk/wp-content/uploads/1991/02/Woolf-report-summary-of-findings.pdf.
300. D. Scott, 'Remembering and Forgetting the Woolf Report: Comment', Centre for Crime and Justice Studies, London, 2020.
301. M. Day, A. Hewson, C. Spirpoulos, *Strangeways 25 Years On: Achieving fairness and justice in our prisons* (Prison Reform Trust, London, 2015).
302. Special edition on 'Evidence-based practice', *Prison Service Journal*, 2024;271: www.crimeandjustice.org.uk/publications/psj/prison-service-journal-271 [accessed 2 September 2025].
303. Prison Reform Trust, 'Written response to the Prisons Strategy White Paper', 2022: prisonreformtrust.org.uk/wp-content/uploads/2022/02/Prisons-Strategy-White-Paper-PRT-response.pdf [accessed 2 September 2025].
304. J. Turner, H. Johnston, 'Female prisoners, aftercare and release: Residential provision and support in late nineteenth-century England', *British Journal of Community Justice*, 2015;13:35–50.
305. A. Gregory, '"Cell, street, repeat": Thousands of prisoners being set up to fail with release into homelessness', *Independent*, 28 December 2023.
306. Special edition on 'Rehabilitative Culture', *Prison Service Journal*, 2019;244: www.crimeandjustice.org.uk/publications/psj/prison-service-journal-244 [accessed 2 September 2025].

307. R. E. Mann, 'Rehabilitative cuture part 2: An update on evidence and practice', *Prison Service Journal*, 2019;244:3–10.
308. D. Gauke, 'Beyond prison, redefining punishment', speech to Ministry of Justice, London, 18 February 2019.
309. UK Government, 'Independent Sentencing Review: Final report and proposals for reform', 2025: www.gov.uk/government/publications/independent-sentencing-review-final-report [accessed 2 September 2025].
310. H. Mills, '"Stopping short?" Sentencing reform and short prison sentences', UK Justice Policy Review Focus, Centre for Crime and Justice Studies, London, 2019.
311. E. Courea, 'Labour to abolish most short prison sentences in England and Wales', *Guardian*, 24 August 2025.
312. H. Pidd, 'Jail cells without toilets persist in England despite "slopping out" law', *Guardian*, 25 October 2023.
313. *The Lammy Review: An independent review into the treatment of, and outcomes for, Black, Asian and Minority Ethnic individuals in the Criminal Justice System* (London, 2017): www.gov.uk/government/publications/lammy-review-final-report [accessed 2 September 2025].
314. D. Etherington, M. Gray, L. Buckner, *Still Digging Deeper: The impact of austerity on inequalities and deprivation in the coalfield areas* (University of Staffordshire, Stoke-on-Trent, 2025).
315. M. Fisher, *Capitalist Realism: Is there no alternative?* (Zero Books, Winchester, 2009).
316. D. Graeber, 'Against Economics', *The New York Review of Books*, 5 December 2019.
317. R. Costanza, 'To build a better world, stop chasing economic growth', *Nature*, 2023;624(7992):519–21.
318. K. Pickett, 'Forget about GDP: It's time for a wellbeing economy', *Open Democracy*, 18 March 2018.
319. R. Costanza, I. Kubiszewski, E. Giovannini, et al., 'Development: Time to leave GDP behind', *Nature*, 2014;505(7483):283–85. doi: 10.1038/505283a.
320. L. Fioramonti, *The World After GDP* (Polity Press, Cambridge, 2017).

321. D. Pilling, *The Growth Delusion: The wealth and well-being of nations* (Bloomsbury, London, 2019).
322. J. Blewitt, R. Cunningham, *The Post-Growth Project: How the end of economic growth could bring a fairer and happier society* (Green House, London, 2014).
323. H. E. Daly, *Beyond Growth: The economics of sustainable development* (Beacon Press, Boston, 2014).
324. T. Jackson, *Prosperity Without Growth: Economics for a finite planet* (Routledge, Abingdon, 2009).
325. N. Klein, *This Changes Everything: Capitalism vs. the climate* (Allen Lane, London, 2014).
326. R. F. Kennedy, 'Remarks at the University of Kansas, March 18, 1968', Robert F. Kennedy Speeches (John F. Kennedy Library and Museum, 1968).
327. R. Costanza, L. Daly, L. Fioramonti, et al., 'Modelling and measuring sustainable wellbeing in connection with the UN Sustainable Development Goals', *Ecological Economics*, 2016;130:350–55. doi: doi.org/10.1016/j.ecolecon.2016.07.009.
328. K. Ura, S. Alkire, K. Wangdi, T. Zangmo, *GNH 2022* (Centre for Bhutan and GNH Studies, Thimphu, 2023).
329. D. Pillay, 'Happiness, wellbeing and ecosocialism – A radical humanist perspective', *Globalizations*, 2019;17:380–96. doi: 10.1080/14747731.2019.1652470.
330. Wellbeing Economy Alliance: weall.org/wego. [accessed 2 September 2025].
331. D. H. Meadows, J. Randers, D. L. Meadows, *The Limits to Growth* (Club of Rome, Geneva, 1972).
332. G. Herrington, 'The Limits to Growth model: Still prescient 50 years later', Earth4All Deep Dive Paper, Club of Rome, Geneva, 2022.
333. G. Herrington, 'Update to limits to growth: Comparing the World3 model with empirical data', *Journal of Industrial Ecology*, 2021;25(3):614–26. doi: doi.org/10.1111/jiec.13084.
334. S. D. Levitt, S. J. Dubner, *Freakonomics* (Penguin, London, 2006).
335. K. Jensen, J. Call, M. Tomasello, 'Chimpanzees are rational maximisers in an ultimatum game', *Science*, 2007;318(5847):107–9.

336. A. Sánchez-Amaro, F. Rossano, 'Chimpanzees and bonobos use social leverage in an ultimatum game', *Proceedings of the Royal Society B: Biological Sciences*, 2021;288(1962):20211937. doi: doi:10.1098/rspb.2021.1937.
337. E. Fehr, U. Fischbacher, 'The nature of human altruism', *Nature*, 2003;425(6960):785–91. doi: 10.1038/nature02043.
338. J. B. Silk, B. R. House, 'Evolutionary Foundations of Human Prosocial Sentiments', in J. E. Strassman, D. C. Queller, J. C. Avise, F. J. Ayala, et al. (eds), *In the Light of Evolution: Volume V: Cooperation and Conflict* (National Academies Press, Washington, DC, 2011).
339. E. Walker, 'Symbolic Violence in Neoliberalism', in M. Wheeler (ed.), *Emptywheel*, 2018: www.emptywheel.net/2018/01/20/symbolic-violence-in-neoliberalism/ [accessed 2 September 2025].
340. K. Raworth, *Doughnut Economics: Seven ways to think like a 21st-century economist* (Penguin, London, 2022); https://doughnuteconomics.org/tools/the-evolving-doughnut [accessed 5 November 2025].
341. J. Rockström, W. Steffen, K. Noone, et al., 'A safe operating space for humanity', *Nature*, 2009;461(7263):472–75. doi: 10.1038/461472a.
342. W. Steffen, K. Richardson, J. Rockström, et al., 'Planetary boundaries: Guiding human development on a changing planet', *Science*, 2015;347(6223):1259855. doi: doi:10.1126/science.1259855.
343. K. Richardson, W. Steffen, W. Lucht, et al., 'Earth beyond six of nine planetary boundaries', *Science Advances*, 2023;9(37):eadh2458. doi: 10.1126/sciadv.adh2458.
344. Confluences asbi, 'Downscaling the Donut at 4 levels in Brussels', Doughnut Economics, 30 March 2021: doughnuteconomics.org/stories/downscaling-the-donut-at-4-levels-in-brussels [accessed 2 September 2025].
345. J. O. Kenter, S. Martino, S. J. Buckton, et al., 'Ten principles for transforming economics in a time of global crises', *Nature Sustainability*, 2025;8:837–47. doi: 10.1038/s41893-025-01562-4.
346. S. J. Buckton, University of York, drawn from: J. O. Kenter, S. Martino, S. J. Buckton, et al., 'Ten principles for transforming economics in a time of global crises', *Nature Sustainability*, 2025;8:837–47.

347. J. Aked, N. Marks, C. Cordon, et al., *Five Ways to Wellbeing* (New Economics Foundation, London, 2008).
348. H-J. Chang, *23 Things They Don't Tell You About Capitalism* (Allen Lane, London, 2010).
349. 'Circular economy in practice: Case studies and company examples', 18 October 2021: www.ellenmacarthurfoundation.org/topics/circular-economy-introduction/examples [accessed 2 September 2025].
350. J. Pretty, D. Garrity, H. K. Badola, et al., 'How the concept of "Regenerative Good Growth" could help increase public and policy engagement and speed transitions to net zero and nature recovery', *Sustainability*, 2025;17(3):849.
351. F. Cortez, *Homo Integralis: A new possible history for humanity* (Leya, São Paulo, 2022).
352. E. Ostrom, *Governing the Commons: The evolution of institutions for collective action* (Cambridge University Press, Cambridge, 1990).
353. E. Ostrom, 'A general framework for analyzing sustainability of social-ecological systems', *Science*, 2009;325(5939):419–22. doi: doi:10.1126/science.1172133.
354. D. N. F. Roe, C. Sandbrook (eds), *Community Management of Natural Resources in Africa: Impacts, experiences and future directions* (Natural Resource Issues, International Institute for Environment and Development, London, 2009).
355. B. J. Thorsen, N. Strange, J. B. Jacobsen, M. Termansen, T. Lundhede, 'Auction Mechanisms for Setting Aside Forest for Biodiversity', IFRO Report, No. 267, University of Copenhagen, Copenhagen, 2018: static-curis.ku.dk/portal/files/194648689/IFRO_Report_267.pdf [accessed 2 September 2025].
356. M. Palahí, M. Pantsar, R. Costanza, et al., *Investing in Nature as the True Engine of Our Economy: A 10-point action plan for a circular bioeconomy of wellbeing* (European Forest Institute, 2020): efi.int/sites/default/files/files/publication-bank/2020/EFI_K2A_02_2020.pdf [accessed 2 September 2025].
357. G. Standing, *Plunder of the Commons: A manifesto for sharing public wealth* (Penguin, London, 2019).

358. G. Standing, *The Blue Commons: Rescuing the economy of the sea* (Penguin, London, 2022).
359. S. J. Buckton, J. O. Kenter, N. Mukherjee, et al., 'Reform or transform? A spectrum of stances towards the economic status quo within "new economics" discourses', *Global Social Challenges Journal*, 2024;3(3):382–421. doi: 10.1332/27523349y2024d000000025.
360. S. Dixson-Declève, O. Gaffney, J. Ghosh, et al., *Earth for All: A survival guide for humanity* (New Society Publishers, Gabriola Island, BC, 2022).
361. M. W. Doyle, J. E. Stiglitz, 'Eliminating extreme inequality: A Sustainable Development Goal, 2015–2030', *Ethics and International Affairs*, 2014;28(1):5–13.
362. Common Sense Policy Group, 'A Green New Deal', in Common Sense Policy Group (ed.), *Act Now: A vision for a better future and a new social contract* (Manchester University Press, Manchester, 2024).
363. D. Orrell, *Economyths: Ten ways economics gets it wrong* (Icon Books, London, 2010).
364. M. J. Sandel, *What Money Can't Buy: The moral limits of markets* (Farrar, Straus and Giroux, New York, NY, 2012).
365. M. Johnson, K. Pickett, D. Nettle, et al., *Basic Income: The policy that changes everything* (Policy Press, Bristol, 2025).
366. N. Foster, *The Guarantee: Inside the fight for America's next economy* (New Press, New York, NY, 2024).
367. Give Directly, 'Early findings from the world's largest UBI study', 6 December 2023: www.givedirectly.org/2023-ubi-results/ [accessed 2 September 2025].
368. S. D. Agarwal, B. L. Cook, J. B. Liebman, 'Effect of cash benefits on health care utilization and health: A randomized study', *JAMA*, 2024 doi: 10.1001/jama.2024.13004.
369. N. Wilson, S. McDaid, 'The mental health effects of a Universal Basic Income: A synthesis of the evidence from previous pilots', *Social Science & Medicine*, 2021;287:114374. doi: doi.org/10.1016/j.socscimed.2021.114374.
370. A. Rizvi, M. Kearns, M. Dignam, et al., 'Effects of guaranteed basic income interventions on poverty-related outcomes in high-income

countries: A systematic review and meta-analysis', *Campbell Systematic Reviews*, 2024;20(2):e1414. doi: doi.org/10.1002/cl2.1414.
371. R. Hasdell, *What We Know About Universal Basic Income: A cross-synthesis of reviews* (Basic Income Lab, Stanford, CA, 2020).
372. R. Bregman, 'The solution to (nearly) everything: Working less', *Guardian*, 18 April 2016.
373. G. Bangham, *The New Wealth of Our Nation: The case for a citizen's inheritance* (Resolution Foundation, London, 2018).
374. V. Mathur, L. Roberts, Z. Bezeczky, et al., *Basic Income for Care Leavers in Wales, Pilot Evaluation: Second annual report, 2024 to 2025*, GSR report number 20/2025 (Welsh Government, Cardiff, 2025).
375. J. Ludwig, K. Schnepel, 'Does nothing stop a bullet like a job? The effects of income on crime', *Annual Review of Criminology*, 2025;8:269–89. doi: doi.org/10.1146/annurev-criminol-111523-122257.
376. B. Peters, 'How basic income can support climate tech solutions', basicincome.org: Basic Income Earth Network, 2024.
377. A. Coote, *Universal Basic Services: Provisioning for our needs within a fair consumption space*, Hot or Cool Institute, Berlin, 2023.
378. M. Maslin, S. Lewis, 'Universal basic income could fight climate change and end poverty', Global Citizen, 17 May 2019.
379. T. MacNeill, A. Vibert, 'Universal Basic Income and the Natural Environment: Theory and policy', *Basic Income Studies*, 2019;14(1) doi: doi:10.1515/bis-2018-0026.
380. P. Brown, 'How a global universal income could help poverty and the planet', *Geographical*, 27 November 2024.
381. E. de Lange, J. S. Sze, J. Allan, et al., 'A global conservation basic income to safeguard biodiversity', *Nature Sustainability*, 2023;6(8): 1016-23. doi: 10.1038/s41893-023-01115-7.
382. H. R. Reed, M. T. Johnson, S. Lansley, et al., 'Universal Basic Income is affordable and feasible: Evidence from UK economic microsimulation modelling', *Journal of Poverty and Social Justice*, 2023;31(1):146–62. doi: 10.1332/175982721X16702368352393.
383. H. R. Reed, E. A. Johnson, G. Stark, et al., 'Estimating the effects of Basic Income schemes on mental and physical health among adults aged 18 and above in the UK: A microsimulation study',

PLOS Mental Health, 2024;1(7):e0000206. doi: 10.1371/journal.pmen.0000206.

384. M. Johnson, E. Johnson, D. Nettle, 'Are "Red Wall" constituencies really opposed to progressive policy? Examining the impact of materialist narratives for Universal Basic Income', *British Politics*, 2023;18(1):104–27. doi: 10.1057/s41293-022-00220-z.

385. A. Coote, A. Percy, *The Case for Universal Basic Services* (Polity Press, Cambridge, 2020).

386. I. Gough, 'Universal Basic Services: A theoretical and moral framework', *The Political Quarterly*, 2019;90(3):534–42. doi: doi.org/10.1111/1467-923X.12706.

387. Office for Budget Responsibility, 'International demographic trends: Fiscal risks and sustainability', OBR, 2022, obr.uk/box/international-demographic-trends/ [accessed 2 September 2025].

388. M. Mazzucato, *The Entrepeneurial State: Debunking public vs. private sector myths* (Anthem Press, London, 2013).

389. B. Cox, 'Look at Donald Trump and his gang of broligarchs – and tell me we don't need a wealth tax', *Guardian*, 25 February 2025.

390. W. McCallum, A. Hamid, et al., 'Open letter to Chancellor: taxing the super-rich at the Budget', Greenpeace UK, 2024: www.greenpeace.org.uk/resources/open-letter-to-chancellor-taxing-the-super-rich-at-the-budget/ [accessed 2 September 2025].

391. A. Advani, A. Summers, 'Fair and Square: A reasonable approach to splitting bills and taxing wealth is key to sound finance and fair taxes', in C. Efford, L. Byrne (eds), *The Change We Need: How a Starmer government can transform Britain* (Tribune Group, London, 2022).

392. R. Murphy, *The Joy of Tax: How a fair tax system can create a better society* (Bantam Press, London, 2015).

393. J. Burke, S. Fankhauser, A. Kazaglis, et al., *Distributional Impacts of a Carbon Tax in the UK* (Grantham Institute, London, 2020).

394. K. Pickett, A. Gauhar, R. Wilkinson, et al., *The Spirit Level at 15* (Equality Trust, London, 2024).

395. Y. Oswald, J. Millward-Hopkins, J. K. Steinberger, et al., 'Luxury-focused carbon taxation improves fairness of climate policy', *One Earth*, 2023;6(7):884–98. doi: doi.org/10.1016/j.oneear.2023.05.027.

396. C. Moran, *Why We're Getting Poorer: A realist's guide to the economy and how we can fix it* (William Collins, London, 2025).
397. L. Byrne, *The Inequality of Wealth: Why it matters and how to fix it* (Head of Zeus, London, 2024).
398. S. Lansley, D. Dorling, J. Ryan-Collins, et al., 'Should we tax wealth to fund social care?', Progressive Economy Forum, 14 September 2021: progressiveeconomyforum.com/blog/should-we-tax-wealth-to-fund-social-care/ [accessed 2 September 2025].
399. D. Nettle, J. Chrisp, E. Johnson, et al., 'What do people want from a welfare system? Conjoint survey evidence from UK adults', *Poverty & Public Policy*, 2025;17(2): e70018. doi: doi.org/10.1002/pop4.70018.
400. J. Meade, *The Structure and Reform of Direct Taxation* (Institute for Fiscal Studies, London, 1978): ifs.org.uk/sites/default/files/output_url_files/meade.pdf [accessed 2 September 2025].
401. P. MacLeod, R. Johnson, *Democracy's Second Act* (University of Toronto Press, Toronto, 2025).
402. R. Wilson, D. Levaï, 'How a New Global Citizens' Assembly Can Revive Climate Action', European Democracy Hub, 2025: europeandemocracyhub.epd.eu/how-a-new-global-citizens-assembly-can-revive-climate-action/ [accessed 2 September 2025].
403. K. McKenzie, 'Using Participatory Budgeting to Improve Mental Capital at the Local Level', in L. Newby, N. Dennison (eds), *'If You Could Do One Thing . . .' Nine local actions to reduce health inequalities* (British Academy, London, 2014).
404. *Brazil: Toward a More Inclusive and Effective Participatory Budget in Porto Alegre, Vol. 1 of 2. Main Report*, World Bank, Washington, DC, 29 January 2008: documents.worldbank.org/en/publication/documents-reports/documentdetail/778301468019774995/main-report [accessed 2 September 2025].
405. 'Participatory Budgeting', Local Government Association, 2025: www.local.gov.uk/topics/devolution/devolution-online-hub/public-service-reform-tools/engaging-citizens-devolution-5 [accessed 2 September 2025].

406. 'Methods, Participatory Budgeting', Involve, 2024: www.involve.org.uk/resource/participatory-budgeting [accessed 2 September 2025].
407. The Baptist Union of Great Britain, the Methodist Church, the Church of Scotland and the United Reformed Church, *The Lies We Tell Ourselves: Ending comfortable myths about poverty*, Joint Public Issues Team, London, 2013: jpit.uk/wp-content/uploads/Truth-And-Lies-Report-smaller.pdf [accessed 2 September 2025].
408. Media Reform Coalition, *Who Owns the UK Media?* (Goldsmiths, University of London, London, 2023).
409. K. Woodsome, 'Jeff Bezos has a very billionaire-ish idea of what freedom means', *The New Republic*, 6 March 2025.
410. D. Hind, *The Return of the Public* (Verso, London, 2010).
411. H. Popović, 'Croatia', in B. Petković (ed.), *Media Integrity Matters: Reclaiming public service values in media and journalism* (South East European Media Observatory, Peace Institute, Ljubljana, 2014).
412. J. Cagé, *Saving the Media: Capitalism, crowdfunding, and democracy* (Harvard University Press, Cambridge, MA, 2016).
413. Reporters Without Borders, 'World Press Freedom Index', 2025: rsf.org/en/index [accessed 2 September 2025].
414. A. Stevens, 'Telling policy stories: An ethnographic study of the use of evidence in policy-making in the UK', *Journal of Social Policy*, 2011;40(2):237–55. doi: 10.1017/S0047279410000723 [published online first: 10 November 2010].
415. S. D. Pearson, M. D. Rawlins, 'Quality, innovation, and value for money: NICE and the British National Health Service', *JAMA*, 2005;294(20):2618–22. doi: 10.1001/jama.294.20.2618.
416. Centre for Health Economics, University of York: www.york.ac.uk/che/about-us/.
417. W. Hutton, 'Britain must harness the social sciences to fight post-pandemic deprivation', *Guardian*, 15 April 2021.
418. M. Kakutani, 'The death of truth: How we gave up on facts and ended up with Trump', *Guardian*, 14 July 2018.
419. P. Shrivastava, L. Jackson, T. Ghneim-Herrera, et al., 'Science in crisis times: The crucial role of science in sustainability

and transformation', *PLOS Sustainability and Transformation*, 2024;3(10):e0000132. doi: 10.1371/journal.pstr.0000132.

420. A. T. Geronimus, J. P. Thompson, 'To denigrate, ignore, or disrupt: Racial inequality in health and the impact of a policy-induced breakdown of African American communities', *Du Bois Review: Social Science Research on Race*, 2004;1(2):247–79.

421. T. Schrecker, 'Can health equity survive epidemiology? Standards of proof and social determinants of health', *Preventive Medicine*, 2013;57(6):741–44. doi: doi.org/10.1016/j.ypmed.2013.08.013.

422. M. Marmot, 'Inequalities in health: Causes and policy implications', *The Society and Population Health Reader*, 2000;2:293–309.

Index

Page references in *italics* indicate images.

abortion 297–8
Academy of Social Sciences 313
Acheson, Sir Donald 50
active transport 26
adultification bias 105
Advani, Professor Arun 291–4
adverse childhood experiences (ACEs) 97, 217–21, 228
Age UK 122
ageing population 76, 88, 122–3, 128, 130, 202, 286
Alaska, US 278, 285
Alphabet 306
Amazon (online retailer) 239, 293, 306
Antisocial Behaviour Orders (ASBOs) 15, 212–13
anxiety 7, 21, 33, 60, 68, 77, 98, 111, 150, 158, 190, 206, 281
Apples and Honey (intergenerational preschool and day care), Wandsworth 73, 75
apprenticeships 84, 112, 158, 178–9
arc of progress 199–200
attachment theory 78

attention deficit hyperactivity disorder (ADHD) 174, 205
austerity, fiscal 57, 118, 177, 178, 191–2, 240, 242, 252, 312
Australia 46, 73, 86–7

Bank of England 90
banks 10, 11, 44, 90, 192, 202, 208, 241–2, 285
Barr, Ben 65, 110
Basic Income Earth Network 281
Basic Income Health 283
basic income schemes *see* universal basic income
Beck, Allen 195
Becker, Gary 211, 228
Behavioural Control Orders 213
Belong Chester 73, 75
Benn, Melissa: *Life Lessons: The case for a National Education Service* 175–7
Bennett, Alan 167
Bennett, Dr Davara 100–101
Beveridge, William 2
Bezos, Jeff 289, 306
Bhutan 11, 245–7, 257, 258

birth rate 87, 286
birth weight 52
Black, Sir Douglas 49–51
Black Report (1980) 49–51
Black, William K. 207
Blackpool 20, 103
Blair, Tony 90n, 212
Blue Zones 27
Blumstein, Alfred 195
Blunkett, David 212, 213
body of persons 295–6
body size difference, social class and 62–4
Bottrill, Stephen John 1
Bourdieu, Pierre 251
Bowlby, John 78
Bradford 99, 315
  Born in Bradford (BiB) 315–17
Brazil 11, 27, 261, 300, 302
Bregman, Rutger 279
British Academy 301–2
British Columbia, Canada 298
British Medical Journal 5–6
'broligarchs' 289
Bromley by Bow Centre 28–9
Bronfenbrenner, Urie: model of child development 139–41, 140
Brussels Capital Region, Belgium 256
Building Human Capital Fund 177–8
Burgess, Simon 172
Burke, Naomi 209
Burnett, Dr Ros 211–12
burnout 25, 26, 56

Cagé, Professor Julia 307
Callaghan, Jim 48–9
Cameron, David 109, 129, 167
Canada 26, 27, 36–7, 64, 73, 103, 246, 298–9
capabilities approach 137–9, 274
capitalism 19, 120, 131, 239, 271, 306
  end of, imagining 239, 240–41, 264
  neoliberal *see* neoliberalism
Cardiff University 108, 205, 281
care homes 20, 73, 75, 77, 102, 121, 123–30, 133, 135, 219, 235
Care Quality Commission 123–4, 131
Carer's Allowance 122
Cartwright, Professor Nancy 33
Casey, Dame Louise 130
causal chains/causes of the causes 31–4, 39–47, 69, 105, 223–4, 273, 279, 286, 306
Census, UK (2021) 76, 204
Centre for Crime and Justice Studies 230–31
Centre for Criminology, University of Oxford 211
Centre for Health Economics (CHE), University of York 311
Chandler, Daniel 13
Change We Need, The (Tribune group of Labour MPs) 289–90
Child Benefit 56, 94, 275, 283
Child of the North 104
  All-Party Parliamentary Group 102–4

INDEX

Evidence-based Plan for Improving School Attendance (2024) 159
Child Tax Credit 56
Child Trust Fund 44, 45
childcare 10, 11, 75, 76, 78–92, 106, 134, 168, 279, 282, 312
  attachment theory and 78
  availability 81–2, 84
  Children's Gilts and 90
  enrolment rates and weekly hours 83–4
  free 81–2, 85, 87, 90, 92
  gender equality and 80, 87–8, 89
  household income spend on 81
  National Children's Service and 86–7, 88, 90, 91
  National Wealth Fund and 91
  parental leave and 83–4, 88–90, 92
  quality of 80, 82–6, 89–90
  return on investment, government 85, 90
  Social Impact Bonds and 90–91
  teaching and learning theory, optimal application of 91
  tech-influenced hypermasculine conservatives and 79
  very young children and 78–9
  widely available, affordable, need for 79–81
  workforce 79, 82–4, 91
children
  adverse childhood experiences (ACEs) 97, 217–21, 228
  child wellbeing 6, 28, 86, 87, 143, 151, 247

childcare *see* childcare
Childhood Vulnerability in Numbers (2019 report), Children's Commissioner 218–19
children's social care *see* children's social care
Convention on the Rights of the Child, UN 165
criminal justice and *see* criminal justice
economic thinking and 243, 244, 247, 249, 255
education *see* education
Good Childhood Report (2024) 149–50
healthcare *see* healthcare
Ministers for Children 86, 87
National Children's Service 86–7, 88, 90, 91, 286
poverty *see* poverty
UBI and 275, 279–83
children's social care / children in need of care 92–109
  adoption 92–3
  basic income for all young people leaving care, Welsh government pilots 108–9
  blueprints for 105–9
  Child of the North All-Party Parliamentary Group, report on, presented to (2024) 102–4
  child poverty link to children entering care 102–3, 106
  child protection orders 94
  children's social services 92–3, 97

children's social care/children in
    need of care – *cont.*
  cost of 98–102
  educational outcomes and 93,
    95–7
  family court and 93
  foster care 92, 93, 95, 101–2
  homelessness and 98
  Independent Review of
    Children's Social Care (2022)
    99, 105–7
  inequalities in 95–7, 102–3, 106
  Institute for Fiscal Studies
    Deaton Review of Inequalities
    and 95–6
  kinship foster care 92
  local authorities financial
    support to families 104
  Mia (case study) 93–6
  outcomes for children with
    experience of UK care system
    94–7
  private equity/foreign sovereign
    wealth funds and 107
  profit-making privatised 'care',
    dependence on 99, 102, 107
  racism and 104, 105
  Regional Care Cooperatives 107
  youth justice system and 97
Children's Society, The 149
chimpanzees 250
chronic social stress 7, 25, 26
Chung, Heejung 88
citizens' assemblies 264, 297–301,
    304, 308, 313
citizen's inheritance 280

City of Research 315
City University 292
civil service 18, 308–9
Clarke, Ken 210, 214
class, social 1, 4, 7–8, 289, 307
  criminal justice and 191,
    194, 204
  education and 142, 155, 168, 173
  health and 27, 44, 48–9, 51, 54,
    62–3
  social care and 95, 108, 114
  social mobility and 6, 142–3, 168,
    170, 173
Climate Assembly UK 299
climate change 3, 19, 21, 22, 38, 53,
    58, 265, 266, 273, 313, 314
  carbon emissions 260, 268, 285,
    292, 295
  carbon taxes 285, 292, 295
  citizens' assemblies and 298–9,
    300
  discounting and 53
  GANE project and 256, 260
  New Zealand Wellbeing Budget
    and 27, 28, 247
  planetary boundaries model
    and *see* planetary boundaries
    model
  UBI schemes and 281–2
  UN Sustainable Development
    Goals and 245
Club of Rome
  The Limits to Growth 247–9,
    255
  Transformational Economics
    Commission 262, 265

INDEX

coal mines 239–40, 271
COBRA 16–17
Cochrane, Dr Archie 310
co-housing 132–5
comfort eating 7
Common Sense Policy Group 268, 276, 295
'commons' 135–6, 261–2
'commons of care' 135–6
community conservancies, Namibia 261
Community Council for Somerset 135
community hubs 28–9, 56, 176
Community Justice Scotland 221
community ownership 261, 307
Competition and Markets Authority 102
Conservative Party 46, 49–50, 129, 209–11, 213–14, 234–6, 274, 285, 293, 295
  Conservative–Liberal Democrat Coalition (2010–15) 57–8, 128–9, 168, 213
Coram Family and Childcare 81–2
Cortez, Fe 261
cost of living crisis 57, 63, 79, 101, 110
Costa Rica 11, 27
Cottam, Hilary 134
Covid-19 pandemic 16–17, 59–62, 89, 100, 129–30, 145, 157–8, 160, 164, 208, 239, 256, 275, 312–13, 317
Cox, Brian 289

criminal justice 4, 20, 32, 54, 94, 97, 105, 184–236, 272, 284–6, 296, 308, 321
  adverse childhood experiences (ACEs) and 217–21, 228
  arc of progress and 199–200
  blueprints for reducing imprisonment 224–6
  children in custody/youth justice system 97, 186–7, 199, 200, 204–5, 218
  control fraud 207
  Crime, Justice and Protecting the Public (1990 White Paper) 210
  crime rates 3, 20, 56, 178, 189, 191, 195, 201
  Criminal Justice and Public Order Act (1994) 210
  Crown Prosecution Service 208, 214
  day in the life of average prisoner 185–6
  death penalty 198–9
  digital infrastructure 233
  European Convention on Human Rights and 188
  exemplary systems 195–9
  government policy and long-term trends in imprisonment in UK 209–17
  His Majesty's Inspectorate of Prisons 188, 189–90, 205
  imprisonment rates 188–9, 194–6, 199–200, 202, 209, 210, 213, 214

criminal justice – *cont.*
  inequality and 191–5, 204, 209, 221, 223–4, 234–5
  international partners refuse to cooperate with UK 187–8, 190
  Lammy Review (2017) 234–5
  'lethal but legal' business practices 207
  mental health problems and 188, 189, 195, 202, 203, 206, 207, 218, 219, 227, 228
  Mexico and South Africa and link between crime and income inequality 192–4
  Ministry of Justice Certified Normal Accommodation policy 189–90
  Nelson Mandela Rules/Standard Minimum Rules for the Treatment of Prisoners 232–4
  neurodivergent conditions and 205–6
  Nordic system of open prisons 196–8
  Out of Court Resolutions 220–21
  patient participation in health care model and 235–6
  prison efficacy 200–202, 208–14
  prison estate, transforming 231–4
  'prison works' slogan 209–14
  Prisons Strategy White Paper (2021) 236
  probation services 203, 230, 236
  procedural justice 227–8
  psychological toll of living with crime/fear of crime 190–91
  public health approach to criminal justice 221–4
  racial/ethnic bias and 204–5, 234–5
  recidivism 199, 202–4, 206, 209, 211, 216, 224
  rehabilitative culture 197, 227–9, 232, 234, 235, 286
  release from prison 197, 198, 200, 203, 204, 211, 214, 215, 224, 226–9, 231
  Scandinavian Prison Project housing unit, 'Little Scandinavia' 197–8
  sentencing 97, 189, 194–5, 200, 203–4, 206, 209–12, 214–17, 221, 224–6, 228–31, 235
  staffing 224, 226, 231, 233–4
  'tough on crime and tough on the causes of crime' slogan 212
  vulnerability in prison system 220–21
  white-collar crime 194, 207–8
  Woolf Report (1991) 225–6, 232
Croatian Ministry of Culture 307
cycling 26, 27

Dahlgren, Göran *38*, 39
Dartmoor Prison Museum 185
Davis, Dr Jahnine 105

INDEX

deaths
  'deaths of despair' 46
  infant mortality 6, 9, 51, 59, 60, 67, 68, 77, 88, 316
  premature 6, 25, 52
  rates 5, 17, 35, 36, 41, 46, 48, 59, 60, 64, 76–7, 95, 120–22, 310
  social class differences 48
Deaton Review of Inequalities 95, 173
Delaney, Rob 120
dementia 121, 126, 129
democracy 21, 46, 59
  deliberative democracy 134, 261, 264, 297–301, 304, 308, 313
  democratic malaise 296–7
  media and 306–8
  participatory democracy 264, 296–301, 313
  wealth taxes and 287
  see also tax
  workers' rights and 267
Democratic Party, US 46
Denmark 11, 27, 73, 83, 133, 142, 145, 149, 188, 197, 261, 308
Department for Education Science Advisory Council 182–3
Department of Health 49, 77
Department for Work and Pensions 71, 119
dependency ratio 286–7
depression 7, 58, 59, 60, 68, 158, 206, 217, 240, 284
deprived areas 29, 51, 62, 68–9, 98, 101, 110, 168, 177–8, 183, 191, 193–5, 202, 205, 212, 323, 324

DFN Project SEARCH 112, 114
Dilnot, Sir Andrew: 'Commission on Funding of Care and Support' 128–9, 130, 132
disabilities 3, 57, 73, 75, 82, 101, 109–20, 122, 130, 134, 274, 280
  Access to Work programme 111, 115
  criminal justice and 199, 205, 206, 219
  disability benefits 110, 114, 117–19
  education and 111, 113, 114, 144, 158, 160, 165
  employment and 111–15, 119–20
  Equality Act (2010) 111, 115, 119
  housing and 111, 112, 114, 115–17, 119
  improvement in aspects of living with 110–11
  Paralympics, Summer (2012) 109–10
  parity of esteem 117–20
  Personal Independence Payment (PIP) 110, 118–19
  poverty, rise in proportion of adults with disabilities living in ('Great Leap Backwards') 110
  Think Work First (2024 report) 113–15
DMG Media 305
Dorling, Professor Danny 312
doughnut economics 253–6, 254
  Doughnut 3.0 model 253, 254
  Doughnut Economics Action Lab (DEAL) 255, 256

drug use 6, 7, 46, 100, 190, 202, 206, 207, 219, 226, 236, 305
Dudamel, Gustavo 162
Duflo, Esther 290

Earth4All 265–9, *268*
Ebola 16
ecological principles 258–60
Economic and Social Research Council 220
economics/economic thinking 3, 239–69
  capitalism, alternatives to/imagining end of 239–41, 264
  care economy, economic benefits of investment in 135
  circular economy 260
  coal mining and 239–40, 271
  commons and 135–6, 261–2
  community conservancies 261
  doughnut economics 253–6, *254* see also doughnut economics
  Earth4All and 265–9, *268*
  ecological principles 258–60
  'Five Ways to Wellbeing' framework 258
  Global Assessment for a New Economics (GANE) *see* Global Assessment for a New Economics
  global financial crisis (2008) 207, 208, 239, 241–2, 269
  Gross Domestic Product *see* Gross Domestic Product
  Gross National Happiness *see* Gross National Happiness
  Gross National Product *see* Gross National Product
  growth delusion 248–9
  Homo economicus (economic man) and *Homo integralis* (integrated man) 249–52, 260–61
  Institute for New Economic Thinking (INET) 252–3
  Limits to Growth, The, Club of Rome 247–9
  natural capital 259–60
  neoliberalism and *see* neoliberalism
  Palma Index 266–7
  planetary boundaries model 253–6, *254*, 258–60
  political economy principles 263–9, 292
  Progressive Economy Forum 252, 293, 312
  'the real economy' 243
  regenerative good growth 260
  Rethinking Economics 252
  reverse auction 261–2
  social principles 260–63
  'symbolic violence' 251
  'Too Little, Too Late' scenario 265–6
  Transformational Economics Commission 262, 265
Economist, The 202
ecosystem services 259

INDEX

education 3–8, 10, 11, 18–20, 137–83, 285, 288, 301, 303, 314, 316, 317
  absenteeism/school refusal 21, 154, 156–60
  arts and humanities 151, 162, 179–80, 271
  balance and 161–3
  Bronfenbrenner's model 139–41, 140
  Building Human Capital Fund 177–8
  capabilities approach 137–9
  care and 76, 85, 87–92, 94–6, 100, 105, 106, 111, 113–14
  child wellbeing and 151
  criminal justice and 197, 203, 204, 205, 217, 217, 223–4, 232, 233, 234
  current education system and flourishing individual children 141–3
  curriculum, national 141, 143, 147, 151–3, 156, 162, 165, 166, 176
  economic thinking and 243, 244, 246, 263, 268, 271
  Education, Health and Care plan (EHC plan) 174–5
  Educational Maintenance Allowance 177
  El Sistema/opportunities for creative development 162–3
  employers and 165–6
  'exam factory culture' 149
  exclusions, school 157, 160–61, 228
  fantasy education system (Finland) 141–4, 156, 175
  funding 141, 160, 176, 177–80, 182
  GCSE 55, 96, 173, 174
  Good Childhood Report (2024) and 149–50
  graduate tax to replace university tuition fees 177
  health inequalities and 27, 32, 33, 42, 51, 54–5, 57, 63, 68
  higher education 144, 177–80, 234
  inequalities in 167–8, 170, 172–4, 178, 181, 183
  Labour government announces independent review (2024) 164–5
  life satisfaction and 149–51
  life skills 150
  low attainment designation 154–5
  maths, reading and science attainment 163–4
  mental wellbeing and 150–51
  multi-age classroom 146–8
  narrative counselling 161
  National Education Service 175–7, 181, 286
  'Not in Employment, Education or Training' (NEET) 105, 160
  Ofsted schools inspection *see* Ofsted
  physical wellbeing and 150–51
  PISA rankings 144–5, 149, 149n, 150–51, 163–4
  poverty and 159, 181–2

education – *cont.*
  private education 166–71, 173, 176, 178, 180, 183
  Progress in International Reading Literacy Study (PIRLS) 164
  Pupil Premium 177
  Pupil Referral Unit 96, 160
  return on investment, government 178
  schools *see* schools
  SEND, inequities faced by children in England with 174–5
  skills wellbeing and 151
  social mobility and 142–3
  soft skills 166–7
  starting school age 144–6
  state school system, uneven playing field in 171–5
  STEAM subjects 180
  STEM subjects 180
  student loans 179
  three Cs, three Rs and 152–5, 157, 165, 180, 181
  Timpson review of school exclusion (2019) 160–61
  TIMSS (Trends in International Mathematics and Science Study) 164
  tuition fees 144, 177, 179, 271
UBI and 276, 279, 280, 282, 284
UK Department for Education Science Advisory Council 182–3

United Nations Convention on the Rights of the Child and 165
universities *see* universities
Education Policy Institute 174
Edwards, Dr Simon 161
El Sistema 162–3
elderly care 3, 10, 11, 25, 72–7, 120–36, 240, 243
  ageing population and 76, 88, 122–3, 128, 130, 202, 286
  amount of care being given 122
  bed blocking 77
  blueprints for 126–30
  broken system 122–3, 132
  care homes with worst ratings receive grants for care from local authorities 123–4
  Care Quality Commission and 123–4, 131
  Carer's Allowance 122
  Casey review 130
  co-housing 132–5
  'commons of care' 135–6
  Covid-19 and 129–30
  death 120–22
  Dilnot commission 128–32
  economic benefits of investment in care economy 135
  family members providing care 76
  gender problem 123
  inequality problem 123–4
  intergenerational care facilities 73–5
  market failure/dysfunctional system 124–5

mutual care networks 132–4
National Care Service 127, 128, 130, 286
non-residential care networks 134
nursing homes 75, 77, 122, 127
reablement 77
Royal Commission on Long-Term Care of the Elderly (1998) 126–7
universal basic income and 132, 279, 280
Universal Quality Social Care 131
Wanless Social Care Review (2006) 127–9, 130, 131
ElderSpirit project 134
empathy 5, 112, 251
Employment and Support Allowance 119
Ennals, David 48–9
Enron (energy company) 207–8
enterprise safety nets 266, 268–9
environment 2, 3, 4, 8, 9, 11, 14, 21, 27, 90, 207
  economic thinking and 245, 247, 249, 252–3, 258–9, 261, 265–7, 269, 274, 281–2, 288, 289, 296, 300, 312
  UBI and 281–2, 288, 289
  see also climate change
Equal Right 282
Equality Act (2010) 29, 111, 115, 119
Equality and Human Rights Commission (EHRC) 116, 119
Equality Trust 292

Estonia 27, 145, 151, 308
European Committee for the Prevention of Torture (CPT) 189
European Congress of Psychology 31–2
European Convention on Human Rights (ECHR) 188
European Union (EU) 300–301, 302
executive stress 48
experts, Gove on 17
Eyjafjallajökull, eruption of (2016) 16

Farage, Nigel 102
Farrall, Stephen 209
Femicide Census 191
Financial Times: 'How to Spend It' 301
Finland 6, 11, 26–9, 63, 84, 91, 142–3, 145, 149, 153, 156, 175, 187, 188, 195, 234, 246, 308
First World War (1914–18) 47, 184
Fisher, Mark 239, 241
Five Ways to Wellbeing framework 258
Forster, E. M.: *Howards End* 69–70
Fort Pampus 256
Foucault, Michel 269
Franklin, Benjamin 120
Freudenberg, Professor Nicholas 207
Friedman, Sam: *Born to Rule* 169
friendship 38, 65, 70, 73, 151, 158

INDEX

Future Generations Commissioner 52
Future Generations Minister 53

Gauke, David 229
GB News Radio 102
gender equality 80, 87–8, 89, 123–4, 164
general election
  (1950) 296
  (2017) 129
  (2019) 296
  (2024) 151, 182, 285, 296
  voter turnout 296
genetics 38, 39, 52, 316
geographic inequalities 64, 178
Germany 11, 27, 56, 184, 187, 188, 190
Global Assessment for a New Economics (GANE) 256–9, 257, 260–64
Global Citizens' Assembly Network 300
global financial crisis (2008) 207, 208, 239, 241–2, 269
good society
  blueprints for 25–236
    see also care; criminal justice; education; healthcare
  'body of persons' proposing and discussing how to build 295–7
  boundaries of 14
  building 237–69
    see also economic thinking, new
  defined 1–3
  fantasy society 10–12, 27, 58, 307, 317
  imagining 9–14
  Pickett version 3–5
  policy-making and 15–16
    see also policy-making
  Simms version 10
  social sciences and 16–17
    see also social sciences
  time for 21–2
  Veil of Ignorance and 12–14
Google 306
Gove, Michael 16, 163
Government Office for Science 17
Graaf, John de 297
Graeber, David 242
Grantham Research Institute for Climate Change and the Environment, Imperial College, London 292
Greater Manchester Independent Inequalities Commission 12
Greaves, Ellen 172
Greece 6, 27, 59
Green Bonds 90
Green New Deal 268
Grenfell Tower fire (2017) 208
Gross Domestic Product (GDP) 11n, 27, 61, 67, 127, 239–45, 247
Gross National Happiness (GNH) 11, 245–7, 246, 258
Gross National Income (GNI) 11, 11n

INDEX

Gross National Product (GNP) 244
Guardian 9–10, 123, 124, 174–5, 188, 304

Hackney Council 154
Ha-Joon Chang, Professor 258
  23 Things They Don't Tell You About Capitalism 269
Hart, Dr Julian Tudor 37
Hay, Colin 209
health/healthcare 25–71
  Black Report 49–51
  childhood, investing in early and 55–6
  'deaths of despair' and 46
  good society that prioritises health and wellbeing of its population, imagining 26–9
  governmental use of health evidence 47–58
  Health Divide, The (Whitehead report) 50
  health impact assessments 67–8
  health indicators 59–61
  health paradox 34–7
  Health and Social Care Act (2012) 117
  healthy standard of living for all 66
  inequalities in 3, 8, 8, 17, 19, 20, 27, 28, 30, 32, 33, 40, 43, 48–51, 53, 56, 57, 61–4, 66–8, 97, 126, 209, 279, 301, 304, 305, 312
  lifestyle drift 40–45
  money and 64–7

National Health Service (NHS) *see* National Health Service (NHS)
  political right and left and 45–6
  prevention and root causes 30–34
  rainbow model 37–40, *38*
  social determinants of health 2, 26, 37–41, *38*, 50, 60, 69, 71, 106, 139, 140
  social relationships and 69–71
  spa treatments, residential 25–7, 56
  Sure Start 51–7, 65, 176
  wellbeing budgets 27, 28, 67–8, 69, 241
  Wellbeing Economy Governments alliance and 26, 27–9
  Wilkinson discovers widening class differences in 48–50
Health Action Zones 56
Health Equity North 68–9
Health Foundation 134
heart attacks 31, 41 48, 121
Heckman, Professor James 55, 178
hierarchy of evidence pyramid *321*, *321*, *322*, *324*
Himmelweit, Susan 72, 125, 134
Hind, Dan 306–7
Homecare Association 124
House of Commons Select Committee on Science and Technology 16
House of Lords 113, 114, 119, 214, 289

household income 63, 81, 169
housing 4, 15, 240, 260, 262, 287
  care and 85, 94, 104, 106, 111–12, 114–17, 119, 132–5
  co-housing 132–6
  community housing 27
  criminal justice and 191, 197, 203, 227, 232, 233, 236, 240
  disabilities and 111, 112, 114, 115–17, 119
  health and 26, 27, 35, 47, 56, 63, 66, 70, 71
  Housing Benefit 15, 94, 275
  right to 115–17, 119
  social housing 111, 117, 191, 262
  UBS and 282, 286
Howard, Elizabeth Jane: *Cazalet Chronicles* 62
Howard League for Penal Reform 231–2
Howard, Michael 210, 211, 213–14
human capital 6, 177, 259
human rights 21, 116, 119, 168, 188, 213, 225, 231, 270
Humanitas 73, 75

Iannucci, Armando 15
Iceland 11, 16, 25–8, 56, 67, 188, 195–7, 246
Imogen (employment and learning difficulty case study) 112–13, 115, 116
Imprisonment for Public Protection (IPPs) 212

income support 26, 275, 280
Independent Inquiry into Inequalities in Health (1998) 50
Independent Review of Children's Social Care (2022) 99, 105–7
Independent Review of Sentencing (2025) 229–30
India 27, 104, 105, 282
inequality 4, 123–4
  chronic social stress and 7, 26, 52
  death rates and 6
  democracy and 296–7
  economic thinking and 262–3, 265–7
  education and *see* education
  health and *see* health/healthcare
  tax and 284, 287, 288–94
  UBI and 276, 279, 280
  Veil of Ignorance and 12–14
  Wilkinson and Pickett first link to wide range of problems 5–9
infant mortality 6, 9, 51, 59, 60, 67, 68, 88, 316
infrastructure 11, 85, 86, 91, 100, 225, 226, 231, 233, 286, 288, 302, 312
inheritance, citizen's 280
inheritance tax 291, 294
innovation safety nets 266–8
Institute for Education, University College London 154
Institute for Fiscal Studies (IFS) 39, 54–5, 57, 95, 129, 173

Institute for New Economic
  Thinking (INET) 252–3
Institute for Public Policy
  Research (IPPR) 67–8
inverse care law 37
Iran 278, 285
Ireland 6, 97, 104, 144, 160, 214,
  297–8
Israel 6
Iswe Foundation 300
Italy 6, 27

Japan 6, 27, 59, 61, 73, 188, 298
Jeffery, Professor Charlie 178–9
Jenkin, Patrick 49–50
Johnson, Boris 109, 129, 236
Johnson, Richard 299, 300
Joseph Rowntree Foundation 58,
  118, 120
Joseph Rowntree Housing Trust
  133

Kakutani, Michiko 313–14
Katelin (young woman in care
  case study) 98
Kennedy, Robert F. 244
Kenway, Emily: *Who Cares* 131–2,
  135–6
Kenya 278
King, Dr Martin Luther 199
King's College London 88
King's Fund 127
Koch, Robert 35
Kotoen intergenerational care
  facility, Japan 73, 75
Kuznets, Simon 244

Labour Party 285, 291n, 293–5,
  299, 312
  care policy 91, 127, 130
  criminal justice policy 212–15,
    224, 229
  education policy 164–5, 168,
    170
  health policy 48–9, 51, 56, 57
  New Labour 51, 56, 57, 127, 168,
    170, 212–13
  Tribune group of MPs
    290–91
Lai, Eric 65
Lammy Review (2017) 234–5
Lansley, Stewart 312
Law, Victoria: *Prisons Make Us
  Safer: And 20 other myths about
  mass incarceration* 206–7
legal aid 191–2, 208
'lethal but legal' business practices
  207
Levaï, David 300
Leyen, Ursula von der 300–301
*Lies We Tell Ourselves: Ending
  comfortable myths about poverty,
  The* (2013 report) 305
life expectancy 8, 21, 36, 51, 59, 63,
  67, 68, 69, 76, 315
life satisfaction 67, 149–51
life skills 150
lifestyle drift 40
Lindley, Paul: *Raising the Nation*
  84, 90, 91
Local Government Association
  135, 303
London Proms (2007) 162

London School of Economics 169, 252, 291
London Violence Reduction Unit 223
loneliness 70, 77, 112, 113, 116
longevity 21, 128

Mackenbach, Johan 36
MacLeod, Peter 299–300
Major, John 210, 213, 216, 270, 274
malnourishment 47
Mandela, Nelson 1, 184, 232–4
Marçal, Katrine 87–8
Marks & Spencer 112
Marmot, Sir Michael 25, 28, 50, 66, 304
Marmot Review: *Fair Society, Healthy Lives* 50, 66, 304
Marmot Review 10 Years On, The 50, 66
Maruna, Dr Shadd 211–12
MASS LBP 299
Massachusetts Institute of Technology 248
May, Theresa 129, 229
Mazzucato, Mariana 288
McCluskey, Karyn 221
McKenzie, Dr Kwame 301–3
McKeown, Thomas 34–6, 41
Meade, James 290
media
  democracy and 216, 304–8
  disinformation and 313–14
Media Reform Coalition 305
Meehan, Genevieve 83

mental health 3, 6, 9
  criminal justice system and 187–90, 195, 202–3, 206–7, 209, 217–20, 223, 225, 227–8
  disabilities and 111, 112, 116–18
  economic theory and 240, 247, 257, 259
  education and 146, 150–52, 154, 156, 158–60, 164, 165, 168, 175
  healthcare and 25–8, 32–4, 39, 43, 44, 51, 52, 59–61, 64, 65, 302, 316
  social care and 93–5, 107–8
  UBI and 281
Meta 306
meta-analysis 310, 321, 322
Metro newspaper 185–6, 305
Mexico, inequality in 192–4
Mia (child social care case study) 93–6
Miliband, Ed 129, 167
Mills, Helen 230–31
Minimum Income Guarantee 26, 66
Minimum Income for Healthy Living 66
Minimum Income Standard 28, 43, 66, 89, 279–80, 283–6
minimum wage 56, 66, 126
Ministers for Children 86, 87
Ministry of Justice 188–90, 205
Mondragón cooperative, Spain 11
Morrison, Reverend William 226
Mujica, José 10
Multiple Risk Factor Intervention Trial (MRFIT) 41

Murphy, Richard 292
Musk, Elon 5, 289

narrative counselling 161
National Audit Office 152
National Care Service 127, 128, 130, 286
National Children's Service 86–7, 88, 90, 91, 286
National Education Service 175–7, 181, 286
National Education Union 149, 151, 182
National Health Service (NHS) 2, 34, 37, 48, 57, 71, 77, 85, 86, 115, 117, 126, 127, 167, 240, 282, 286, 301, 303, 310, 316
National Institute for Health and Care Excellence (NICE) 309–12
National Institute for Social Change 311, 313
National Insurance 126, 284
National Planning Policy Framework 117
National Wealth Fund 91, 285
natural capital 259–60
Natural Capital Committee 259
Navigator programme 222–3
Nelson Mandela Rules/Standard Minimum Rules for the Treatment of Prisoners 232–4
neoliberalism 20, 240, 242, 251, 252, 258, 263, 288
Netherlands 11, 27, 61, 64, 73, 83, 133, 149, 187, 189, 195, 196, 202, 308

neurodiversity 75, 120, 134, 205–6
New Economics Foundation (NEF) 85, 131, 132, 258, 281–2, 286
New Ground community, Barnet 133
New Labour 51, 56, 57, 127, 168, 170, 212–13
New Society 48–9
New South Wales, Australia 46
New Zealand 26–8, 67, 146–7, 246–7
News UK 305
Nightingale House 73
non-profit media organization (NMO) 307
Nordic countries 6, 61, 64, 86, 142, 149, 196–8, 234
see also individual nation name
Norway 6, 64, 83, 142, 188, 195–8, 285, 294–5, 308
Nuffield Trust 126
nursery care 73, 78–9, 81–3, 84, 90
nursing homes 20, 75, 77, 121, 122, 127
Nussbaum, Martha 138–9

Obama, Barack 14
Obama, Michelle 183
obesity 6, 41–2, 59, 61, 62, 68, 70, 150, 317
Office for Budget Responsibility 313
Office for National Statistics (ONS) 67, 201
Office for Social Responsibility 313

INDEX

Ofsted 82–3, 97, 151–2, 154, 161, 172–3, 176, 181, 205
Open University 125, 225
Organisation for Economic Co-operation and Development (OECD) 21, 58–61, 81, 103, 142–5, 149, 151, 163, 193, 267
Orrell, David 269
Ostrom, Elinor 261
Out of Court Resolutions 220–21

Pakes, Francis 197
Palma Index 266–7
Paralympics, Summer (London 2012) 109
parental leave 83–4, 88–90, 92
Paris, cycling in 27
Paris Institute of Political Studies 307
Parliamentary Office of Science and Technology (POST) 216
participatory budgeting 11, 301–4, 308, 313
patient participation 235–6
Patriotic Millionaires 287, 289, 290
Payscale 84
Peasants' Revolt (1381) 1
pedagogy 91
Pennsylvania State University 314
pensions/pensioners 56–8, 87, 112, 207, 213, 275, 280, 283, 291
Perry, Ruth 151–2
physical wellbeing 150–51

Pickett, Kate
  good society, version of 3–5
  Inner Level, The 7
  Spirit Level, The 6
Piketty, Thomas 290
  A Brief History of Equality 167–8
planetary boundaries' model 253–6, 254, 258–60
policy-making
  Conservative Party and *see* Conservative Party
  economic *see* economic thinking, new
  evidence-based 15–18, 30, 181, 222, 223, 229, 235, 258, 295–7, 305, 308–9, 311–12
  governmental use of evidence available 47–58
  haphazard nature of 15–16
  Labour Party and *see* Labour Party
  wellbeing at centre of 26, 67, 68
political economy principles 263–9, 292
Porto Alegre, Brazil 302–3
Portugal 6, 59, 103, 149, 187
poverty 4, 14, 17, 19
  care and 87, 102–3, 106, 110, 112, 113, 117, 118, 132
  child poverty 21, 34, 56–8, 68, 102–4, 106, 181, 182, 283
  criminal justice system and 191, 193–5, 202, 205, 212, 218, 219, 223–4
  deep relative 58

economic thinking and 265–6,
    272–4, 276, 280
education and 159, 181–2
health and 34, 40, 43, 56–8, 63,
    65–6, 67, 68, 70
*Lies We Tell Ourselves: Ending
    comfortable myths about poverty,
    The* 305
media and 305
participatory budgeting and 303
relative 57, 58, 68
tax and *see* tax
UBI and 276, 280, 281, 283–4,
    288, 297
Power, Dr Maddy 42
pregnancy 51, 52, 84, 88, 222
Presidential election (2024), US
    79, 289
prevention
  care systems and 78, 94, 100,
    105–7, 112, 135
  criminal justice and 191–2, 195,
    199, 204, 206, 213, 217, 222–5,
    228, 281
  economic thinking/UBI and
    262–3, 273, 279, 281, 284, 286
  education and 159, 161, 175
  public health and 3, 26, 30–34, 37,
    41, 50, 54, 56, 64, 68, 69
Prince's Trust 112
Prison Reform Trust 215, 226,
    236
prisons *see* criminal justice
Programme for International
    Student Assessment (PISA)
    144–5, 149, 149n, 150–51, 163–4

Progressive Economy Forum 252,
    293, 312
Proust, Marcel 1
public health perspective 30–34
public spending 11, 49–51, 57, 67,
    69, 276, 293, 302
Pybus, Dr Katie 42

quality of life 4, 20, 34, 36, 56
Quality-Adjusted Life Year
    (QALY) 310
Quick, Dr Laura 154

racial bias/racism 104, 105, 151,
    204–5, 234
rainbow model 38–40, *38*, 45, 57,
    70, 139–41, *140*
randomised controlled trials 310,
    322
rational maximisers 250
Rawls, John 12–13
Raworth, Kate: *Doughnut
    Economics: Seven ways to think
    like a 21st-century economist* 253,
    254, 255
Reach Plc 305
Reay, Professor Diane 180–81
Reeves, Aaron: *Born to Rule* 169
rehabilitation programmes 25, 31,
    195, 196, 199, 212, 216, 225, 227
rehabilitative culture 197, 227–9,
    232, 234, 235, 286
Reporters Without Borders 308
Republican Party, US 46
Resolution Foundation 280
Rethinking Economics 252

INDEX

return on investment 54, 60, 90, 178
reverse auction 261–2
Rikowski, Glenn 166
root causes 33–4, 39, 40, 222, 223
Rothermere, Viscount 305
Royal Commission on Long-Term Care of the Elderly (1998) 126–7

Sandel, Professor Michael 269
Scandinavian countries 6, 61, 86, 142, 149, 197–8
see also individual nation name
Scandinavian Prison Project 197–8
schizophrenia 39
schools
  absenteeism/school refusal 21, 154, 156–60
  academy schools 96, 154
  exclusions 157, 160–61, 228
  free school meals 26, 27, 29, 106, 158, 172–4, 182, 183, 205
  private/public 166–71, 173, 176, 178, 180, 183
  state school system 29, 168–9, 171–6
  see also education
science checks 314
Scientific Advisory Group for Emergencies (SAGE) 16–17
Scotland
  baby box provided in 29
  'Big Noise' 162
  Future Generations strategy 53
  GDP and 67

Minimum Income Guarantee considered in 66
National Care Service and 127
participatory budget pilot scheme in Govanhill 303
prison population 188
Royal Commission on Long-Term Care of the Elderly (1998) and 126–7
Scottish Parliament 53
sentencing in 230
universal care offering 127
Violence Reduction Unit 221–3
Wellbeing Economy Government 27, 28
Scott, Dr David 225
Second World War (1939–45) 47, 62, 142–3
secondary prevention 31–2
self-enhance 7
self-esteem 7, 146, 171, 276
Sen, Amartya 138–9, 274
shared lives schemes 116
sheltered housing scheme 116
Shrigley, David 180
Shrivastava, Professor Paul 314
Simms, Andrew 10–11
Simón Bolívar Youth Orchestra 162
Sinclair-Gieben, Wendy 226
Skilling, Jeffrey 207–8
skills wellbeing 151
Slovak Republic 83–4
smoking 32, 38, 41, 43, 70, 185, 243

384

INDEX

social capital 6, 227, 259
social care 4, 19, 20, 21, 32, 50, 55, 72–136, 176, 217, 224, 234, 263, 272, 282, 284–6, 293, 310, 312, 316
  'care' and 'caring' defined 72, 75
  care economy 76, 135
  childcare 78–92
    see also childcare
  children's social care 92–109
    see also children's social care
  disabilities 109–20
    see also disabilities
  elderly care 72–7, 120–36
    see also elderly care
  ethics of care 98, 106, 132, 138, 152, 274
  healthcare see health/healthcare
social epidemiology 2, 18, 70
social evaluative threat 7
social gradients 8, 104, 105
Social Impact Bonds 90–91
social isolation 70, 111, 116
social mobility 6, 142–3, 168, 170, 173
social principles 260–63
social relationships 6, 70, 259
social safety net 266–7
Social Science Advisory Group (SSAG) 312–13
social sciences 17–18, 46, 50, 149, 220, 296, 301, 304, 311–13
social security 26, 29, 66, 106, 118, 275–6, 279
social stress, chronic 7, 26, 52
social workers 18, 75, 99, 102, 106
socialism 62

soft skills 166–7
Somerset Carers 135
Soros, George 252
South Africa, inequality in 192–4
sovereign wealth fund 102, 107, 285
spa treatment, residential 25–7, 56
special educational needs and disabilities (SEND) 55, 96, 158, 160, 174–5, 178, 218
Standing, Professor Guy 125–6, 262, 279
Starmer, Keir 130, 214, 215
Stevens, Alex 308–9
Stevenson, Gary 293
Stiglitz, Joseph 242, 290
Stockholm Resilience Centre 253
Strangeways prison, Manchester riots (1990) 224–5
suicide 46, 60, 68, 119, 150, 190
Summers, Andy 291–2
supported living services 116
Sure Start 51–7, 65, 176
Sutton Trust 180
Syme, Professor Len 40–41
systematic reviews 310, 321–2
Szreter, Professor Simon 29, 35

tax
  bedroom tax 15, 94
  carbon taxes 285, 292, 295
  credits 56, 57, 66
  dementia tax 129
  Denmark and 11
  graduate tax 177

tax – *cont.*
  health inequalities and 43
  income tax 49, 135, 283–4, 286, 295
  inheritance tax 291, 294
  joy of 294–5
  land tax 282, 292
  Minimum Income Standard and 283–4
  National Insurance 126, 284
  personal allowances 283
  progressive 43, 266, 267, 285–90
  VAT, independent schools and 170, 178
  wealth taxes 267, 269, 285–95, 296, 297
Taylor, Charlie 226
Taylor-Robinson, David 65, 110
Thatcher, Margaret 4–5, 49, 50–51, 148, 209–10, 271
therapeutic breaks 25–7, 56
Thick of It, The (TV series) 15
Timpson, James 214–15
Timpson, John 214
Timpson review of school exclusion (2019) 160–61
TIMSS (Trends in International Mathematics and Science Study) 164
tipping points 255
Tower Hamlets 28–9, 303
trade unions 112, 264, 266, 267, 308
Transformational Economics Commission 262, 265

Treasury Executive Institute, US Department of the Treasury 5
Treasury, UK 44, 47, 85, 87, 127
Tribune group of Labour MPs 290–91
Trump, Donald 79, 208, 289
'truth decay' 314
tuberculosis 35, 47
Tyler, Wat 1

Ultimatum Game 250–51
United Nations (UN) 232, 244
  Convention on the Rights of the Child 165
  Sustainable Development Goals 244–5, 267
  UNESCO (United Nations Educational, Scientific and Cultural Organization) 256, 314
  UNICEF (United Nations Children's Fund) 103, 143, 150–51
universal basic income (UBI) 28, 66, 108, 132, 241, 269, 274–86, 296, 297
  care sector and 108–9, 132, 275, 279–83
  climate change/environment and 281–2, 288, 289
  education and 276, 279, 280, 282, 284
  inequality and 276, 279, 280
  paying for 283–5

poverty and 276, 280, 281, 283–4, 288, 297
prevention and 262–3, 273, 279, 281, 284, 286
universal basic services (UBS) 281–2, 286
Universal Credit 42, 85, 119, 275
Universal Quality Social Care 131
universities 18, 73, 91, 95–6, 144, 158, 162, 167, 168, 172, 177, 178–80, 182, 272, 315
see also individual university name
University of Cambridge 29, 35, 169, 172, 180, 181, 211, 252, 271–2
University College London 154, 288
University of Edinburgh 40, 43
University of Kent 308–9
University of Liverpool 65, 100, 110
University of Northumbria 268, 283
University of Nottingham 48
University of Oxford 169, 180, 211
University of Portsmouth 161
University of Warwick 114, 291
Uruguay 10–11
USA
  criminal justice system 187, 195–8, 217, 219, 222, 223
  global financial crisis and 207–8
  Head Start programme 139
  healthcare in 36–7, 41
  homicide rate 6, 46
  inequality in 5, 6, 14, 142
  media in 308

Vance, J. D. 79
Varadkar, Leo 298
Veil of Ignorance 12–14
Victoria, Australia 86–7
Vignoles, Anna 172
village agents 135
Voltaire 72
Vulnerability & Policing Futures Research Centre 220–21

Wages for Housework movement 79
Wales
  age of criminal responsibility 187
  basic income pilot scheme 108–9, 280–81
  GDP, moves beyond 67
  Royal Commission on Long-Term Care of the Elderly (1998) and 126
  Wellbeing Economy Government 27, 52–3, 87, 246, 247
  Wellbeing of Future Generations Act (2015) 52–3, 87, 247
walking 26, 27, 29
Wanless Social Care Review (2006) 127–9, 130, 131
Wealth Tax Commission 291

welfare state 2, 47, 168
wellbeing budgets 27–8, 67, 69, 241, 247
Wellbeing Economy Governments 26–8, 246–7, 258
wellness industry 64–5, 303
What Works Network 309
Whitehead, Professor Dame Margaret 38, 39, 50, 65, 110
Wilkinson, Richard 48–9, 162
  inequality, first links to wide range of problems 5–9
  Inner Level, The 7
  Spirit Level, The 6
Williams, Zoe 5
Wilson, Rich 300
women
  childcare and 79, 80, 83, 87–90, 121, 123, 125, 131
  criminal justice and 186–7, 191–2, 226, 230
  democratic malaise and 296
  domestic abuse / domestic violence / violence against 103, 184–5, 191–2, 194, 200, 202, 208, 213, 217–18, 223, 281
  education and 167, 179
  gender equality 80, 87–8, 89, 123–4, 164

life expectancy 20, 69
lung cancer rates 121
Women's Budget Group 131, 132, 135
Woodsome, Kate 306
Woolf Report (1991) 225–6, 232
workers' rights 266–8
working week, length of 10, 11, 26, 27, 80
work–life balance 11, 26
World at One (radio programme) 167
World Economic Forum Social Mobility Index 142
World Health Organization (WHO) 60, 123
  Regional Office for Europe 39
  violence as 'a public health concern', declares (2002) 222
World Press Freedom Index 308
World3 (computer model) 248, 249
Wright, Professor John 315–16

X Corp 306

York Castle Museum 184, 185
York Crown Court 184